BIG
TIME

Murry R. Nelson

BIG
TIME

The History of Big Ten
Basketball, 1972–1992

RED  LIGHTNING BOOKS

Red Lightning Books
1320 East 10th Street
Bloomington, Indiana 47405 USA

redlightningbooks.com

Manufactured in the United States of America

First printing 2024

Cataloging information is available from the Library of Congress.

ISBN 978-1-68435-218-0 (paperback)
ISBN 978-1-68435-220-3 (ebook)

CONTENTS

PREFACE

As the 1972–73 NCAA men's college basketball season began, UCLA was the dominant team, having won eight of nine NCAA titles since 1964 (and would go on to win two more in the next three years before the retirement of legendary coach John Wooden, a former All-American player at Purdue 1929–32). The Big Ten had teams in the NCAA Final Four in 1964, 1965, 1968, and 1969, but that was the only impact from the conference since Ohio State University had been in three straight championship contests (winning one) from 1960 to 1962. One of the players on those OSU teams was Bob Knight, and his return to the Big Ten for the 1971–72 season as head coach of men's basketball at Indiana University would alter the conference and college basketball for the next thirty years.

Knight would not only be the key factor in the resurgence of Indiana basketball but also would affect the coaching patterns of every team in the Big Ten, if not beyond. Certainly, the 1970s and 1980s were Knight's years of dominance in the Big Ten as well as nationally, winning three NCAA titles and taking his teams to two other Final Fours in the 1972–1992 period, the years covered in this volume. Other great coaches were hired in the Big Ten during this period and took their squads to the Final Four, but Knight's influence and impact was unmatched. Between 1972 and 1992, no fewer than five Big Ten coaches were voted national coach of the year by either the National Association of Basketball Coaches or the Associated Press. The Big Ten was truly a coaches' conference during this period and was recognized for the genius of its leaders, four of whom (Jud Heathcote, Lou Henson, Gene Keady, and Knight) were subsequently voted into the Naismith Memorial Basketball Hall of Fame for their coaching successes.

The Big Ten was represented in the first three Final Fours, starting in 1939 (winning two championships), then made four appearances in the 1940s, six in the 1950s, and seven in the 1960s, including the Ohio State run, before UCLA made the tournament its own. Knight's hire brought some hope to the conference and would also lead other Big Ten schools to seek top coaches to compete with his Indiana teams as the Big Ten became, once again, the best conference in the country in the 1970s.

This book captures the intensity of the years 1972 to 1992, as the Big Ten put five, six, and even seven teams in the increasingly expanding NCAA tournament field. National championships were won by three different Big Ten teams during this period with twelve Big Ten appearances in the Final Four (detailed in Appendix 2).

This was also a time of significant alterations to the college basketball game itself, with the additions of a shot clock and the three-point shot. Player eligibility also changed as the NCAA allowed freshmen to be eligible to play varsity football and basketball starting in the 1972–73 academic year. These changes were coupled with a number of Big Ten and NCAA academic requirements for being eligible to play varsity basketball, which had a major effect on recruiting and continued eligibility.

The college basketball fan base grew exponentially during this time period, thanks in large part to the growing practice of broadcasting college sports on television in the 1970s. TV exposure was key to popularizing the college game, and the Big Ten was a major part of that, ultimately resulting in the formation of the Big Ten Network in 2006 under Commissioner Jim Delaney, who had replaced Wayne Duke as commissioner in 1989. This was a dynamic period in college basketball and, particularly, the Big Ten, and it is described in detail in this book, as are many games and the conference races from 1972 to 1992.

As in my previous book, *Big Ten Basketball, 1943–1972*, I have relied heavily on newspaper accounts, mostly from the *Chicago Tribune*, which was considered by some as the Big Ten's "mouthpiece," but I have also used other newspapers, basketball annuals, and, of most insight, interviews with former players and coaches. My hope is that the picture I paint of these Big Ten years reflects the excitement that I felt in reliving and writing about this period of time in Big Ten basketball.

BIG
TIME

CHAPTER 1

THE EARLY 1970s
The Big Ten Asserts Its Strength as a League

The appointment of Bob Knight as head basketball coach at Indiana University in 1971 changed Big Ten basketball immediately, with Knight's emphasis on defense. His first Indiana team, mostly with holdovers from former head coach Lou Watson (minus George McGinnis), finished 9–5 in conference, good enough to finish in a tie for third place and to secure a slot in the National Invitational Tournament (NIT). Indiana lost in the first round. In the coming years, Indiana basketball would fare much better.

Prospects for 1972–73

The 1972–73 Big Ten basketball season began with no clear favorite, but overall prospects for the league looked excellent, especially according to sportswriter Roy Damer of the *Chicago Tribune*. He noted that the conference "could post a winning nonconference record of 75 percent, and that would border on the astounding." He based his prediction on a number of factors: first, 78 percent of the starters from the previous season were returning, including thirty-nine of the top fifty scorers and the league's overall leading scorers, which included Mike Robinson of Michigan State (27.2 ppg), Henry Wilmore of Michigan (23.4), and Allan Hornyak of Ohio State (23.3); second, Damer called attention to the number of "extraordinarily tall men," with twelve at 6 feet, 10 inches or taller; third was the addition of some top transfers; and fourth was the number of "super sophomores" in the league, led by Campy Russell of Michigan.[1]

Knight commented that "this league will be very physical. But we will not be a physical team—that's for sure." In response to a reporter's joke about when he would open up his offensive attack, Knight responded, "I bought a book over the summer by the name of *How to Coach the Fast Break*. I really didn't understand all of it."[2] With four returning starters and the addition of freshman Quinn Buckner, Knight's squad was predicted to be a highly ranked team.

1

Bob Knight, the youngest coach in Division I Basketball at the age of thirty-one in 1971.
(*Courtesy of Indiana University Archives*)

Johnny Orr saw his Michigan squad as "the strongest all-around team that I've had at Michigan. We have four starters returning, a suspended player back (Terry Tyler, a junior guard), and some outstanding sophomores. If we get it all jelled, we could be an outstanding team."[3]

As defending champion, Minnesota was seen as a slight favorite but was also "the least liked team in America because of the terrible scene in Minneapolis the previous January, when some of their players physically assaulted Ohio State players after it was evident that the Buckeyes had won the game."[4]

As for Ohio State, the Buckeyes were generally rated just behind Minnesota, but Damer was picking OSU to edge Minnesota in the upcoming season.[5]

Preconference Games

In early nonconference play, it was too soon to determine each team's strengths. Michigan State edged Toledo 98–96 on November 28. Ohio State lost to Washington in Seattle 67–63. Wisconsin was pounded by defending NCAA champion UCLA 94–53 in the Badgers' opening game. Kentucky topped Michigan State 75–66. Indiana toyed with Harvard, winning 97–76. All this occurred in the first week of the season, making it difficult to tell how good teams would really be.

Kentucky lost to the young Indiana squad, in the traditional "border rivalry" contest between the teams, by a score of 64–58.[6] The win catapulted the Hoosiers forward to a big 69–67 win in the next contest, this time over traditional rival Notre Dame in South Bend.

Defending Big Ten champion Minnesota went to 4–0 with a hard-fought 87–81 victory in Chicago against Loyola. Minnesota would remain unbeaten in the preconference schedule, finishing with a victory over Oregon State 83–80 in the Far West Classic on New Year's Eve in Portland.[7]

Indiana was upset 74–65 by University of Texas-El Paso (UTEP) in the Sun Bowl Classic Final that same night, but they recovered three days later to rout Ball State back in Bloomington by a score of 94–71. Balanced scoring by Ritter (24), John Laskowski (23), and Downing (19), on top of Buckner's leadership, made the win an easy transition to the opening of Big Ten play.[8]

The Big Ten Conference Season Opens

It didn't take long for upsets to roil the Big Ten season. Iowa knocked off undefeated Minnesota 65–62 on opening night of conference play in Iowa City. In Columbus, Ohio State was upset 68–62 by Michigan. The Wolverines took it to the Buckeyes, who had only Alan Hornyak scoring in double figures with 28. Indiana opened by defeating Wisconsin 78–64 in Madison, as Ritter and Laskowski topped the scoring with 24 and 18 points, respectively.[9]

Michigan continued its strong start in conference play with a 71–59 home win over Iowa, as the Wolverines showed the balanced scoring that would prove so valuable during the season. Michigan relied on a pressure overplay man-to-man defense. Guard Steve Grote noted that the team always went into full-court press after free throws were made, played "over the top" on picks, and didn't change their style for anyone. The Michigan offense was a motion offense against man-to-man defense and a 1-3-1 setup against a zone. With no shot clock, almost all games ended with some sort of "keep-away" situation that would run out the clock. Their thinking was that whoever scored the most layups would win the game, and Michigan just happened to be a fast-break team.[10]

The next week, Illinois extended Iowa's swoon with an 80–78 last-second win in Champaign.[11] That same evening, Michigan struggled to edge Michigan State 78–71 in East Lansing, despite MSU dominating the boards 34–26. Turnovers were a key factor in the contest, as MSU had 25 to Michigan's 11.[12] After two weeks, the Big Ten was down to three undefeated teams in conference play: Michigan (3–0), Indiana (2–0), and Purdue (2–0).

In Minneapolis, the Minnesota Golden Gophers topped powerful Marquette 64–53 before a crowd of 17,987, a number made even more impressive by the fact that the game was being shown on closed-circuit television at the hockey arena next door before another 4,002.[13] In their next contest, however, the Gophers were upset 83–71 in Bloomington by Indiana, as the Hoosiers closed out the game with eight straight points for the win. John Ritter had 22 and John Laskowski had 17 off the bench. Turner had 30 and Brewer 23 for the Gophers. Earlier that week, Coach Knight had praised Laskowski for being his "super sub," as he came into games "to rectify a mistake or straighten out a problem" for the team and promptly did so. Damer noted that Knight had "done an outstanding job in a season and a half at Indiana."[14]

The next week, in a crucial game for both squads, Indiana defeated Michigan 79–73 in Ann Arbor, keeping the Hoosiers undefeated in the league and handing the Wolverines their second loss. Indiana had great balance, with five players in double figures, led by Steve Downing with 22. Michigan's Wilmore had 31, but Campy Russell was held to just 4. Ohio State knocked Purdue from the undefeated ranks in conference with a 79–73 win in West Lafayette. Alan Hornyak was superb with 34 points.[15]

The Race Tightens in the Second Half of the Conference Season

Indiana, now the only undefeated team in conference play, had risen to #5 in the AP national poll.[16] Indiana hurt themselves with a 70–69 loss to Ohio State in Columbus, as Hornyak sank the decisive free throw with five seconds remaining. Both teams underperformed at the free throw line with OSU going 8 of 14 and IU 17 of 26.[17] The Big Ten race was becoming increasingly muddled, as Damer had predicted in his preseason assessment.

On February 10, Ohio State hosted Minnesota (in their first match since the infamous melee of the previous year), while Indiana visited Purdue: these games would go a long way toward clarifying the conference race. The former game was televised, not just regionally on WGN in Chicago, but also nationally. In a contest as tight as anticipated, Minnesota edged the Buckeyes 80–78 before 13,489 Ohio State fans.[18] In West Lafayette, the Boilermakers slipped by Indiana 72–69 in a hard-fought but sloppy contest. Purdue had 26 fouls and 23 turnovers, while Indiana had 20 fouls and 26 turnovers, which was uncharacteristic of Knight-coached teams.[19]

With Indiana's and Purdue's records tied at 6–2, Minnesota at 5–2, and Illinois 4–2, the next week would be key. Knight knew it and acted accordingly. First, he shuffled his lineup for the game against Illinois, and the result was a crushing defeat of the Illini, 87–66. Overall, it was an ugly win: Indiana had 37 turnovers to Illinois's 28, both of which were far too many for a well-prepared team. Knight had decided to start freshman Tom Abernathy and sophomore Steve Ahlfeld and consigned Ritter and Buckner to the bench, either to fire up the latter two or to provide a different rhythm to the game. The result was a big win but a bad offensive flow, as evidenced by the many turnovers noted.[20]

This was clearly not what Knight had hoped to see, even after he had called an early morning drill on Sunday, two days before the Illinois game. The prior games were both losses, one to Ohio State and the other to Purdue: this did not sit well with Knight, and "the 33-year-old coach verbally tore into his athletes . . . and held an unusual 8 a.m. practice on Sunday morning following the loss at Purdue." Knight explained that "we don't talk about winning; we talk about how to win."[21]

Damer noted how strange this team was for Knight because it was built on offensive—not defensive—abilities. For three years prior to Knight coming to Bloomington, his Army teams had led the nation in defense, but that was not happening at Indiana.[22] The Hoosiers would have another chance to please Knight with their next contest against Minnesota in Williams Arena. In anticipation of an overflow crowd (more than the eighteen thousand seating capacity), the game was shown on closed-circuit television in the hockey arena next door, which seated another seven thousand.[23] The home crowd was not disappointed, as Minnesota toppled the Hoosiers 82–75 in a hard-fought but well-played game. Minnesota had six players in double figures, led by Turner with 20 and Nix with 16, and they shot 49 percent from the floor and sank 16 of 20 free throws. Indiana was led by Downing with 23, followed by Laskowski and Buckner with 12 points each. The Hoosiers shot 54 percent from the floor and made 13 of 19 free throws. The big key, however, was rebounding, where Minnesota more than doubled Indiana 47 to 23.[24]

In his weekly evaluation of the Big Ten, Damer credited freshmen for changing the tenor of the league, as well as significantly affecting the standings. His first "frosh" was Coach Fred Schaus of Purdue, who had returned to college coaching after being the general manager and coach of the Los Angeles Lakers. He was joined by another freshman of note: his guard Bruce Parkinson. The other freshmen who impressed Damer the most were Wayman Britt of Michigan and three Indiana players: starting guards Buckner and Jim Crews and forward Tom Abernathy.[25]

Both Purdue and Indiana kept pace. In West Lafayette, the Boilers won 74–66 over Iowa, with Frank Kendrick and John Garrett leading the way with 22 and 20 points, respectively. The Hoosiers were slowed by the Badgers but managed to eke out a 57–55 victory. Steve Downing had 18, while three teammates—Green, Laskowski, and Buckner—contributed 10 points each.[26] The five Big Ten games had also set a one-day attendance record for the conference with 70,720 fans at the five sites, an average of 14,144 per site, even though every game had been televised locally.

Down to the Wire

With two weeks left in the season, the conference race was still wide open, with at least three teams in close contention for the championship. The standings had Minnesota at 8–2, Indiana at 9–3, and Purdue at 9–3. February ended with a stunning 71–63 Purdue loss in Madison, putting the Boilermakers two games behind the Minnesota Golden Gophers, who coasted to a 90–74 victory at home against the hapless Wildcats of Northwestern.

The matchup between Purdue and Minnesota would be telling. The Gophers shot .582 for the game, with most coming from 15 to 20 feet, rather than from inside the paint. Meanwhile, Purdue was saddled with 39 percent shooting.[27]

With a week to go in the season and Minnesota in the proverbial driver's seat, the Golden Gophers crashed with a 79–77 loss to Iowa. It was Minnesota's first home loss of the season, and the timing could not have been worse.[28]

Amid the tight race, the Big Ten was rife with rumors about coaching futures and decisions on player eligibility. The jobs of three Big Ten coaches seemed in trouble: Brad Snyder at Northwestern, John Powless at Wisconsin, and Dave Schultz at Iowa—although only Snyder was let go after that season. In a more far-reaching decision, the Big Ten voted to approve the "redshirt" rule, allowing a player five years, rather than four, to complete their eligibility. The Big Ten was the last major conference to abandon the four-year rule. The conference also agreed to comply with the NCAA's decision to drop the 1.6 predicted grade point average (GPA) requirement based on high school grades and SAT scores and, instead, allow freshmen to be eligible as long as they had achieved at least a 2.0 GPA in high school.[29]

Both the Gophers and the Hoosiers were 10–3, so a tie, leading to a one-game playoff in Champaign on March 12, seemed likely. Minnesota seemed the clear favorite, but then it all came apart for the Gophers. The Northwestern Wildcats played what may have been their best game of the season while the Golden Gophers were probably looking beyond the 'Cats to possible NCAA competition, all of which led to a 79–74 NU victory. The Gophers, meanwhile, were overly aggressive with thirty team fouls and four starters fouling out.[30]

In Bloomington, 17,436 fans (an attendance record) squeezed into Assembly Hall and helped their favorites topple Purdue, 77–72. Knight thought the crowd was "good" and, more important, so was the balance of his team. A noteworthy difference was free-throw shooting, where the Hoosiers were 19 of 24, while the Boilers were just 6 of 8.[31]

The final standings for 1972–73 had Indiana at 11–3 and Minnesota at 10–4. Within a week, a couple of coaching events became newsworthy in the conference. First, Brad Snyder resigned at Northwestern after four seasons and a conference record of 26–70. The second was Bob Knight being named the first winner of the Big Ten Coach of the Year Award; he was also the youngest head coach at a major college. His Hoosiers would open NCAA tourney play against Marquette, coached by Al McGuire.[32] The tourney then included just twenty-five teams, with no more than one team from any conference.

The Big Ten in the 1973 Postseason

Minnesota was invited to the still-prestigious NIT in Madison Square Garden, where they defeated Rutgers 68–59 to advance to the semifinals against Alabama, where they lost 69–65 to the Crimson Tide. An encouraging sign was that the Gophers finished with their first-ever twenty-win season (21–5).

The opening NCAA game for Indiana (after a first-round bye) would be played in Nashville against the rugged Marquette Warriors. A late surge saw the Hoosiers win 75–69, after being down 53–43 with 14:22 to play. Steve Downing was a monster for Indiana, going 12 of 17 from the floor with 29 points and 10 rebounds.[33] The win sent Indiana into the Mideast Finals against Kentucky. Indiana rallied to defeat the Wildcats 72–65. After being down 61–59 with 7:30 to go, Knight switched Quinn Buckner to the high post against the Kentucky zone, and the guard responded with 16 points and 11 rebounds, complementing Steve Downing's 23 points and 13 rebounds.[34]

The NCAA Semifinals would first pit Providence, the East champion, against Memphis State, the Midwest champion. Then the Hoosiers took the court against a UCLA team that had gone 203–5 over the past seven years, led by NCAA Players of the Year Lew Alcindor (later known as Kareem Abdul-Jabbar) and Bill Walton. This was a veteran UCLA team, coached by John Wooden, while Indiana had a young coach and a lineup that included three freshmen and two sophomores in significant roles. The game seemed like a decisive UCLA victory with the Bruins leading 46–24 with eighteen minutes to go. Then the Hoosiers rallied behind Downing (26 points) and Ritter (13) to close to 57–55 with 5:48 left, when a controversial call allowed UCLA to slide to victory, 70–59. Knight recalled the play in this manner: "We got it to 54–51—we had scored seventeen straight points—when Walton posted up along the baseline, turned to his right shoulder to drive, and drove his forearm into Downing's chest. The call was a foul on Downing—not Walton's fifth. Downing's fourth. Within a minute, Downing had his fifth foul and was out of the game." He went on to note that "I've always considered that fourth foul on Downing one of the two worst calls my team ever had."[35]

Ritter agreed with Knight: "I'm prejudiced. I was on the floor when the play happened. I was sure that it was going to be called on Walton and then I couldn't believe it happened the other way. I think you see that in basketball at every level, and Bill was certainly a star."[36] Not surprisingly, Walton saw it differently. In recalling the play, he noted Knight's opinion that the call was one of the worst he'd ever seen, but Walton felt that "the ref was in perfect position, had the clear angle and made the right call."[37]

The Hoosiers would not be in the championship game. They did, however, overwhelm Providence to take third in the NCAA tournament. The Hoosiers routed the Friars to end the season at 22–6 but with high hopes for the next year. Downing was named Honorable Mention All-American, as well as Indiana's MVP and MVP of the Big Ten conference, as Knight had hoped. Knight subsequently heaped praise on Downing, saying, "We were blessed to have Steve Downing."[38]

The Off-Season into 1973–74

The first team to make a significant move in preparing for 1973–74 was Northwestern, who hired "Tex" Winter as their new basketball coach. The fifty-one-year-old Winter had been head coach at Kansas State for fifteen years, following three years at the University of Washington and a year and a half as head coach of the San Diego Rockets of the NBA. He retained Rich Falk and Dan Davis as his top assistants at Northwestern. Winter would be inducted into the College Basketball Hall of Fame in 2010 and into the Naismith Memorial Hall of Fame in 2011, but his work was certainly going to be challenging at NU.[39]

With Indiana's excellent finish and the return of nearly the entire team (minus Downing), plus the addition of two "nonqualifiers" from the prior season (Scott May and Bobby Wilkerson), the Hoosiers seemed poised to repeat as Big Ten champions. Their closest competition promised to be within the state, at West Lafayette, where Purdue returned John Garrett, Bruce Parkinson, and Frank Kendrick and would welcome Tom Scheffler, a six-foot-nine freshman, to spell Garrett in the middle. Damer thought that the conference as a whole would not be as rugged as 1972–73 but that its teams might be just as competitive outside the conference. Indiana was ranked #3 in preseason polls behind UCLA and North Carolina State. Purdue was also mentioned as a top-twenty team.[40]

Preconference Games

Big Ten teams won almost all their preconference games, often against much weaker opponents, except for a few notable exceptions. Indiana topped Kansas 72–59 before a crowd of seventeen thousand in Bloomington, but Purdue lost to Clemson 81–80 in West Lafayette. South Carolina beat Michigan State 74–63 in East Lansing, and Michigan was surprised by Detroit 70–59 in Detroit. Purdue was upset 86–85 by Miami of Ohio at Oxford.[41]

Indiana topped Kentucky in Louisville 77–68, led by John Laskowski and Steve Green, with 23 and 18 points, respectively. Kevin Grevey had 25 for the Wildcats. But less than a week later, the Hoosiers lost at home to Notre Dame before the largest crowd in IU history (17,463). John Shumate led the Irish with 26, while Green and May topped IU, scoring 21 and 14 points, respectively.[42]

The Big Ten Season Opens

After the preconference results were in, the league did not look as strong as in previous seasons. As conference play began on January 5, Wisconsin ran by Northwestern 87–53, as expected, but the rest of the opening games were less predictable. Illinois edged Ohio State in Columbus 75–73; Michigan surprised Indiana 73–71; Purdue rallied to beat MSU 77–75 after being down 24–6 early in the game; Iowa won in Minnesota.[43]

After the Michigan victory, Knight spoke up for Michigan coach Johnny Orr in the postgame press conference. "A lot of people up here have been on

John Orr's ass who don't know a damn thing about college basketball. . . . It's easy for a coach when he's lost a game like this to come out and say, 'We played poorly,' but that's not the case. Michigan really deserved a lot of credit because they just beat us."[44]

The various outcomes pushed Wisconsin into a top-twenty ranking—at #16. This would seem to be a season of greater parity.[45] The Badgers looked even better in defeating Ohio State in their next game in Madison, extending the record of the Badgers to 9–1. A bigger and more surprising story was one that Damer carried through over two days. He exposed the lack of African Americans on the Illinois roster, seventeen years after the Illini had added its first Black basketball players to the Land of Lincoln's land grant university.[46] Damer first asked Coach Harv Schmidt for his comment on this situation, and Schmidt felt that it was "as much a coincidence as anything," since three years earlier there were six African Americans players, two of whom used up their eligibility, one graduated, two flunked out, and one transferred. Schmidt felt that he had great rapport with Black players, noting that when he played at Kankakee High (just south of Chicago), he was the only white starter.[47] By the next season, the Illini roster included five African Americans, most of whom had been recruited by Schmidt; but Schmidt was now gone, having been replaced by Gene Bartow at the end of the season.

Meanwhile, heavy conference favorite Indiana struggled to defeat emerging power Wisconsin, in Bloomington, 52–51. Michigan stayed unbeaten in the conference by stopping MSU 84–82 in Ann Arbor. Purdue also stayed unbeaten by topping Northwestern 89–76 in Mackey Arena, while Wisconsin and Indiana were close behind with just one loss each to Illinois and Iowa, respectively.[48]

This set up an early season battle of note when Purdue hosted Michigan. The game was worthy of the preliminary hype as Purdue edged the Wolverines in overtime 85–84, leaving the Boilers as the only undefeated team in the conference. The contest was rugged, as evidenced by the free throws, which saw Purdue making 23 of 37 and Michigan 22 of 26 from the line.[49]

By the last week of January, the standings were still tight among the "haves" (Purdue, 6–0; Michigan, 5–1; Indiana, 4–1; MSU, 5–2; and Wisconsin, 3–2) and the "have nots" (Illinois, Iowa, OSU, and Minnesota, all at 1–4; Northwestern, 1–6). Many of the contests were very close "with 14 of the 28 league games to date, undecided until the final 30 seconds."[50]

February brought the electric atmosphere that the impending NCAA tournament generated, and Michigan State harnessed that electricity by shocking Purdue in East Lansing, 76–74.[51]

Govonor Vaughn, one of the first Black players for the University of Illinois.
(*Courtesy of University of Illinois Athletics*)

The Race Tightens and Pretenders Vanish

Michigan, Indiana, and Purdue notched easy victories to start the next week, before Purdue was upset 112–111 in triple overtime at Iowa. Michigan barely edged Northwestern 50–48 in Ann Arbor to maintain their slim Big Ten lead, while Indiana destroyed Wisconsin 81–63.

The latest AP poll found the Big Ten leaders, Indiana and Michigan, ranked just #12 and #15, respectively, so the league's seeming parity was working against higher rankings. Damer was impressed with Knight's ability to adjust quickly to teams that Indiana had already played once, which was different from the previous season. Now Indiana had changed to a running team from a "cautious defensive-oriented philosophy." Knight said that they were practicing more full-court work than ever before and credited much of their improvement to Buckner (adjusting after the football season where he played as a top defensive back) and freshman center Kent Benson.[52]

It was most fortuitous, then, that Indiana would be meeting Michigan in Bloomington that week. The largest crowd in the history of IU basketball was expected at Assembly Hall. Knight hoped that Indiana would be better than they were in the Big Ten opener at Michigan, where the Wolverines triumphed 73–71. Despite Indiana increasing its game pace, Michigan coach Johnny Orr said (and guard Steve Grote agreed) that they didn't expect a big running game but rather about the same pace as the last meeting. Orr called his squad "the most conservative that I've had at Michigan."[53] Orr's expectation regarding pace was certainly wrong, as the Hoosiers blasted the Wolverines 93–81 behind a career game for Steve Green (17 of 24 field goals, 11 rebounds, 4 assists, 37 points). Kent Benson was also brutally effective, scoring 20 points on 9 of 13 shooting.[54]

Purdue beat Wisconsin 107–80 to tie Michigan with just two losses with two weeks to go in the conference season, but once-beaten Indiana clearly had the edge at this point. All three kept winning the next week, but Michigan and Purdue met on February 23 in a battle for second in Ann Arbor, with the home team winning easily 111–84. Indiana, meanwhile, won its eleventh game in a row, this one a 91–85 win at home against Michigan State. Indiana now had a full one-game lead on Michigan and two games on Purdue.

March brought more action, both on and off the court.[55] On the Big Ten coaching carousel, Dick Schultz quit at Iowa after going 40–55 in four years, and Gene Bartow was announced as the new Illini head coach, leaving Memphis State.[56]

In game play, perhaps most startling was the Indiana loss in Columbus to a mediocre OSU team, 85–79. Knight, never one to hide his feelings, said after the game, "That was the most gutless, atrocious job of officiating that I've ever seen in college basketball! And you can quote me on that!" The Buckeyes shot 62 percent from the floor after going into the contest with a 44 percent mark for the year. OSU played a zone defense, and the Hoosiers could not sink enough baskets to keep up.[57]

So the Big Ten race was deadlocked. Both Indiana and Michigan won on March 9, with Indiana edging Purdue 80–79 and Michigan crushing MSU 103–87 in East Lansing to set up a playoff in Champaign on March 11. Russell had 36 points, 13 rebounds, and 7 assists "leading UM to a share of its first Big 10 championship in eight years." Russell, though pleased, was not satisfied, saying, "I want to play for the big one—the NCAA."[58]

The Postseason

On the same day as the Big Ten title playoff, the NIT announced that Purdue had accepted a bid, leaving the loser of the Big Ten playoff out of the tourney at Madison Square Garden. Michigan, behind a great performance by C. J. Kupec (22 points, 15 rebounds), defeated Indiana 75–67 to secure the NCAA bid. After the game Knight said, "Without any question, Michigan deserved to win. . . . On this night a better basketball team beat us."[59] In his own version of graciousness, Knight began his press conference with a question: "Would the Michigan writers who have been on John Orr's ass please stand up? I think we've seen a pretty good coaching job from a darn good coach."[60]

So Michigan was off to the NCAAs; for Purdue it was the NIT. As for Indiana, "Knight was obliged by his IU bosses to play in a made-for-television post season tournament called the Collegiate Commissioners Association tournament, instead of his beloved NIT. The Hoosiers won it, drubbing No.15-ranked USC by 25 points in the finale in St. Louis."[61]

At the NCAAs Michigan defeated Notre Dame, 77–68. Campy Russell had 36 points—24 in the second half. Coach Orr heaped effusive praise on his star, calling him "the greatest all-around player in the United States." Michigan outrebounded the bigger Irish 53–49 and held star Adrian Dantley to just 1 of 7 field goals. John Shumate had 34, however, for Notre Dame.[62]

Purdue won its first three NIT games, against UNC (82–71), Hawaii (85–72), and Jacksonville (78–63) before toppling Utah 87–81 to win the tourney and bring more prestige to the Big Ten. Michigan endured poor shooting all night in a loss to Marquette in the Mideast regional finals 72–70, as Michigan had just one field goal in the last seven minutes and shot just 37.5 percent for the game (24 of 64). Russell had 21 and Johnson 15 in the loss. Despite this tough loss, it had still been an excellent year for the Big Ten.[63]

Campy Russell, All-American at Michigan. (*Courtesy of Bentley Historical Library, University of Michigan*)

Johnny Orr was named Big Ten Coach of the Year. He would finish fourth in the national balloting behind Norm Sloan of North Caroline State, Al McGuire of Marquette, and Digger Phelps of Notre Dame.[64]

Campy Russell was named Big Ten MVP, and he was named first on every ballot, having led the league in scoring while finishing second in assists. He also applied as a junior for the so-called hardship draft of the NBA. He was selected in the first round of the draft by the Cleveland Cavaliers as the #8 pick.

The 1974–75 Season Opens

Basketball News 1975 College Yearbook ranked Indiana #3 and Purdue #16 in its preseason top twenty with Michigan, Minnesota, and Ohio State following in the predicted Big Ten standings. No Big Ten players were selected as part of *Basketball News*'s five-man All-America team.[65] According to *Basketball News*, keys to Indiana's success were Steve Green, Quinn Buckner, and Kent Benson. Scott May was noted as a starter but not as a potential Big Ten first-teamer. *Basketball News* named three blue chippers among Indiana's incoming freshmen, including a lad named "Larry Byrd" from Spring Valley, "another All-Indianan with 30-point and 20-rebound averages."[66] But Bird, who dropped out of school after a month, returned to French Lick, Indiana, and enrolled at Indiana State the following year.

Preconference Play

Preconference play made the predictions seem savvy. Indiana, Purdue, Michigan, and Minnesota all looked tough to beat. Most played less-skilled opponents, but Indiana did have a difficult 74–70 overtime win at #6 Kansas, when May (29), Green (19), and Benson (14) carried most of the scoring. Indiana returned home to pound Kentucky 98–74 three days later (before 17,418) with Benson (26) and May (25) leading the scoring once again.[67]

Purdue was upset by California in Berkeley 76–73 but still maintained a spot in both the UPI (#15) and AP (#16) polls of December 10. Indiana was ranked #3 in both polls.[68] The Hoosiers were 4–0, and Scott May was scoring 24.5 per game with all starters above 45 percent shooting, except for Buckner's 32 percent.[69] Purdue was 5–1 and had a deep bench to complement its starters. Referred to as the "soul patrol," four African American freshmen entered as a unit, while white starter Dick Satterfield stayed in and played with them. Guard Gene Parker, one of the "soul patrol," saw no problem with that, commenting that Satterfield "plays black."[70]

Conference Play Begins

The Big Ten season opened in 1974–75 with Indiana still undefeated and looking consistently powerful. When Purdue was upset by both Florida State and Western Kentucky and dropped from the top twenty, Indiana had overtaken UCLA, Louisville, and NC State to grab the top spot in the country. The Hoosiers solidified that position with their thirteenth win in a row, this time beating Michigan 90–76. The Indiana balance was impressive: Steve Green had 26, Scott May 20, and John Laskowski 19. Minnesota took advantage of the Wolverine loss, dropping Illinois 77–67 before 17,573 in Minneapolis.[71]

As always, Indiana was not the only impressive team in the league, which was viewed by one of its newest coaches as "big and physical." Gene Bartow, who had come from Memphis State, was "amazed at what I've seen as to strength and the overall play in the Big Ten.... I thought the Missouri Valley was physical, but there are more big, strong people here."[72]

Indiana continued to roll, embarrassing Iowa 102–49 for their seventeenth regular season win in a row over two seasons and then crushed Minnesota 79–59 to remain undefeated at 15–0. When Michigan was upset by Michigan State 86–78, Indiana's path to the Big Ten title looked clear. Knight's team was averaging 91.7 ppg and allowing just 64.8 ppg (tops in the nation in scoring margin) and continued to lead the national polls, with UCLA ranked #2.[73] The Hoosiers stormed on, defeating Purdue, Illinois, and then Ohio State 72–66 in Columbus; it was Knight's first win as IU coach on the floor of his alma mater. Indiana was 9–0 in the league with Purdue and Minnesota at 6–3.

No one seemed to have an answer for Indiana's power. And the rest of the conference was literally playing for second place and a possible berth in the NIT. The Indiana team as a whole was as acclaimed as Knight was. Roy Damer named him as the best coach in the country, and both his players and the Indiana athletic director (Bill Orwig) agreed.[74] It seemed Indiana could not be stopped. They powered through Iowa on February 8, Minnesota on February 10, Northwestern on February 15, and Wisconsin on February 17 to go to 14–0 in the conference, upping their in-season winning streak to 28.

With Indiana undefeated and #1 in the country, there was no question that the Hoosiers would be in the NCAA tourney and hold a #1 seed. The question for the rest of the conference was who else would be tournament bound? Bob Knight proposed that the NCAA tourney should be modified: under his plan, the champions of the eight top conferences would get first-round byes, then the remaining thirty-two teams would begin play in eight sectionals, with the survivors playing the eight champions. His suggestion was not well received.[75]

After Indiana went to 14–0 with a rout of Wisconsin, they then defeated Purdue 83–82 but paid a huge price in the victory. Just before the end of the first half, Scott May suffered a broken left arm in a collision. He was through for the season, leaving Indiana at 26–0. The Hoosiers still finished Big Ten play at 18–0. In the Michigan State game, May entered the game with a broken arm, but it was clear that he couldn't do much—it had only been eighteen days since the injury—and was swiftly pulled from the game.

Except for Indiana, the rest of the league was suffering from an inability to win on the road, with Purdue having the best away record at 3–6. In a newly expanded field of thirty-two teams in the NCAA tournament, would any other Big Ten team make it? Michigan was 19–7, Minnesota 18–8, and Purdue 16–10. Ultimately, Purdue was named to the National Commissioners Invitational Tournament and defeated Missouri before losing to Arizona, both games being played in Louisville. Michigan was selected for the West bracket of the NCAA where they would open against UCLA.

Before the NCAA tourney began, the Big Ten and the NCAA each named their Coach of the Year, and Knight won both honors. The Big Ten also named the team MVPs, as voted on by teammates, and May was named as the league's MVP.

The NCAA Tournament

Indiana had ended the regular season undefeated and #1 in the country, but May's loss was obviously significant. Knight said, "I'll always believe that his arm injury at Purdue on February 24 is why the 1974–75 Indiana team isn't among the seven unbeaten NCAA champions."[76] The Hoosiers would play in the Mideast in Lexington, Kentucky, and face UTEP in the first round. Even without May, the game wasn't close, as the Hoosiers sank 17 of 28 second-half field goals to win going away, 78–53.[77]

The next night Michigan nearly ousted UCLA (who would ultimately win the NCAA title, John Wooden's last). The score was tied at 87 at the end of regulation as Michigan missed a shot at the buzzer. In overtime, UCLA pulled away for a 103–91 victory.[78]

Indiana, still undefeated, moved on to the regionals in Dayton where they toppled Oregon State 81–71 behind a 59 percent team field goal average for the game (35 of 59). The Hoosiers would play Kentucky, a 90–73 winner over Central Michigan. There was talk that Scott May would play, possibly even start, just four weeks after breaking his arm.

May did not start, but he did play four minutes and scored two points. "With a cast on his left wrist and the Wildcats playing man-to-man, not zone, May missed his first four shots, turned the ball over three times, and watched

Kentucky's star Kevin Grevey zip past him for seven minutes until Knight pulled him."[79] Kentucky edged the Hoosiers 92–90 to end their thirty-four-game winning streak and avenge a 98–74 loss to Indiana from early December. Kentucky's plan had been to play as aggressively as the Hoosiers, if not more so, and they did. Roy Damer claimed that Kentucky fouled from start to finish in order to deter Indiana.[80] This was not just Damer's view, but, indeed, the Kentucky game plan. Damer said that "Kentucky fouled all game and the officials did little about it and certainly didn't penalize them commensurate to their overzealousness.... (Lou) Soriano and (Robert) Korte called an inept game and should be banned from NCAA tournament competition."[81]

Knight was devastated by the loss, "crying his eyes out, really painfully" in a toilet stall, when he thought the locker room was empty. Freshman forward Mark Haymore, who had forgotten his gym bag, attested to the scene.[82] Knight used the loss the next season for motivation when the Hoosiers played Kentucky early in the season.

Nevertheless, Indiana's season had ended on a very sour note, and there was only next year to look forward to when all the starters would return, and May would have recovered.

Knight and his Hoosiers would get their chances and make the most of them in the next season.

CHAPTER 2

INDIANA ALL THE WAY
Big Ten Basketball between Seasons

Shortly after the NCAA tournament ended in 1975 with the last UCLA victory of John Wooden's career, Big Ten teams were busy changing coaches. Gene Bartow's departure from Illinois, after just three years, to coach UCLA left a number of his players resentful, and the Illini were eager to replace him quickly.[1] Don DeVoe, a former Ohio State player under Fred Taylor—and then-Virginia Tech coach—was announced as the new Illinois coach, but that was a premature prediction made by a number of sportswriters, including Roy Damer of the *Chicago Tribune*. (DeVoe stayed at Virginia Tech but went to Wyoming as head coach the next year.) Two weeks later, Illinois officially announced that its new coach would be Lou Henson of New Mexico State.

Henson was approved by the Illinois Board of Trustees, which did not realize that NMSU was on probation for violating NCAA rules. Illinois athletic director Cecil Coleman didn't inform the board because he was "satisfied Henson was not involved in the violations. The board also expressed a vote of confidence in Coleman."[2]

In the fall, another NCAA investigation broke, this one at Minnesota. Coach Bill Musselman, who had left to coach the San Diego Sails in the American Basketball Association, was involved with an NCAA investigation into more than one hundred alleged recruiting violations in the Gopher basketball program.[3]

In a preseason exhibition game played in Indianapolis, the Indiana Hoosiers crushed the touring Russian national team, 94–78 before 17,377. This was basically the same Russian squad that had defeated the USA for gold at the 1972 Munich Olympics in a controversial game that ended the US streak of Olympic basketball wins since the game had been introduced at the Berlin Olympics in 1936. Indiana exacted revenge in a rough contest with 70 fouls called, 35 on each team.[4] (Both Quinn Buckner and Scott May would see the

Jerry Sichting, All-Big Ten guard at Purdue. *(Courtesy of Purdue University Archives and Special Collections)*

Russian team again in July, when the United States would win the gold medal at the Montreal Olympics and the Soviets the bronze.)

Indiana was named #1 in the preseason AP poll, with Michigan #16, and the Big Ten race was already being conceded to the Hoosiers. Roy Damer, too, saw Michigan as a likely second, led by Rickey Green who, Coach John Orr said, "can do so many things with a basketball." Freshman Phil Hubbard, despite being short for a center (at six feet seven), also excited Orr. Orr noted that Hubbard would be one of the smallest centers in the league but also said, "If he's not the quickest, he's one of the quickest" at the position.[5]

Purdue returned Bruce Parkinson, Walter Jordan, Wayne Walls, and Eugene Parker and added Tom Scheffler to replace the graduated John Garrett. Frosh Jerry Sichting and Kyle Macy looked to be great additions at the guard spots. Michigan State, by contrast, had lost four starters but did return the league's top scorer, Terry Furlow, who had averaged over twenty-one points in Big Ten play the previous season.

Iowa looked like a good team with Dan Frost, Bruce King, and Scott Thompson back to lead the Hawkeyes. Illinois had a new coach in Henson, but they had veteran returnees on the roster. With Bill Musselman's departure, the Minnesota Golden Gophers would be coached by Jim Dutcher, former head coach at Eastern Michigan and, most recently, an assistant to Johnny Orr at Dutcher's alma mater, Michigan. Dutcher hoped that sophomore Mychal Thompson would lift the Gophers into the first division of the conference, with assistance from "Flip" Saunders and Tony Dungy, the latter coming over from the Minnesota football team. Five Minnesota players, including number-two scorer and rebounder Mark Landsberger, were not happy, apparently, with Dutcher's hiring and transferred to other schools.

One early season controversy was the NCAA's cost-saving measure limiting the home team to thirteen players and the travel roster to ten. Bob Knight was vocal in his opposition, and he was joined by North Carolina State's coach, Norm Sloan, who said that the decision would lead to morale problems. Knight predicted that some players might transfer or quit because a coach might be forced to renege on commitments to players.[6] Knight unsuccessfully sued the NCAA to prevent the rule from being enforced.

Preconference Play Begins

In a season-opening game that was significant on many levels, Indiana crushed defending NCAA champion UCLA 84–64 in St. Louis. Scott May, now fully recovered from the broken arm that had ended his previous season, had 33 points; his effort was supported by Kent Benson with 17 and Quinn Buckner with 14.[7] Knight was still excited by the UCLA victory two days later, calling it "kind of a fairy tale experience." Another such experience was probably felt by Tex Winter's Northwestern Wildcats, as they shocked the Kentucky Wildcats 89–77 in McGaw Hall before fifty-five hundred fans—a big crowd for Northwestern. Billy McKinney had 31, Jim Wallace 18, and NU shot 33 of 55 from the field (60 percent) to humble coach Joe B. Hall and his team.[8]

There continued to be a few surprises in the preconference season such as Michigan's loss to Tennessee in Knoxville, 82–81, but the Vols had a tough team with Bernard King's 27 points and Ernie Grunfeld's 22. Phil Hubbard had 27, John Robinson 22, and Rickey Green 12 for the Wolverines in the loss.[9] Despite a few tough losses, the Big Ten was performing very well against all outside competition with a record of 19–5. Bob Knight, still pleased with the UCLA win, "thought his squad will improve. . . . What we will try to do— what we have always tried to do—is simply go out and play up to our potential each time."[10]

Meanwhile, in Minnesota, the proverbial "other shoe" dropped when the university reported 128 cage violations to the NCAA, almost all of them committed under departed coach Bill Musselman. These included inappropriate summer jobs, use of cars, inappropriate air travel, and direct transfers of money totaling $2,500 to $3,000, among the violations.[11]

In another early season "made-for-television" game, Indiana met Kentucky in Louisville. The Wildcats were still smarting from their surprising loss at Northwestern and came out snarling. Indiana was eager to avenge the loss to Kentucky that had knocked the Hoosiers out of the NCAA tourney the previous season, a game that would be called "the most crushing defeat of his (Knight's) career."[12] The contest went back and forth with Kentucky leading by four with just under two minutes to play, but in overtime Indiana put the game away 77–68. The win solidified Indiana's position as #1 in the week's Associated Press poll.[13]

Probably the most unusual Big Ten news that week was that Tex Winter, the new Northwestern head coach, had purchased the Kansas State basketball floor for $7,000 (K-State was installing a new one). Winter had been head coach at K-State for fifteen years (1953–1968) and an assistant coach from 1947 to 1951, so it was obvious that he had warm feelings for the school and the floor, but this seemed a bit extreme. It was not explained what Winter planned to do with the floor.[14] As it turned out, Winter had big plans for McGaw Hall, which was often referred to as "the poorest facility in the Big Ten." Those plans included lowering the court (it had been a raised floor on hard-packed dirt) and adding on the K-State court, which widened the court by forty-four feet and doubled the usable space.[15]

The Holiday Tournament Season

Heading into the holiday tournament season, Indiana was undefeated, Michigan had lost one game by a single point, and the Big Ten was 44–15 as a conference. Minnesota and Iowa were undefeated, Illinois was 6–2, and Wisconsin 5–1. Only Purdue (2–3) was a disappointment, so far.[16] The Illini, in particular, seemed to be rejuvenated under new coach Lou Henson.[17]

Conference performances in various holiday tournaments were impressive. Indiana won the Holiday Festival in Madison Square Garden, Michigan took the Las Vegas Holiday Classic, Michigan State lost to VCU in the finals of the VCU holiday tourney in Richmond, Iowa lost in the Rainbow Classic final to USC, and Purdue finished second to UCLA in the Los Angeles Classic. Other Big Ten teams played well as they prepared for the Big Ten openers on January 3, 1976. Only Michigan State (4–5) had a losing record in nonconference play.

The Big Ten Conference Opens Play

Opening night brought unexpected results. Illinois, a team that looked very much improved, was pounded 84–60 by an Iowa team that had only one loss. Indiana had its hands full with Ohio State before finally prevailing 66–64 in Columbus. In the most exciting game of the evening, Purdue edged Minnesota 111–110 in two overtimes. Mychal Thompson fouled out with 33 points, but Kyle Macy of Purdue was the top scorer for the game with 38, the highest total ever for a Big Ten freshman.[18]

Indiana ripped Northwestern, 78–61, in their next game. Michigan seemed to be getting better as they smashed Minnesota 95–72 despite Mychal Thompson's 26 for the Gophers, while Rickey Green had 32 for the Wolverines.[19]

Terry Furlow made a big impression on the conference when he scored 50 points against Iowa in a 105–88 MSU victory in East Lansing. Just how good was Iowa? And was MSU a team that might contend? It was way too early to do more than speculate.[20]

Indiana came to Ann Arbor to face the Wolverines in an important early conference game. The Hoosiers rose to the occasion, winning 80–74, led by Benson's 33 points on 16 of 18 field-goal shooting. With fortuitous timing, the *Chicago Tribune* ran a feature by Robert Cross on Bob Knight in their *Sunday Magazine* the day after the Michigan win. In that article, Knight discussed his "gruff" behavior and both explained and justified it.[21] Cross noted that Knight's salary of $30,000 a year made him one of the best-paid college coaches in the country. He asked Knight if he thought that his gruffness hurt his team in any way. Knight said that "if it hurt morale, I don't think that we'd be nearly as successful as we are." He continued to note that he yelled at players when they made mistakes and congratulated them on good plays, but felt it was "the things that you're doing poorly that you have to straighten out." As for his noted emphasis on defense, he explained, "Defense can be the most consistent and constant part of the game because you've got more control over it. You can't *will* the ball into the basket, so you work hardest on those things you have the most control over."[22]

The lengthy piece ended with Knight's assertion that "the mental aspect to basketball is to physical as four is to one."[23]

In their next contest, Indiana "held" Terry Furlow to 28 in a 69–57 win in which both Buckner and May fell into foul trouble and played cautiously in the second half. Michigan stayed right on the Hoosiers' heels, sliding by Ohio State 84–81 in Ann Arbor.[24] The two victors were the only Big Ten teams ranked in the latest AP poll: Indiana, holding at #1 and Michigan at #16.

Other teams were having their ups and downs. Lou Henson was pleasing fans and his players as the new Illini coach. Otho Tucker called him "the best coach he's had because he treats everyone the same." Minnesota had lost Mychal Thompson, at least temporarily, because he was accused of selling comp tickets at more than face value, an NCAA violation, but Minnesota was appealing his ineligibility. Losing their leading scorer and rebounder was obviously a huge factor when Minnesota lost to Northwestern the day after Thompson was declared ineligible.

Purdue lost Bruce Parkinson with a broken wrist, but the Boilermakers still managed to hang on to beat Ohio State 84–80, as Purdue remained unbeaten in the conference.[25] Minnesota then caught a break as Thompson was reinstated under a temporary restraining order pending a hearing on January 28, after the NCAA had declared him ineligible for the rest of the season. (Thompson told Minnesota officials that he hadn't known it was against the rules to sell tickets for more than face value.[26])

In a hard-fought battle in Bloomington, Indiana eked out a victory over Purdue 71–67, with May scoring 32.[27] In a surprising development for an undefeated and #1-ranked squad, Bob Knight noted that he might pull starting point guard Quinn Buckner from the starting lineup. The coach felt that "his stamina has been poor," and in the past six games, Buckner had scored just 27 points and shot 31 percent from the floor. The previous year he had shot 56 percent, leading all Big Ten guards in field goal percentage.[28]

The drama did not seem to adversely affect the Hoosiers as they won their twenty-sixth Big Ten game in a row with an 85–76 victory in Minnesota. But it wasn't an easy victory. The Gophers led 50–40 at the half, but the Hoosiers rallied in the second half. Michigan kept pace with an 84–80 win at Purdue.[29]

Indiana tied the consecutive conference win mark at Iowa 88–73, with Buckner not starting for the second game in a row but coming off the bench to play tough defense. Iowa coach Lute Olson said that the IU defense "just wears you down ... [it's] physical and they never stop coming at you."[30]

Indiana easily beat Wisconsin 114–61 to set a new Big Ten consecutive victory mark of twenty-eight wins and maintain their hold on #1 in the national polls. Michigan was upset by Illinois, on a tip-in with thirty-eight seconds left.[31] Despite the loss, the Wolverines remained in the top twenty at #15.

Michigan came back with wins against Iowa and Wisconsin before facing the Hoosiers, once again, this time in Bloomington. In a sloppy but intense contest, Indiana triumphed in overtime, 72–67. Johnny Orr said, "I can't tell you how disappointed I am. ... I thought our defense was excellent. We couldn't ask for more than what our players gave us today."[32] Michigan sealed its own fate with twenty-eight turnovers in the game.[33]

Knight became a sort of "national ogre" when he grabbed Jim Wisman, who had thrown away two passes in a row, by the jersey during a time-out, "his face mottled in rage." The next morning, a photo of this episode made the front page of the *Indianapolis Star* and was covered by papers nationwide. Most of the players were not surprised by Knight's action as such incidents had been a common occurrence in IU practices. But this was the first time this kind of behavior was captured in a game photo and in the *Bloomington Herald*. Knight did apologize three days later for his temper tantrum and showed that he bore Wisman no ill will by playing him for twenty-four minutes in the next game, as Indiana took out their aggression on Michigan State, 85–70.[34]

Meanwhile, Purdue awoke to win its third in a row, blasting Northwestern, 86–58. Michigan stayed solidly in second with a 90–66 victory over a disappointing Ohio State team. The Wolverines were 9–3, behind IU's 11–0 and ahead of Purdue, who was at 7–4.

Other teams had some rough patches, too. Wisconsin was 2–10 in the conference and 8–12 for the season, which led to head coach John Powless's resignation at the end of the season. He had had just two winning seasons, and his overall record at the end of his tenure was 88–108, simply not good enough to compete in the Big Ten.[35]

Indiana continued to win, and Michigan stayed right on their heels, although the Wolverines did drop two games on last-second tip-ins to Illinois and Indiana, respectively, before crushing Michigan State, 81–64 in East Lansing. Johnny Orr noted, "We're at our best when we're running."[36]

Purdue pounded Ohio State 98–73 as Fred Taylor closed out what had been a sterling coaching career. Rick Talley explained why Taylor's scruples demanded that he resign at age fifty-one. Noted Talley, Taylor simply refused to cheat to get players. He hadn't wanted to resign but was given the "win or get out" ultimatum, a sad comment after what Taylor had accomplished in his years of coaching. Talley felt that Taylor had received little support from his athletic director after the infamous Minnesota attack on the OSU players at the end of the 1972 season. Taylor never fully recovered from that.[37]

What seemed to be the last hurdle in Indiana's Big Ten title quest was a game against Purdue, a winner of four in a row and just a game behind Michigan. Purdue had narrowly lost to Indiana 71–67 in Bloomington, and this game was a chance for redemption and an end to the IU win streak. The game was all that it was hyped to be, but the result was a 74–71 Indiana victory.[38]

Michigan established itself as the clear #2 power in the league with a 92–81 victory over Purdue. In East Lansing, Terry Furlow set an all-time MSU season scoring mark as he scored 27 in the 69–59 win over Illinois. Iowa continued Ohio State's sad season, winning in Columbus 69–66 with six straight free throws in the last forty-nine seconds. It was OSU's sixteenth loss of the season, the most ever for a Buckeye squad.[39]

Indiana clinched at least a title tie in their next contest, defeating Iowa 101–81. It was heartening for Quinn Buckner, who had a season-high 24, as he recovered from what was termed a "long illness." The win broke Iowa's modest five-game win streak. The rest of the conference performed pretty much as expected with Minnesota crushing Ohio State 89–73 and Michigan routing Illinois 90–75. Only MSU was a mild surprise, defeating Purdue 89–76. In Michigan's victory, there was an interesting "forewarning" as assistant coach Bill Frieder led the team while Johnny Orr was out with the flu. In 1980, Orr would resign to take the reins at Iowa State and Frieder would become head coach.[40]

Three nights later Indiana won the title outright as Scott May soared for forty-one points in a 96–67 win in Madison over the Badgers. Michigan then clinched second in the conference and Purdue third, with wins over Iowa and Illinois.[41]

The title was won, but the season wasn't over yet. Indiana still had to play Northwestern, whom they beat soundly, 76–63, and Ohio State, whom they overwhelmed 96–67. In the latter contest, Knight had very mixed emotions, since it was his former coach Fred Taylor's final game, closing his OSU coaching career with a record of 297–157.[42]

This great Indiana senior class included Buckner, Tom Abernathy, and Jim Crews and was 108–12 as well as the winner of four Big Ten championships or co-championships. Scott May and Bobby Wilkerson were with them the last three years, and those teams were 86–6. No Big Ten team ever matched those records.[43] Indiana was also the first Big Ten team to win all their thirty-six Big Ten games two years in a row, as well as fifty-six in a row in the regular season. Despite Indiana's blowout of OSU, Knight said the game was special for him, since he had played for Taylor and "wasn't very pleased with the way Ohio State had treated him in his last few years."[44]

The final Big Ten standings had IU at 18–0 and Michigan at 14–4. Purdue was third at 11–7. Scott May was, again, the Big Ten's MVP.

Tournament Time

As Indiana headed into the thirty-two-team NCAA tourney, ranked #1 and undefeated, Roy Damer tried to find out what qualities this team had, besides physical talent, that made them so good. One interesting aspect was that Coach Knight had help in recruiting by letting his players speak to the character of recruits and assess whether the current players would want the recruits as teammates. Steve Green played a bigger part in recruiting than Knight, as the recruits spent more time with the current players and less time "having a good time" while on campus.[45]

By contrast, a story appeared the next day reporting that Minnesota was put on NCAA probation for three years as a result of ninety-eight recruiting violations from 1971 to 1975 while Bill Musselman was head coach. The Gophers would not be allowed in any postseason tournaments and could award only three new scholarships for 1976–77 and 1977–78.[46]

The NCAA selected Indiana as the #1 seed in the Mideast for the tournament but also picked Michigan as a #4 seed in the Midwest. Indiana would open against St. John's in South Bend, Indiana, on the Notre Dame court. Michigan would start with Wichita State in Denton, Texas, on the court of the University of North Texas. Roy Damer called Michigan "perhaps the most underrated team in the tournament." His observation would prove very prescient.[47] On the eve of the tournament, the Associated Press announced its national Coach of the Year Award. For the second straight year, it went to Bob Knight, ahead of Tom Young of unbeaten Rutgers, and Al McGuire of Marquette.[48]

Both Big Ten teams started the tournament with victories. Indiana won in a 90–70 rout while Michigan eked out their game 74–73 over Wichita State. In the former contest, Scott May had 33, and Kent Benson had 20 with 13 rebounds to lead the Hoosiers.[49]

Before the next game, Big Ten coaching situations were in flux. Gus Ganakas was fired at Michigan State after seven years as head coach. He

Bill Cofield, the first Black coach in the Big Ten. (*Courtesy of University of Wisconsin Athletics*)

compiled a record of 89–84. Ganakas expressed surprise, thinking that "the review of the season would merit a reward." As a tenured employee, he was reassigned in the sports department as an assistant athletic director. At Wisconsin, Bill Cofield was hired to replace John Powless. Cofield, thirty-six, had been an assistant coach at Virginia. He would be the first African American head coach of a major sport in the Big Ten. He agreed to a five-year contract with a $25,000 salary for the first year.[50]

Meanwhile back at the NCAA tourney, there was speculation about who should be favored in a prospective tournament match-up between Indiana and Marquette. John Powless, whose Wisconsin team had played both squads twice, favored Indiana because of their physical strength. Both would need to win two games against top opponents in order to meet in the Mideast Finals in Baton Rouge.[51]

In Louisville, there was action both on and off the court for the Big Ten. In on-court action, all five Michigan starters scored in double figures, but the many steals by the Wolverines were crucial in topping Notre Dame 80–76. Off the court, Indiana's attorneys got a temporary restraining order to allow the Indiana game to be televised to Bloomington and Indianapolis, despite the fact that there had been no sellout in Louisville.[52]

Indiana also won, beating Alabama 74–69 after trailing 69–68 with four minutes to go. Marquette achieved a 62–57 victory over Western Michigan.[53] This set up a battle between Indiana and highly ranked Marquette for the Mideast title and a berth in the Final Four. Michigan would take on Missouri for the Midwest title.

Both Big Ten teams were triumphant in tough battles. Indiana won by nine, 65–56, behind Benson's 18 and May's 15, but the difference was largely field goal percentage. Indiana was 27 of 47 (57 percent), while Marquette was 25 of 66 (38 percent). Michigan won 95–88, behind their big three: Green (23 points), Robinson (21 points, 16 rebounds), and Hubbard (20 points, 18 rebounds).[54]

In the West, UCLA defeated Arizona, 82–66; and in the East, Rutgers was champ after beating VMI, 91–75. The Final Four was set, with Michigan to face Rutgers and Indiana to meet UCLA in Philadelphia. UCLA was looking to avenge their 84–64 loss to IU in November, while Michigan hoped to hand Rutgers its first loss and to then defeat Indiana, whom they had lost to twice during the Big Ten season. This would be the first Final Four with two unbeaten teams, as well as two teams from the same conference.[55]

The tournament was producing big money, with television revenue at $2.5 million and $5 million assured by 1979. First-round teams would be receiving $25,000 each, second-round teams would bring $70,000 each, and the Final Four teams, $140,000 each. The financial growth of the tourney was summarized by Roy Damer, who noted that in 1953, the entire tournament generated $159,000, which grew to $347,000 by 1960 and $1.03 million by 1969. The prior year (1975), $3.4 million was generated with $133,000 to each Final Four team. In the Big Ten, 50 percent of the team receipts went to the actual team that played, and the other 50 percent was split with the rest of the conference.[56]

The Ohio State coaching vacancy was still a prime topic, and Don DeVoe was no longer viewed as the likely choice. Instead, Eldon Miller, who did not play for Fred Taylor, was now seen as the candidate of choice. Miller, who had played and coached at Wittenberg, was the coach at Western Michigan and had a record of 86–68 in six years, including a record of 25–3 in 1975–76. He was announced as coach on March 27.[57]

The Final Four became an all–Big Ten affair after Michigan crushed Rutgers 86–70 and Indiana repeated its early season victory by defeating UCLA 65–51. Bob Knight said that an all–Big Ten final was "an indication of the kind of basketball we play in the Big Ten."[58] Michigan's win was aided by Robinson with 20 points and 16 rebounds and abetted by Hubbard and Green with 16 points each. In assessing the play of junior college transfer Rickey Green and freshman Phil Hubbard, Johnny Orr said, "We had no idea Green and Hubbard would play so well."[59] For Indiana, the key was defense, as UCLA shot just 34 percent from the floor. IU scoring was spread around, with Benson getting 16, while May and Abernathy had 14 apiece. Bobby Wilkerson had 19 rebounds from his guard spot.[60]

During the one-day hiatus between the semis and the final, there was more Big Ten news. First, Johnny Orr was named Coach of the Year by the National Association of Basketball Coaches (NABC). Second, the Big Ten was assured of its fifth NCAA title (Indiana, 1940, 1953; Wisconsin, 1941; Ohio State, 1960),[61] and Indiana would try to become the seventh team to win the NCAA title with an undefeated record. The others had been University of San Francisco in 1956, University of North Carolina in 1957, and four UCLA teams: 1964, 1967, 1972, and 1973.

Indiana handled Michigan for the third time in the season and came away with the NCAA championship by a score of 86–68. Kent Benson had 25 points for the Hoosiers and was named Most Outstanding Player of the Final Four.[62] But Scott May led the scoring with 26, and Quinn Buckner had 16. Rickey Green led the Wolverine scoring with 18.[63] In his postgame remarks, Knight praised Fred Taylor (his college coach), Clair Bee, and Pete Newell (Hall of Fame coaches who had become informal mentors to Knight), John Havlicek (a former OSU teammate of Knight's who had spoken to his squad that day), as well as the athletic directors who had employed him: Ray Murphy at the US Military Academy and Bill Orwig at Indiana.[64]

The season was over, but Big Ten action continued. On April 5, Michigan State announced its new head coaches. Darryl Rogers would replace Denny Stoltz in football and Jud Heathcote, former Montana head coach, would be the new basketball coach, succeeding Gus Ganakas. Heathcote would receive $25,000 per year.[65] Heathcote said that "we're hoping to be competitive as soon as possible"[66] and that his primary task, once on campus, was "to recruit Earvin Johnson, better known as Magic, a superstar in the making from nearby Lansing."[67]

The Big Ten had shown its superiority in 1975–76,[68] but the Hoosiers would lose key players the next season. Michigan was already being touted as the favorite for 1976–77.[69] But that was next year. Meanwhile, Indiana and the Big Ten had time to savor a season to remember.

CHAPTER 3

COACHING IN THE 1970s IN THE BIG TEN
The Knight Effect

Bobby Knight was a new and relatively unexpected choice to lead the Indiana Hoosiers when he was hired for the 1971–72 season on March 27, 1971. There was no question that he had achieved great success as head coach at United States Military Academy (known as West Point or Army) despite facing the unusual strictures that Army placed on its potential recruits. At Army, Knight's teams, limited by military height requirement of six feet, six inches went 152–102 in his six years as head coach, with no NCAA tournament appearances. He had shown that he could shape winning teams, despite the lack of a real superstar. Mike Silliman, a six-feet-six forward (recruited under head coach Tates Locke, who had hired Knight as an assistant coach, then worked for Knight as an assistant coach at Indiana from 1987–89), had led Army to the NIT semifinals in 1964, 1965, and 1966, Knight's only tournament head coaching appearances at a time when the NCAA tournament was limited to twenty-two to twenty-five teams, conference champions, and a few top independents.

At Army, Knight set about altering the team's play and that of college basketball at large through his emphasis on intense defense. Knight hired a number of young coaches who went on to head coaching jobs and brought the lessons they had learned to their new assignments. Before that, however, Knight took the head coaching position at Indiana University, and a number of his Army assistants followed him there. The style of play Knight emphasized could directly or indirectly be from his experience as a player at Ohio State (1959–62), which included an NCAA championship and two runner-up finishes, under Fred Taylor. The most significant change in teams and leagues was in the intensity that the coaches brought to their teams and the "ball-man-you" defensive scheme that Knight and his disciples practiced.[1] Some of this Knight picked up from Taylor; some was refined by an assistant coach, Al Lobalbo, hired from the successful Belleville (New Jersey) High School team.

What effect did Knight have on coaching philosophy and practice from 1965 until his exit from Indiana in 2000? Dave Bliss was Bob Knight's "enlisted assistant" at Army and then went with him when Knight was hired at Indiana. Bliss asserted that, before Knight, the coaches in the Big Ten were a more "laid back" club of competitors but that Knight's entrance into the league as a coach ramped up the intensity and caused the rest of the conference's universities to hire better coaches who could recruit more aggressively and compete more intensely. "No one had Knight's recruiting and coaching intensity," said Bliss, "but, over time, the entire conference changed."[2]

The rest of this chapter examines two major issues: first, coaching hires in the Big Ten and where/how they were found and selected; second, recruiting of players, an increasingly important nationwide function of coaches and their assistants, especially after John Wooden recruited his national "superclass" of 1965 that led to national titles in 1967–69 at UCLA and continued through Wooden's retirement after the 1975 national championship.

Knight's hiring broke a pattern at Indiana that extended back to 1924, when Everett Dean was hired to be the head coach of his alma mater where he had starred from 1918 to 1921 and was named a Helms All-American in 1921. After three years as the head coach at Carleton College, Dean returned to Bloomington, where he remained as head coach until 1938. Dean was succeeded by Branch McCracken, another Indiana All-American who had starred from 1928 to 1930 and then spent eight years as head coach at Ball State University in Muncie, just over one hundred miles away. McCracken was the "dean" of Big Ten coaches when he retired in 1965 after twenty-seven years. He was succeeded by one of his former players, Lou Watson, who had been an All-America while playing for Indiana from 1947 to 1950. Watson coached freshman ball at IU before becoming a McCracken assistant in 1958.

Watson won the Big Ten championship in 1967 (with mostly McCracken recruits), but his overall record in Bloomington (65–60) was not up to Indiana's standard. He resigned before the end of the 1970–71 season, pressured by alumni concerns about lack of wins, player claims of favoritism by coaches, and his own health issues. Watson transferred into the IU athletic administration before retiring in 1987. Jerry Oliver, who had filled in for Watson twice when Watson had health issues, seemed to be his natural successor, but Indiana decided on Ohio State alum Knight.

With his success at Indiana, Knight had a significant effect on the Big Ten and on college coaching more broadly. His top assistant coaches (and their subsequent institutions where they became head coaches) included:

- Steve Alford (SW Missouri, Iowa, Arizona, UCLA, Nevada)
- Bob Bender (Illinois State, Washington)
- Dave Bliss (SMU, Oklahoma, New Mexico, Baylor)
- Jim Crews (Evansville, Army, St. Louis)
- Dan Dakich (Bowling Green)
- Gale Daugherty (Ohio Northern)
- Mike Davis (Indiana, University of Alabama–Birmingham, Texas Southern, Detroit Mercy)
- Don DeVoe (Wyoming, Tennessee, Florida, Navy)
- Bob Donewald (Illinois State, Western Michigan)
- Gerry Gimelstob (George Washington)
- Mike Krzyzewski (Army, Duke)
- Al Lobalbo (Fairleigh Dickinson)
- Tom Miller (Cornell, Colorado, Army)
- Lionel Sinn (Southern Indiana)
- Kohn Smith (Utah State)
- Ray Swetalla (Marycrest, Wisconsin-Milwaukee)
- Royce Waltman (DePauw, Indianapolis, Indiana State)
- Bobby Weltich (Mississippi, Texas, Florida International, South Alabama)
- Joby Wright (Miami of Ohio, Wyoming)

Knight had been a player and a student of basketball under Fred Taylor, who coached OSU for eighteen seasons and took home seven Big Ten championships. According to Dave Bliss, Knight learned how to coach talented players.[3] Taylor returned to OSU in 1951 as a volunteer assistant basketball coach under Floyd Stahl and became the university's first full-time freshmen baseball and basketball coach in 1953. As the chief OSU recruiter, Taylor got to know high school coaches and prospects as he crisscrossed the state of Ohio. Taylor was Stahl's obvious replacement because of Taylor's insider knowledge of the players on the OSU varsity and of Ohio State athletics overall.

But Taylor had lost his love for the game and chose to retire in 1976, four years after he had previously stated he would step down as coach. (He put in his resignation after members of the University of Minnesota basketball team attacked the Ohio State squad in 1972.)[4] Soon the university was looking elsewhere for a head coach. Perhaps influenced by Indiana's hiring of Knight, Ohio State also found an "inside/outsider" in Ohio native Eldon Miller, who had played and coached at Wittenberg in Springfield, Ohio, before finding great success at Western Michigan University. There he went 86–68 in seven seasons but 25–3 in 1975–76, taking his underrated squad to the NCAA Sweet Sixteen. OSU had broken its tradition of hiring alumni but retained the practice of hiring coaches from the state of Ohio.

Fred Taylor, Ohio State coach, 1959–1976. (*Courtesy of Ohio State Athletics*)

During this period, the Minnesota coaching situation was in turmoil. Longtime Minnesota and Minneapolis Lakers coach John Kundla, Gopher alum, had retired from coaching at the age of sixty-one, and he was succeeded by Bill Fitch in 1968. Fitch was a young coaching vagabond, who had recently gone 18–7 at Bowling Green University before accepting the Minnesota position. An Iowan, he seemed to have good skills and Midwestern connections, but after two seasons, he snatched the opportunity to be an NBA head coach for the expansion Cleveland Cavaliers in 1970.

Minnesota, caught by surprise, hired alum George Hanson, who was an assistant coach for Fitch after being initially hired by John Kundla. The fit was not good for either Hanson or the Gophers: the team went 11–13; and Hanson was not that interested in running a big-time basketball program, his real passion being adaptive physical education. Thus, a parting of the ways after the 1970–71 season was mutually agreed upon. Now the Minnesota athletic administration had to make a decision on whether to continue pursuing coaching prospects with a state or university connection or follow the new pattern of looking for a young, dynamic outsider to lead the basketball team. They chose the latter, hiring thirty-one-year-old Ohio native Bill Musselman, who had been head coach at Ashland College for the previous six seasons, compiling a record of 109–20, setting a record for defense, averaging 33.9 points allowed per game, and earning a reputation for intensity both on and off the court.

The University of Iowa also followed the "young coach with no prior institutional affiliation" approach in 1974 with the hiring of Lute Olsen as head coach. A native of North Dakota, Olsen had coached at Minnesota and California high schools and then for four years at Long Beach City College and one year at Long Beach State, where he led his team to a 24–2 record and the Big West title. He was thirty-nine when selected as the new head coach of the Hawkeyes.

Three Big Ten teams (Illinois, Northwestern, and Purdue) followed what one might call a middle path when their coaching positions opened in the early 1970s. The latter two hired former NBA coaches who also had extensive college coaching experience outside the Midwest. Tex Winter was fifty-one when tapped as the new coach at Northwestern, coming directly from the Houston Rockets after stints as head coach at Marquette, the University of Washington, and Kansas State. Fred Schaus, forty-seven, had also coached in the NBA after enjoying six years as head coach at West Virginia, before being hired by Purdue in 1972. Jerry Sichting, who played for Schaus for three of his four years at Purdue, referred to him as "old school" in his defensive and offensive sets and patterns. After Schaus left in 1978, Purdue hired Lee Rose from the University of North Carolina–Charlotte, who stayed at Purdue only two years before going to South Florida. Sichting emphasized what a great coach Rose was and how surprising it was that Purdue didn't do more to retain him. Sichting noted that Rose had great ideas, employed a variety of offensive and defensive strategies, and related well to players. Rose

Lee Rose, Purdue coach, 1978–1980. *(Courtesy of Purdue University Archives and Special Collections)*

worked them harder, got them in great physical condition, conceived a variety of 1–3–1 traps on defense, and taught his team to play deliberate or "fast paced" ball.[5]

When Rose left after only two seasons, Gene Keady, a native of Kansas and the head coach at Western Kentucky, was hired. He did not fit the Big

Ten alum nor former pro pattern, but the hire proved to be visionary in the long term: Keady remained at Purdue for twenty-five seasons, retiring in 2005 after winning six Big Ten titles and being named National Coach of the Year five times.

Illinois selected Gene Bartow, who had coached with great success at the Missouri high school level, as well as at three colleges, including Memphis State. Bartow led Memphis State to Missouri Valley Conference championships and to the 1973 NCAA championship game. He had excellent high school connections and was one of the first Illinois coaches to recruit African Americans from Chicago during his one year in Champaign. Then he was lured to UCLA to replace John Wooden after an 8–18 record in 1974–75 at Illinois.

Lou Henson, who replaced Bartow, also had no prior Illinois connections. But Henson was, at forty-three, another "young" college coach on the way up when the Illini hired him. He had spent four years as head coach at Hardin-Simmons and nine years at New Mexico State before coming to Illinois.

In 1976, the University of Wisconsin set off on a new course for the Big Ten and its basketball coaches by hiring Bill Cofield, a thirty-six-year-old African American assistant coach at the University of Virginia under head coach Terry Holland. Cofield had no prior affiliation with the University of Wisconsin or the state. He had been a high school coach in Cleveland and a head coach at three different historically Black colleges and universities (HBCUs) before taking the head coaching and athletic director jobs at the predominantly white College of Racine in 1973, where his assistant coach was Bo Ryan, the future Wisconsin coach. Unfortunately, the College of Racine was on very shaky financial footing and closed in 1974; Cofield moved to the University of Virginia (along with Ryan) as an assistant coach. There was some irony in Wisconsin's hiring of the first African American basketball coach, since the Badgers were the last Big Ten school to integrate their basketball roster with the addition of Ken Barnes in 1963. The hope was that Cofield would recruit top African American players, especially from Cleveland, because of his contacts; however, success did not materialize. Cofield was fired in 1982 after compiling a record of 63–101, with his highest Big Ten finish a tie for seventh in 1976–77 and only one season above .500 (1979–80). A year after being fired, Cofield died of cancer in Madison aged forty-three.

These changes at Wisconsin would not have occurred had the Wisconsin administration not jumped the gun in 1968 after offering the head coaching position to Bob Knight. Knight tentatively accepted, but he wanted a bit more time to check with his mentors and consider the offer. "He was all set to go to

Wisconsin after his third season (at Army) in the spring of 1968, but backed out when the athletic director, Ivy Williamson, announced it before Knight gave him a final commitment."[6] Instead of Knight, the university hired John Powless, who was also the head tennis coach. Powless was "a real gentleman," and that made his recruiting of top players that much easier, according to Dale Koehler, who played for him from 1972 to 1976; all schools offered the same package to potential student-athletes.[7] That assessment was replicated by Brian Colbert, who called Powless "a good man" who was a "major reason why I chose Wisconsin, (admiring) his personality, values, respect from his peers in the Big 10 and throughout the nation, his honesty and his loyalty."[8]

Cofield and Ryan successfully recruited James Gregory, Joe Chrnelich, and Arnold Gaines but neglected the top returning players in order to play the new recruits. Rather than blending his team, Cofield alienated some of the older players and lost them. Brian Colbert, an African American and also the leading returning scorer, left the team and the university and finished his career at Carthage College, a Division III school. Al Rudd, second-leading returning scorer in 1976–77, lost his starting position and also left the team. Steve Yoder, head coach at Ball State took the Wisconsin position after Cofield was relieved of his duties. Yoder had no prior Wisconsin connections, but he did possess a solid Midwest background as a high school and college coach, most recently at Ball State, where he was head coach from 1977 to 1982. He led Wisconsin to its first postseason tournaments in forty years (the NIT) in both 1988–89 and 1990–91.

At Michigan, Johnny Orr had taken the Wolverine head job in 1968 after serving for four years as an assistant coach of the Wolverines under Dave Strack. Orr was a native of Illinois who had starred at the University of Illinois in his freshman year before joining the US Navy and fighting in World War II. Rather than return to the Illini after the war, he enrolled at Beloit College, where he received his degree and played under Dolph Stanley, his high school coach. Stanley had convinced other members of Orr's Taylorville (Illinois) state high school champions to enroll at Beloit—most notably Ron Bontemps, who captained the 1952 US Olympic basketball team, and John Erickson, who was Wisconsin head coach from 1959 to 1968.

In 1959, Orr was hired as an assistant coach at Wisconsin. Then in 1963 he was hired as head coach at the University of Massachusetts, where his team went 39–33 in three seasons. Orr had made a name for himself as John Erickson's top recruiter and as a scout for other coaches, namely Joe Lapchick at St. John's. Massachusetts hoped to capitalize on Orr's reputation.[9]

In 1967 Orr began his tenure as an assistant coach for Dave Strack, an appointment that led to Orr's hiring as head coach when Strack became business manager of the Michigan athletic department in 1968 when as the department reorganized under athletic director Don Canham following the retirement of Fritz Crisler.[10] Orr would remain in Ann Arbor through the 1979–80 season, and then he was hired as head coach at Iowa State. He was almost immediately succeeded by Bill Frieder, one of his assistant coaches and a Michigan alum (having earned two degrees there) in addition to serving seven years as an assistant to both Orr and Strack.

Orr's team enjoyed playing for him. C. J. Kupec said that "playing for Johnny Orr was like playing for your dad."[11] Orr's practices, unlike those of most other coaches at the time, were relatively short, no more than ninety minutes, but the players ran the whole time. Steve Grote believed that his team was fresher for games since they had not slogged through three-hour practices four or five times a week.[12] Kupec agreed, claiming that "we were the best conditioned team of any that I was ever on."[13]

Michigan State's approach to coaching hires was a combination of the patterns followed elsewhere. In 1950 the Spartans persuaded a West Coaster, Pete Newell, who had just taken his University of San Francisco team to the NIT championship, to take the MSU head coaching position. At thirty-five, Newell was one of the relatively young coaching phenoms, and he led the Spartans for four seasons before returning to the West Coast as coach at the University of California at Berkeley. The Spartans looked past their own region again to snare Fordy Anderson, an Indiana native, who had played and starred at Stanford before and after World War II. He then found coaching success at Drake and Bradley, taking the latter squad to the NCAA and NIT runner-up position in 1950.

When Anderson left MSU in 1965, former Michigan State assistant coach John Bennington, who had coached under both Pete Newell and Anderson, was hired. Bennington had left MSU in 1956 to become head coach at Drake for two seasons, and then at St. Louis University for seven, leading the Billikens to four NIT berths (at a time when that tournament's status was more widely respected than today). Unfortunately, Bennington died of a heart attack at age forty-seven, while jogging in MSU's Jenison Fieldhouse, and Gus Ganakas, a former player and assistant coach for the Spartans (1966–69) was hired because of his experience and contacts in the state of Michigan.

After compiling a record of 89–84 in seven seasons, Ganakas was relieved of his coaching duties on March 16, 1976, the same day that Cofield was hired at Wisconsin. Ganakas was "chiefly criticized for poor recruiting" and, as a tenured employee, was reassigned to assistant athletic director in the athletic department. Ganakas said that the reassignment was "a surprise" and that he "thought the review of the season would merit a reward."[14]

The reassignment of Ganakas left MSU with a choice. Having tried the MSU assistant coach / Michigan State alumnus path and finding it wanting, the Spartans' new athletic director, Joseph Kearney, chose the successful outsider Jud Heathcote as the next coach. Kearney had just been hired from the same position at the University of Washington, so he was familiar with Heathcote's successes at Washington State as an assistant basketball coach and, for the previous five years, as head coach at the University of Montana. Heathcote was forty-eight but had experience and energy, as well as a strong supporter in Kearney. He was named head coach on April 6, 1976, less than a month after Ganakas was reassigned and the same day that Darryl Rogers was named head football coach. Heathcote would receive $25,000 per year as his salary.[15]

The Duties of a Coach

Obviously, a coach's job is to coach, but in college, a key to a coach's success is recruiting. Without good players, success is unlikely, so finding the best players and convincing them to come to one's institution is a matter of convincing seventeen- and eighteen-year-old young men why a particular institution is the place for them to matriculate and play basketball. Since all schools are officially limited by the NCAA as to what they can offer a prospective student-athlete, recruiters must rely on other factors. These would include the beauty of the campus, the quality of one's education, how the player would fit with the program, and how the program might prepare him for a professional career (which many high school basketball players expect would be their next step after college). A lot of this was shaped by the high school prospect's perception of and relationship to the assistant coach, who was doing the recruiting and was key in securing a young athlete's promise to matriculate at a particular university.

A big difference in the "old" Big Ten and the new one that came with Knight's arrival was the emphasis on recruiting. Knight got into schools and homes not just via reports and letters to kids: "We worked hard at recruiting; we worked twice as hard," said Knight. In recruiting, Indiana sought great players with great character—players who were interested in winning as a team and not just for personal glory. In turn, players "had great faith in Knight, but he drove them together."[16]

Another big factor for young recruits was the desire to have family and friends see them play, this at a time when few college basketball games were televised other than on weekends and during the postseason tournaments. Most prospective college players grew up hoping to star in the high school state tournament, often held at the state flagship university's arena; most programs in the 1970s still offered the opportunity to play at those prestigious state venues.

This commitment to localism was still in place when Knight arrived in Bloomington. In 1960 Ohio State won the Big Ten and NCAA championships. The OSU roster, headed by Jerry Lucas, John Havlicek, and Mel Nowell, had sixteen listed players, with all but one (Gary Milliken of Waynesburg, Pennsylvania, just east of the Ohio border) from Ohio. In 1965 Indiana's roster was composed almost exclusively of players from the state of Indiana, except for five nonstarters. This was the common pattern both in the Big Ten as well as nationally.

But when Knight came to Indiana, he pushed his assistants to work harder and look farther afield for top talent. Dave Bliss recalled piling into a car with Weltich, Gimelstob, and Smith and dropping each of them off at a different high school. They'd meet with players, watch a game, and then head back to Bloomington. That doesn't sound unusual by today's standards but was not common practice then.[17]

A new factor to be considered was race. The civil rights movement in the mid-1950s and 1960s began to slowly result in wider recruitment of African American players; that effort accelerated after the success of teams like Cincinnati, Loyola of Chicago, and Texas Western in that period, all of which had recruited Black players. Certainly, one of the most impactful recruitment years at one institution was accomplished at UCLA by John Wooden and his staff. In 1965, the "fabulous frosh" class (freshmen could not play varsity ball until 1972) included future stars Lew Alcindor from New York City and Lucius Allen from Kansas City. When UCLA won national championships in 1964, 1965, 1967–73, and 1975, it certainly had to influence coaches and institutions to seek players nationally, as well as to more aggressively recruit African Americans.

These lessons were not lost on the new Big Ten coaches of the 1970s as the conference had been integrated with African American players since 1963. But Knight more aggressively recruited talented Black players. Knight's first recruiting class included two African Americans—Quinn Buckner, from the Chicago area, and Scott May, from Sandusky, Ohio, who would both end up being key players. Bobby Wilkerson, an African American from Anderson, Indiana, also joined the team. Knight was able to maintain his program's superiority without extending beyond Indiana, Illinois, and Ohio because of the successful recruiting by assistant coaches Bob Donewald and Bob Weltich (who were former high school coaches from the region and had great contacts), and assistants Dave Bliss and Mike Krzyzewski (a native Chicagoan), who both came with Knight from Army. Indiana University's reluctance to recruit African Americans became a thing of the past with Knight's arrival. The successful recruitment of Ray Tolbert, Landon Turner, and Isiah Thomas continued this trend into the 1980s when all three joined Knight, from Anderson (IN), Indianapolis, and Chicago, respectively.

Other Big Ten schools followed this pattern. Gene Bartow at Illinois followed the first efforts of his predecessor, Harv Schmidt, by pursuing African Americans from the Chicago area and hiring Tony Yates as an assistant coach. Yates had been a starter on the two-time University of Cincinnati Bearcats that won back-to-back NCAA championships in 1961 and 1962 with four African American starters. After Lou Henson came on as Illini coach, he continued this pattern, recruiting from Chicago and Peoria, as well as expanding to include African Americans from Grandview, Texas (James Griffin); West Palm Beach, Florida (Derek Harper); and Flint, Michigan (Craig Tucker).

Under coach Bill Perigo, Michigan had not had great success at signing top African Americans and probably didn't make a huge effort to do so. But Dave Strack began to change that with an impact player, Bill Buntin, from Detroit. Buntin's presence greatly influenced the later signings of Oliver Darden from Detroit and Cazzie Russell from Chicago's Carver High School. Carver would also produce Ken Maxey, who followed Russell to Michigan in 1966. Chief recruiter for Dave Strack and Johnny Orr in the late 1960s and early 1970s was assistant coach Fred Snowden, an African American who had played at Northwestern High School in Detroit (as well as Wayne State before a coaching stint at his old high school) before being hired by Strack.

At Michigan State, Greg Kelser was already on the team when Jud Heathcote was hired, but Heathcote and his staff managed to convince two other African Americans, hometown high school heroes Jay Vincent and Earvin Johnson, to stay in town and combine with Kelser to lead the Spartans to the NCAA title in 1979.

Other Big Ten schools tried to emulate this pattern. Northwestern had recruited Chicago Marshall High product Jim Pitts after he led his team to the Illinois high school championship two years in a row in 1960 and 1961. A gradual progression of African American players began to arrive at Northwestern after Pitts. The 1961 and 1962 NCAA champion Ohio State Buckeyes had an African American starter named Mel Nowell. At Iowa, George Peeples started in the early 1960s. Two years later, Sam Williams and Gerry Jones led the Hawks in scoring. Purdue had no African American players of note until Herm Gilliam led the team in scoring in 1966–67. At Wisconsin Ken Barnes began in 1963 and was followed by Joe Franklin a year later.

Finally, Minnesota had Archie Clark and Lou Hudson starting in 1963–64. Slow but sure progress.

Recruiting and Retaining Players

Of course, each coach had their own ways of recruiting (personal visits, local contacts, etc.), but the first step was to identify players and how they might fit into a particular program. Such identification would come in a number of forms. One way was through summer basketball camps held on campuses for various age groups. Most of the camps were linked with the head coach leading each camp, but almost all were run by an assistant coach or former assistant who now had full-time employment as camp director with other athletic duties worked in. The head coach would usually make a daily appearance at these camps, staying from a few minutes to much of the day, depending on his and the camp's schedule. The important thing was "face time": the head coach had to be seen and needed to interact in some way with campers, including observing scrimmages and seeing how players performed in various situations. One variable that could not be controlled, of course, was the physical growth of a camper from year to year. A young star center or forward who might not have grown as much as predicted could be, for example, relegated to a guard spot where he was not as adept at ball handling or defense. Thus, getting to know these young players and their families was useful in making reasonable predictions on physical growth as well as on the kind of encouragement that the camper might receive from family members regarding basketball fundamentals and lifestyle choices.

Of course, it was a challenge getting players to visit a campus—not to mention getting coaches to travel long distances to high schools, especially during winter when the season was in full swing for both coaches and recruits. Bob Knight noted that some of the annoyances were bumpy roads, unpredictable commuter planes, steamy gyms, fickle young people and their parents, and unreliable video conversations. David Israel saw Knight and Johnny Orr as "two of the most adept and honest recruiters," despite these obstacles.[18]

A second way of finding players was through so-called bird dogs. These were usually alumni of a university who were not officially connected to the university's basketball program and had irregular communication with a coach in the program regarding top players in the "bird dog's" locale; these were players who might be missed because of the high school's small enrollment or the lack of overall success of the school, despite the excellent qualities of an individual player. Video might be sent, but that was less common at the time because game footage was not as easily shot in the era before cell phones and smaller, more high-quality video cameras. Even top-quality video could not be relied upon, but it might motivate an assistant coach to make a physical appearance at a game to observe a player or two not already on a list of possible recruits.

A third approach to scouting was simply using media sources. Cultivating friendships with journalists who covered high school games made an assistant coach's job that much easier, because he could be alerted by direct contact with a journalist, or the coach could read stories by sportswriters whose opinions on players were respected by the coach. An advantage of a number of Big Ten universities was that the high school tournament finals in their state were often held on the campus of the specific state university. The players would come to them, as it were, although because of their own college game schedules, many times there would be only one assistant coach available to actually attend such tournament games.

CHAPTER 4

THE BIG TEN IN THE LATE 1970s

1976–77 Preseason Forecasts

Indiana's defense of its Big Ten and NCAA basketball titles would prove to be a tremendous challenge for the Hoosiers, who had lost seniors Scott May, Quinn Buckner, Tom Abernathy, Bobby Wilkerson, and Jim Crews. Only Kent Benson returned as a starter, and he would be joined by Wayne Radford, a junior, and three freshmen—Glen Grunwald, Butch Carter, and Mike Woodson. *Street and Smith's Official College, Pro and Prep Yearbook 1976–77* identified Carter as one of fifteen freshmen of influence being counted on as the six-foot-five forward to fill Scott May's spot.[1] This was not the kind of squad Bob Knight wanted, with so many freshmen starters, but he had no real choice after last season's great senior class had left. Still, one *Chicago Sun-Times* writer commented that there should be no weeping for Knight, who was "probably the best coach in the country."[2] The championship team's hallmarks were defense, discipline, and conservative shot selection, qualities that took more than just a few weeks of practice to instill. The team's progress was hampered by unexpected injuries to Benson (sprained knee), Grunwald (torn knee cartilage surgery), and Carter (cast on right ankle) in the preseason.[3]

Minnesota continued to stumble with an indefinite probation from the NCAA, and specifically, the three-year probation for the basketball program, all related to former coach Bill Musselman and the ninety-eight violations. The NCAA wanted Mychal Thompson, Dave Winey, and Flip Saunders to be declared ineligible because they had been accused of scalping tickets, making illegal visits to a fan's cabin, and making long-distance phone calls without paying. The NCAA also wanted Minnesota to make the declaration. Minnesota would not do all this, so the NCAA ended up putting all Minnesota men's teams on probation and banning them from all postseason appearances. Appeals would follow.[4]

Kent Benson, NCAA Tournament Most Outstanding Player 1976. *(Courtesy of Indiana University Archives)*

Indiana's losses from graduation were exacerbated by transfers. As Delsohn and Heisler note, "In five years at IU, Knight had only two players ... transfer. Now, in 18 months, he would lose six. ... In the summer, within months of winning the championship, sophomore forward Mark Haymore transferred to Massachusetts. Sophomore guard Bob Bender, a coach's son from Quincy, Illinois, and his roommate, sophomore forward Rich Valavicius, a tough rebounder from Hammond, Indiana, thought about leaving that summer, although they both returned for their sophomore year." After Knight heard about their hesitation, he called them in, dressed them down, and, in essence, made their choices for them. The implication was that they'd not be likely to play much unless they showed exemplary play in each practice. Bender left a few weeks later, before the 1976–77 season started. Valavicius departed during the season, as did Mike Miday, another sophomore forward.[5] Nevertheless, Indiana had some top freshmen entering, as Knight himself noted.[6]

Roy Damer saw Michigan and Indiana as the top teams in the Big Ten and Purdue and Minnesota as the top challengers, although he noted that Minnesota's status was unclear with the pending penalties. As for Michigan, Green, Grote, Hubbard, and Robinson all returned, in addition to top sub Stanton, so Damer was high on the Wolverines. Purdue had all five starters returning—Parkinson, Parker, Jordan, Walls, and Sichting—while Minnesota seemed to have Thompson and Williams, along with the NCAA penalties. New coach Eldon Miller at Ohio State welcomed Larry Bolden and freshman Kelvin Ransey as his starting backcourt but was "short" in the front court. Damer was also surprisingly upbeat regarding Northwestern, noting that four starters were returning, including leading scorer Billy McKinney.[7] NU coach Tex Winter said, "I think that we were a pretty good team" (in 1975–76), and he looked to improve.[8]

Preconference Play Begins

The conference had preseason ups and downs that included some minor upsets, but none was bigger than Indiana's 59–57 loss at Toledo on December 1, which ended IU's thirty-three-game win streak, as well as its fifty-seven-game regular season winning streak. Toledo built a 46–33 lead, faltered enough to allow Indiana to tie at 49, and then outscored the inexperienced Hoosiers down the stretch. IU shot poorly (36 percent) and were outplayed. Knight said, "Toledo outhustled us and I don't like to be outhustled."[9]

Minnesota gained a significant off-court victory on December 2 when their appeal was granted, and their men's teams were removed from probation. This greatly enhanced the Gopher prospects for the basketball season.[10]

Indiana's newfound troubles continued in a home contest against Kentucky. Before 17,632, the Wildcats ended the IU home winning streak at thirty-five with a dominant 66–51 win. Indiana played mostly with Benson (who had 21 points) and four freshmen, so there was some hope that the Hoosiers would develop as the season progressed.[11]

The Big Ten was not nearly as dominant as it had been in previous nonconference contests, but it was still one of the toughest conferences from top to bottom.

Wisconsin's new coach, Bill Cofield, attested to the assertion of Big Ten superiority, noting that the Big Ten was more physical while the Atlantic Coast Conference (ACC) was more of a finesse league.[12]

Besides Michigan, Purdue, and Minnesota, at least two other conference teams were impressive in early season games. Iowa was unbeaten, and Illinois was 7–1. Minnesota enhanced the conference aura by toppling top-ranked Marquette, 66–59 as Ray Williams (19 points, 11 rebounds, plus nine assists) and Mychal Thompson (23 points, 16 rebounds) both had double doubles.[13]

The holiday basketball tournaments followed with no great surprises on the won-loss side for the Big Ten. Ohio State beat Rochester in the Kodak Classic, Holy Cross topped Michigan State in the Gator Bowl Classic, New Mexico defeated Iowa in the Lobo Classic, and Purdue won over Georgetown and Manhattan in the Holiday ECAC Fest at Madison Square Garden. As the conference season loomed, it was hard to tell what any of this really meant. One notable game was Michigan's 90–86 win over South Carolina, notable because Michigan had to overcome the loss of three starters to personal fouls and Phil Hubbard's ejection with 6:58 to play.[14]

The Big Ten Season Opens

The Big Ten season began with a game featuring traditional rivals. The Boilermakers pounded IU in an 80–63 Purdue win. The loss ended Indiana's Big Ten winning streak at thirty-seven and was their worst defeat in their six years at Assembly Hall. Purdue used both a press and a zone defense to thwart the IU offense.[15]

The next night, Purdue got good news. Bruce Parkinson, who had broken his wrist the previous year and played in just two games, was granted eligibility for a fifth year in 1977–78. According to Jerry Sichting, the whole team was thrilled by this development since Parkinson was not only a great shooter and smart player but an overall great guy.[16] Purdue's first sophomore MVP in a decade in the 1974–75 season would now be able to team with shot-blocking centers Tom Scheffler, in his senior year, and highly regarded freshman Joe Barry Carroll.[17]

The heat of the Big Ten season started early with Johnny Orr raging against the referees after the Wolverine win over Wisconsin. It was not a pretty game, as Michigan shot just 29 percent in the first half and Wisconsin 20 percent, with UM leading 27–22. The second half was only slightly better as Wisconsin finished with 38 percent from the floor and Michigan 36 percent, but the Wolverines did hang on for the victory, 66–63. Orr claimed that he had witnessed "the most incompetent job of refereeing I've ever seen," calling out officials Richard Weller, Gary Muncy, and Phil Robinson for giving Michigan a technical foul on a dunk, which was illegal at that time.[18]

Having been released from NCAA purgatory, Minnesota had now won eleven games in a row, including two in conference against Iowa and Illinois. But Purdue ended that string at Mackey Arena, 66–64 in overtime.[19] Michigan continued to be the class of the league, if not the nation, by humbling Iowa in Iowa City, 99–75. The Wolverines shot 59 percent from the floor.[20]

Indiana, by contrast, continued to tumble, losing 61–60 to Michigan State in Assembly Hall. Jud Heathcote observed, "I'm not saying the best team won. . . . I'm very happy to win a game on the road—any place."[21]

At this early point of the conference season, Michigan continued to be the conference leader after toppling Purdue, 82–76, in Ann Arbor. In the next game, Hubbard had 29 to power the Wolverines to a win over the Illini, the sixteenth win in a row at home for Michigan.[22]

Purdue and Minnesota stayed right on Michigan's heels, the Boilers topping MSU 76–70 and the Gophers downing Wisconsin 82–64. When both kept winning, Roy Damer speculated about what might happen if Minnesota finished first or second in the Big Ten since Minnesota was ineligible for postseason play. He posed two unanswerable questions (at least at that point in the season). The first was "Would the NCAA reject a #2 Big Ten team and just have one in post-season play?" The second was "If Minnesota does win the Big Ten, will they get to keep the championship?"[23]

Halfway through the Conference Season

At this juncture, the Big Ten standings had Michigan at 8–0, Purdue at 6–1, and Minnesota at 5–1. The top four scorers were Benson (IU) and Kelser (MSU), each at 21.8, Thompson (MN) at 21.4, and McKinney (NU) at 21.3.

Billy McKinney of Northwestern had a "perfect" game against Michigan State, going 6 of 6 from the floor and 10 of 10 from the line to lead the Wildcats to a 66–58 victory. He followed that up with 29 points to pace Northwestern to a 99–87 stunner over Michigan in McGaw Hall.

McKinney also held Rickey Green to fifteen points. Tex Winter noted that "Billy is the only guy on our team with the quickness to guard Green. I hated to give him a tough assignment like that." But it worked.[24] McKinney's superb shooting inspired his teammates, and the Wildcats shot 61.3 percent from the floor (with six players in double figures), while holding Michigan to 40 percent shooting and handing the Wolverines their first conference loss while avenging a 102–65 Michigan win earlier in the season in Ann Arbor.[25] Winter, in retrospect, claimed that it was the sweetest victory in his thirty years of coaching.[26] Johnny Orr's postgame comment was succinct: "We got outplayed and outshot. We tried everything and it didn't work. We thought if we ever caught them, we'd beat them. The trouble is, we never caught them."[27]

Michigan did bounce back to beat the defending champions, 89–84, led by Green's 32, which was matched by Woodson's 32 for the Hoosiers. Michigan needed the win to maintain distance from Purdue, who defeated Illinois and Northwestern.[28]

Despite the enthusiastic encouragement of 17,504 Gopher fans, Michigan eked out an 86–80 victory in Minneapolis, although Minnesota controlled the boards, 40–31.[29]

Michigan was now 11–1 in conference standings with Purdue at 8–2 and Minnesota at 7–2. But a surprise loss to Wisconsin dropped Purdue to 8–3 and allowed Minnesota to slide past them at 8–2 with an easy 91–65 victory over Ohio State, as the "big three" of Minnesota—Thompson (24), McHale (23), and Williams (21) all had fine games.[30]

Indiana arose from its torpor to stun Michigan 73–64 and seemed to be making its presence felt in the Big Ten. The game was played before 17,654 in Assembly Hall, as well as viewed on national television.[31] Indiana's euphoria didn't last long. Next they went to Minneapolis and lost to Minnesota 65–61. Then Indiana lost to Illinois in Champaign 73–69, despite 25 from Benson and 21 from Woodson. The Hoosiers were an inconsistent squad, and it seemed that Knight could not inspire them to be any better.[32]

Michigan rebounded quickly, beating Iowa 91–80, with six Wolverines scoring in double figures. Michigan's "up and down" play wasn't lost on Coach Orr, who noted, "We haven't been consistent this year."[33] The Wolverines then went into Minneapolis where they crushed the Gophers 89–70 and regained the top spot in the conference.[34] Despite the victory, Orr was rankled by a comment from MSU coach Jud Heathcote, who said that Minnesota had the best five but that Michigan had the best eight. After the victory over Minnesota, Orr said, "We proved we have the best five, and the best team."[35]

Purdue pushed Indiana further back, while continuing to enhance its own chances at postseason play with an 86–78 victory at Mackey Arena. The Boilermakers had six players in double figures and held Kent Benson to just seven shots (though he made six). Benson also injured his back in the contest by taking a charge from Joe Barry Carroll with a minute left, and his college career was considered over.[36]

With just over a week to go, the Big Ten was a three-team race, but Michigan held the inside track over the Gophers and Boilermakers. Minnesota forced its way forward with an 84–78 overtime win over Purdue before 17,581 in Williams Arena.[37] Purdue could still be one of two Big Ten teams in the NCAA tourney, a practice allowed since 1975, if they were to win. They beat Iowa 81–70 but had to beat Michigan State and Michigan to finish the conference season and have a chance at the NCAA tournament. They accomplished the first step with a win over the Spartans 78–69 in Mackey. Minnesota also won that night, edging Wisconsin 64–61, while Michigan clinched at least a tie for the title with an 87–72 win at Illinois. Unfortunately, Ricky Green limped off the court with a bruised hip bone in the first half. The final games would be decisive for all three teams.[38]

In the season finales, Michigan edged Purdue 84–79 to win the Big Ten, in what Coach Johnny Orr called "a great victory without Rickey Green." Coach Fred Schaus of Purdue noted that "they are tough to match up defensively."[39] In a major surprise the next day, Purdue was invited to the NCAA tournament as an at-large team (one that was an independent with no conference affiliation). Minnesota was still suspended by the NCAA, and its appeals had not yet been heard.[40]

The Final Big Ten standings for 1976–77 had Michigan at 16–2, Minnesota at 15–3, and Purdue at 13–5. (Due to its ongoing NCAA suspension, Minnesota was later forced to forfeit all games, making them 0–18 and 0–27 for the season and altering every other team's record.) Iowa and Indiana finished over .500, and Illinois, Wisconsin, Northwestern, and Ohio State finished in that order. In an interesting end to the season, Michigan defeated #1 Marquette 69–68 in a nationally televised game. It led Johnny Orr to immediately proclaim his team #1 in the nation.[41]

The NCAA Tournament

The *Chicago Tribune* awarded its Silver Basketball Award for Big Ten Most Valuable Player to Kent Benson, based on the votes of Big Ten coaches, officials, three *Tribune* writers, and Commissioner Wayne Duke. Benson also was named to the Associated Press All-America First Team.

Heading into the NCAA tournament, Michigan was ranked #1 with Purdue at #20, but injuries, most notably Bruce Parkinson's sprained ankle, threatened to impede Purdue's quest for advancement. That quest was, indeed, stifled swiftly, as the Boilermakers lost in the first round to North Carolina 69–66,[42] leaving just Michigan to carry the Big Ten banner. And they did so, topping Holy Cross 92–81 in Indianapolis. Rickey Green, back at full strength after missing most of three games with a bruised hip, was amazing from the floor, hitting 16 of 20 shots for 35 points; he was ably backed by Hubbard and Robinson with 16 points each.[43] After the game, Orr responded to rumors of his retirement by saying that "as long as [AD Don] Canham stays, I'll stay. I'm not going to retire. I'm not going to quit."[44] An unusual milestone was reached in that game as Steve Grote became the first player to play in four NCAA tournaments, starting his freshman year (1973–74), when freshmen were first eligible for varsity play.

Michigan's second-round 86–81 win over Holy Cross was a relief for the Wolverines. Robinson had 25 points and Hubbard 22, but the latter's 26 rebounds were the key to victory. In the next round, however, the Mideast regional finals, the Wolverines were surprised by UNC-Charlotte, led by Cedric "Cornbread" Maxwell, who scored 25 points and took 13 rebounds in the 75–68 upset of the #1 team.[45] It was a bitter ending for Michigan, especially when Marquette defeated UNC-Charlotte in the NCAA Semis and UNC-Chapel Hill in the NCAA Finals, allowing Al McGuire to retire with his only collegiate title.

The season had ended with disappointment for the conference. So there was new discussion about what the league should do to build on its successes. Those successes included attendance, which was just over 900,000 for the conference, an average of 10,263 per game, with Minnesota (15,910) and Indiana (15,650) leading in this category. There was discussion of a Big Ten end-of-season tournament (after the example of the ACC) to determine the conference title and represent the conference at the NCAA meet, but the coaches and athletic directors voted that down, amid what Commissioner Wayne Duke called "mixed sentiment among Big 10 officials."[46]

1977–78

Heading into the 1977–78 season, there was stability among the coaches in the league, and this was matched by player stability. Minnesota had given up the fight against the NCAA after just over a year and had declared Mychal Thompson and Dave Winey, both seniors, ineligible, hoping that this action would get the NCAA to remove the Gophers from probation and that the two players *might* be able to play before the end of the season. Thompson had led the Big Ten in scoring in 1976–77 and was Minnesota's career scoring leader. As Roy Damer saw it, the Gophers really had no choice left after losing their appeal in the Federal Court of the Eighth Circuit, and many feared that the Big Ten might lose its automatic NCAA bid if the Gophers continued to defy the NCAA.[47]

Mychal Thompson, 1978 Big Ten Player of the Year. *(Courtesy of University of Minnesota)*

But the story wasn't quite over. On November 9, it was announced that the NCAA would rule on the eligibility of Thompson and Winey in five days via a conference call involving the NCAA Subcommittee on Eligibility Appeals, Coach Jim Dutcher, and University of Minnesota Vice President Stanley Kegler. After that session, it was announced that Thompson would be ineligible for seven games and Winey for three. In addition, the basketball program would remain on probation for one year, a ruling that would make the Gophers unable to appear on televised games and be ineligible to play in the NCAA tournament.[48]

A week later, the Big Ten was set to begin play. Purdue seemed solid from top to bottom with Joe Barry Carroll at center, seniors Walter Jordan and Wayne Walls returning at the forward spots, and Jerry Sichting and Eugene

Parker as the starting guards. The bench was not deep, however. Minnesota was tabbed as the likely #2, largely based on their great back line of Thompson, McHale, and Winey. The most heralded freshman in the conference, Earvin "Magic" Johnson (who had been given this appellation because of the amazing things he could do handling the ball), was seen as the key to Michigan State's title hopes. He would be joined by another freshman, Jay Vincent, plus all-conference players Rob Chapman and Greg Kelser with Terry Donnelly, a sharpshooting guard, rounding out the first five. Indiana, Iowa, and Michigan were expected to follow in the middle of the Big Ten. Michigan was devastated by the loss of Phil Hubbard for the year, due to knee surgery.[49]

Street and Smith's predicted the order of finish in the Big Ten: Minnesota, Michigan, Indiana, Purdue, Wisconsin, Ohio State, Michigan State, Iowa, Illinois, and Northwestern. A lot would depend on freshmen, and Johnny Orr of Michigan asserted, "I can't see all these freshmen dominating. Some will be disappointments." Not a really bold assertion. And Jim Cohen of the Milwaukee Journal said that Magic Johnson was "considered by many to be the best high school player in the country."[50]

Preconference Play

It didn't take long for upsets to occur. The most surprising one was Indiana State's rout of Purdue 91–63 in Terre Haute. Former Indiana recruit Larry Bird dominated the floor with 26 points, 17 rebounds, and 8 assists. Joe Barry Carroll had 14 points and 15 rebounds for Purdue, but he fouled out with 9:16 to go in the game.[51]

Purdue showed early mettle by topping Alabama, one of the favorites for the SEC championship in 1977–78. The score was 82–65 as Joe Barry Carroll had 26, 16 rebounds, and 6 blocks to power the Boilermakers before a sold-out crowd at Mackey Arena.[52]

Indiana lost its second game of the season, this time to Kentucky 78–64 in Lexington before 23,521 fans. Woodson led the way with 20 but fouled out with twelve minutes left in the contest. Minnesota lost to defending NCAA champion Marquette 61–44 in Minneapolis. Without the ineligible Thompson, the Gophers' attack was severely hampered. Michigan lost too: they were bested by Louisville in Ann Arbor 88–85. This was the first nonconference loss for the Wolverines at Crisler Arena since 1971.[53]

The Big Ten was not looking as formidable as it had in the previous few seasons. The conference also was making it more difficult for players to transfer within the conference, making them pay to do so. The first to feel the impact was six-foot-eleven Derek Holcomb, who had originally enrolled at

Indiana then, after foot surgery, transferred to Illinois. He had been touted as Kent Benson's successor but was not happy at Indiana under Knight.[54]

Purdue and Michigan State were livening up the preconference season, one because of meeting team expectations, the other because one special player energized his team and his league. On December 8 the Boilermakers traveled to Tucson to play Arizona, who had been the second-place finisher in the Western Athletic Conference the prior year and riding a thirty-eight-game home winning streak. Purdue edged the Wildcats 80–78 behind 19 points from Sichting.[55]

The excitement in East Lansing for Magic Johnson was spreading and leading to Michigan State hopes for a Big Ten title. Jud Heathcote gushed over his freshman star as well as his team, saying Magic has created "great enthusiasm around Lansing. His greatest attribute is his passing." Heathcote also asserted that Magic's teammate Kelser "is the best forward in the conference" and that "Chapman is the best complete guard in the league."[56]

As the holiday tournament season began, the only Big Ten teams nationally ranked were Michigan (#14) and Purdue (#16), so it appeared that the Big Ten would be an afterthought nationally. Indiana, coming back from a disappointing 14–13 season, won the Gator Bowl tourney, defeating Jacksonville in the semifinals and Florida in the championship contest. Mike Woodson asserted himself in both games, leading the team to victory. Michigan State won the Old Dominion Classic in Norfolk, defeating New Hampshire 102–65. Minnesota defeated Air Force 66–50 for the title in the Minneapolis Classic. In Ann Arbor, Michigan fell 91–84 in overtime to a good Toledo team. Uncertainty still ruled as the conference season opened. Ohio State was 7–2, Iowa 6–2, Wisconsin 5–4, and Northwestern, 4–5.

The Big Ten Season Begins

Purdue, Michigan, and Michigan State all won their openers, but only MSU had to struggle, topping Minnesota 87–83 after being down seven with four minutes to play. Magic Johnson had 31 for the Spartans, a total matched by Minnesota's Thompson.[57]

Indiana began with a 69–51 win over Iowa in Bloomington, but Bob Knight's comments might have made one think that the Hoosiers had lost. He said that his "offensive play was the worst I've ever seen since I've been here. Our play was disgraceful." Iowa helped Indiana's cause with 20 turnovers in the first half alone. Next game, Indiana earned the loss that they "escaped" against Iowa, as Illinois rallied to win 65–64 at Indiana, outrebounding the Hoosiers, 38–30. It would be an up-and-down year for the

Hoosiers.[58] Not so for Michigan, Purdue, and Michigan State, who were establishing themselves as the class of the league.[59]

Magic Johnson now began to assert himself even more for his team. He had 17 points and 10 assists in an 82–70 win in Champaign, and his assists set up teammates Kelser (25) and Vincent (19). Coach Heathcote noted, "He's our catalyst, a typical Earvin game . . . teammates are learning to adjust to playing with him."[60] Sometimes the learning was harder than usual, as in the narrow 67–63 MSU victory over Northwestern in their next contest at McGaw Hall in Evanston. The Spartans had 28 turnovers but luckily outrebounded the Wildcats 39–17 for the victory. Iowa helped the Spartans by topping Purdue 66–60, and Illinois rallied to upset Michigan in Champaign.[61]

In an important early season game, Michigan State knocked off Purdue 60–51 in a slow-paced contest. The Spartans decided to ease up the tempo after a sloppy first half, and the result was a nice victory, led by Johnson's 21 points and Kelser's 10. After Purdue coach Fred Schaus saw Johnson in a Big Ten game for the first time, he said, "I was very impressed with Johnson's play. He's the finest freshman I've ever seen." Michigan kept pace with an easy victory over the overmatched Wisconsin Badgers 83–64.[62]

A third of the way through the conference season, Michigan State was undefeated in the league at 5–0 and held a one-game lead on Michigan at 4–1. In a significant battle, Purdue crushed Michigan 80–65, as Jordan (19), Carroll (17), and Walls (14) all scored in double figures, and the Boilers hit 19 of 29 field goals in the second half.[63] The standings now had MSU at 7–1, Purdue at 6–2, and Minnesota tied with Michigan at 5–3 in the conference.

Then came an epic game in East Lansing. Michigan defeated MSU 65–63 with a 25-foot buzzer shot by little-used sub Mark Lozier. Michigan State had its usual good shooting (27 of 54 for 50 percent), led by Johnson with 22 points, 8 assists, 5 rebounds, and 7 steals. But Michigan shot even better, with 30 of 55 from the floor (54 percent), led by McGee's 23 points, to edge the Spartans and turn the conference race into a free-for-all. Purdue asserted itself with a 71–69 win over Ohio State, finding themselves in a tie for first in the conference.[64]

Indiana came into East Lansing on the heels of the MSU loss to Michigan, having beaten the Spartans just a week before in Bloomington. This time it would be Michigan State, although they made it extra hard for themselves by going 8 of 19 from the free throw line with Kelser the biggest "clanker" at 1 for 8. He did make up for that with 21 points and 13 rebounds overall in the 68–59 victory. Coach Heathcote called it "our best team victory."[65] Purdue helped themselves and the Spartans by knocking off Michigan 75–66 at

Mackey Arena, and Purdue and Michigan State were now tied for the conference lead at 8–2, while Michigan dropped to 6–4 behind Minnesota's 7–3 record.[66]

Halfway Home: Can MSU Hold the Lead?

To begin the second half, the Spartans set out on a tough three-game road trip, and Jud Heathcote had lots to say about his team, starting with praise for Bob Chapman and Greg Kelser. "When Chapman and Kelser play well, we're a super team; when one does, we're good. When neither does, then . . . it rhymes with pretty."[67] The Spartans were ranked #10 in the country with Purdue at #13.

The MSU trip had a shaky start with a 71–70 win at Iowa, with Chapman (22) and Johnson (18) leading the scoring for the Spartans. Meanwhile Purdue was edged in Bloomington 65–64 to put MSU back into the lead all alone, at least temporarily. Then MSU won again in a smashing 73–62 victory in Ann Arbor, while Purdue bumbled its way to a loss in Columbus, 91–77. In the Michigan game, Magic had 25 points, 8 rebounds, 6 assists, and 2 steals. Michigan had won 11 of the previous 12 games against MSU so the hope in East Lansing was that the jinx was broken. Johnny Orr was thoroughly impressed by Magic Johnson, noting that "he plays forward, guard, center and even coaches a little, too. And he doesn't do a bad job."[68]

The last game of the MSU road trip was at Mackey, and the Boilermakers were ready as they played a switching defense to combat Magic Johnson's talents. When Magic was on top of the key, Purdue went with a 1–3–1 zone with Walter Jordan on top to defend. When Magic moved to a wing, so did Jordan, as Purdue switched to a 2–3 defense. Obviously, Purdue had spent a lot of time preparing, and the Spartans were caught unawares. On the other end, Purdue's shooting (58 percent for the game to MSU's 33 percent) forced MSU out of their zone, and the Spartans were "not a good man-to-man defense" team, according to their own coach. Purdue had five players with at least 13 points, led by Jordan's 26. The score was not close: 99–80.[69]

Meanwhile, some of the stress of Big Ten competition surfaced when Indiana called out Purdue for unethical recruiting practices. Apparently newspaper articles covering junior Bill Cunningham's decision to quit the Indiana team were sent to current Indiana high school stars, the implication being that Indiana would not be a good school to play for. There was no evidence that Purdue was connected with any of this, but it was an ugly scene.

On the court, Michigan State clinched a share of the conference title with a 89–67 romp over Illinois, Minnesota was routed by Indiana 68–47, and Purdue held on to fading title hopes by defeating Wisconsin 87–78.

Joe Barry Carroll, All-American at Purdue. *(Courtesy of Purdue University Archives and Special Collections)*

Purdue's balance (five players scored in double figures) was the key to their win.[70] Heathcote was pleased and, he said, a bit surprised at the Spartan title, noting that although he thought they had a chance at the title, "realistically, as young as we were, I didn't think we'd beat out Minnesota and Purdue."[71]

On March 1, both All-America and Big Ten all-conference teams were announced. Only Mychal Thompson represented the conference on the ten-member All-America squad of the USBBWA. Former Indiana enrollee Larry Bird was also a member. The Big Ten first team included Thompson, Magic Johnson (MSU freshman), Walter Jordan (Purdue senior), Ronnie Lester (Iowa sophomore), and Kelvin Ransey (Ohio State sophomore). The second team included Mike McGee (Michigan), Mike Woodson (Indiana), Greg Kelser (Michigan State), Wayne Radford (Indiana), and Osborn Lockhart (Minnesota). Third team included Eugene Parker (Purdue), Joel Thompson (Michigan), Kevin McHale (Minnesota), Jerry Sichting (Purdue), Herb Williams (Ohio State), and Joe Barry Carroll (Purdue). Even forty years later it is an impressive group and indicates the strength of the conference when players like Kevin McHale and Joe Barry Carroll are relegated to third team all-conference status.[72]

There was still a conference title to be decided, and Michigan State clinched the title on March 2 by defeating Wisconsin in Madison 89–75. Bill Jauss waxed effusive in regard to the coaching of Jud Heathcote in leading MSU to the top of the Big Ten heap. Deflecting his "in game" coaching ability, Heathcote asserted that "recruiting is the most important part of my job," and he did it well. In the clinching game, Johnson (26 points) and Kelser (23) led the Spartan attack.[73] Johnson's comments after the game summed up his view. "This is the hungriest team I've ever played for. . . . We played hard and all looked for each other on the floor. And we had good coaching."[74]

Minnesota and Indiana also won, keeping solidly in second and third, respectively, while Purdue was idle. The Boilermakers lost to Illinois two nights later, to make Purdue 2–7 on the road and 9–0 at home in conference play. Minnesota then lost to Michigan State in Minneapolis 71–70. Mychal Thompson set a new Big Ten career scoring record with 1,477 points (in four years) and a 20.8 scoring average in the game, breaking Rick Mount's total of 1,461 (set in three years). Indiana won its last eight games to tie Minnesota for second place, while Purdue fell to fourth. The final standings saw Ohio State, Illinois, Iowa, Northwestern, and Wisconsin complete the field.

Individual conference honors in scoring went to Mychal Thompson (22.7), followed by Mike McGee (21.8) and both Ronnie Lester and Magic Johnson (19.8). Rebound leaders were Clay Hargrave of Iowa (11.9), Mychal Thompson (11.6), Herb Williams of OSU (10.8), and Joe Barry Carroll (9.3). The Big Ten MVP was Mychal Thompson of Minnesota.

On the eve of the NCAA tournament, Fred Schaus resigned as coach of Purdue after going 16–11 for the season and 104–60 for his tenure there. He would stay at the university as associate athletic director and be part of the search for his successor. That would be Lee Rose, the coach at UNC-Charlotte, who had taken his team to the Final Four in 1977.[75]

The NCAA Tournament

Both Michigan State and Indiana opened their tournament games with victories, the former with a 77–63 win over Providence in Indianapolis, and the latter with a narrow win over Furman 63–62 in Charlotte.[76] Michigan State then won easily over Western Kentucky 90–69 in the Mideast regional semis, but Indiana was not as fortunate, losing in the Eastern semis to Villanova 61–60. IU led by 10 with 12:37 to go, but the Wildcats were able to catch and then surpass the Hoosiers. Despite the loss, Knight expressed not outrage but pride in his team, which he thought "lived up to its potential as completely as any other team I've ever coached. A coach can't ask for anything more."[77]

Michigan State's victory was a display of great team play, as they had 25 assists on their 37 field goals. Magic Johnson had 14 of those assists and 14 points, despite shooting just 3 of 17 from the floor. Kelser and Chapman had 23 points apiece.[78]

The Mideast championship would pit MSU against Kentucky, and Jud Heathcote told his players that "the winner of this game will win the national championship." He was proved correct, but unfortunately for MSU and the Big Ten, the winner was Kentucky by a score of 52–49, led by Purdue transfer Kyle Macy (who went 10–11 from the free throw line). Michigan State led 31–24, before Kentucky switched to a zone, and the MSU offense slowed to a walk. Johnson said that the 1–3–1 clogged up the middle, and he was obviously pressing, as he ended up with just 6 points on 2 of 10 shooting and had 6 turnovers. MSU shot just 7 free throws (making 5), while Kentucky was 16 of 18 from the line.[79]

Despite Michigan State's exit (losing to the eventual champions), there was still news of interest to Big Ten basketball. The NCAA had increased the amount paid to first-round losers by $10,000 to $36,000, and NCAA finalists would get about $250,000. The increases were due to the larger arenas being utilized, the greater number of teams in the tournament, and the increase in television money. The Big Ten allowed teams in the tournament to get 50 percent of the money that they "earned," with the rest being split eight ways, so IU and MSU each received $70,000 while the other schools in the conference got $12,000 each. The increase sounds quite small compared to what schools get today, but it was a big boost to athletic budgets at that time. Coaches of the Big Ten again considered a postseason playoff or full tournament but voted it down 5–4 with one abstention.[80]

With the end of the season, the big news would be coaching alterations. In addition to Fred Schaus, Tex Winter resigned from Northwestern after five years to coach at Cal State-Long Beach; Rich Falk was swiftly named to replace him. Winter, in resigning, said that "Northwestern has an Ivy League philosophy in a Big Ten athletic conference. 90% of the prospects weren't admissible . . . 80% seemed interested in a business major, which we didn't have. . . . That left us with 20% and everybody was after them."[81]

In addition to the coaching changes, there were concerns about key player departures. Magic Johnson noted in late April that "if the money's right and a few other things are right, I'd probably have to go (pro)."[82] Ultimately, Johnson decided that the money was *not* right and declared that he would stay at MSU for the 1978–79 season, likely his last season there, making the next one of urgency for the MSU Spartans.

CHAPTER 5

THE 1978-79 SEASON
The Big Ten Proves Its Mettle and Tenacity

The Preseason

In 1978, a series of international amateur tournaments were held, with the most notable one being in Vilnius, Lithuania, in August. Since no professionals were allowed, the US team would be all collegiate players. The other teams were mostly veteran players in their own countries, playing in subsidized leagues that allowed them to retain their amateur standing. Following these various tourneys, the team from the Soviet Union began a tour of the United States, playing various American college squads. One of the early stops, in November of 1978, was Champaign, Illinois, where the veteran Soviet squad played a young and middle-of-the-pack Illini squad, which had just started preseason practices.

The Soviets edged the Illini 77–73, but the Illinois faithful were heartened by the play of its Indiana transfer, six-foot-eleven Derek Holcomb, who scored twelve points against the rugged Soviet defense. Optimism was running high in Champaign.[1] That win was impressive enough to have the Illini mentioned in the same breath as four other Big Ten teams who were seen as potential threats to the heavily favored Michigan State Spartans for the 1978–79 Big Ten title. Besides Holcomb, the Illini would rely on six-foot-ten James Griffin and high-scoring Neil Bresnahan as part of a solid front line. Indiana had Mike Woodson and Ray Tolbert, an underrated center, as their leaders. Iowa hoped for big things from a UNC transfer, six-foot-eleven Steve Krafcisin, who was recovering from a hip injury. Michigan also looked for a recovery from a top player, Phil Hubbard, who had missed the entire 1977–78 season after undergoing back surgery. In addition, Michigan returned Mike McGee, who coach Johnny Orr called "the greatest offensive player I've ever had."

Jud Heathcote, the MSU coach, saw his star, Magic Johnson, as "the best player in the open court in all of basketball." The preseason was a time for hyperbole, but Johnson would justify that pronouncement. Because of their lack of depth, the Spartans would play zone on defense.[2]

The other Big Ten teams were also hopeful. Minnesota had lost Player of the Year Mychal Thompson to the NBA, but Kevin McHale returned, joined by a top class of freshmen, that included Leo Rautins, a six-foot-eight Canadian who had played on Canada's national team. Purdue's new coach, Lee Rose, expected help from Steve and Brian Walker, both transfers from North Carolina State, to support veterans Joe Barry Carroll and Jerry Sichting. Wisconsin would have two quality guards in Arnold Gaines and Wes Matthews; however, the key to their success, according to coach Bill Cofield, would be Larry Petty, a six-foot-nine center who had lost thirty-five pounds over the summer after carrying way too much weight to be an effective player the previous season.[3]

Ohio State was showing steady improvement as Eldon Miller began his third season as head coach. The Buckeyes returned two twenty-points-per-game scorers in sophomore Kelvin Ransey at guard and junior Herb Williams at center. They would be aided by returning sophomore starters Carter Smith and Jim Smith. The Bucks had won sixteen games in 1977–78 and were on the cusp of heading into postseason play. Northwestern looked to be cellar dwellers again with the departure of top scorer Tony Allen, their only player to average in double figures the prior season, but the team was young and would be coached by former NU great Rich Falk, so hopes were high that the Wildcats might escape the conference dungeon.

Big Ten sportswriters made MSU their choice for the conference title, followed by Michigan. Purdue fell to third, especially after losing 63–53 to what seemed an inferior team in Indiana State in West Lafayette. Joe Barry Carroll had 22 points and 14 rebounds, but Larry Bird of ISU countered that with 22 points, 15 rebounds, and 4 assists.[4]

Preconference Play

The preconference season brought some early upsets, or so it seemed, since it was still difficult to tell exactly how teams would gel. Pepperdine's victory over Indiana in a tournament in Anchorage, Alaska, was certainly a surprise, but that was followed by a second straight loss by the Hoosiers in Alaska, this one to Texas A&M 54–49. Despite that, the early UPI poll had Indiana ranked as #11 nationally but preceded by two other Big Ten squads, Michigan State at #4 and Michigan at #11. Minnesota was ranked #19. Clearly, the league's successes the prior season had a significant carryover effect.[5]

Illinois started off well with wins over weaker teams like Texas-Arlington and University of Denver, so they still seemed like they would be formidable.

Iowa coach Lute Olson called them "the most improved team in the league," bolstered by Holcomb and freshmen James Griffin and Perry Range.[6] Michigan was heartened by the return of Phil Hubbard. Playing in his first game in twenty months, he scored 25 points in an 87–78 win over Central Michigan. He was supported by Mike McGee's 30 points and 11 rebounds. The Wolverines followed that with a big win over Alabama 99–84: Hubbard had 24 points and 15 rebounds, McGee 27 points, and Alan Hardy 20 points off the bench. Minnesota, whose coach Jim Dutcher claimed to have the best freshmen in the conference, had a signature win over Loyola in double overtime in which freshman Leo Rautins had 31 points. Veteran Kevin McHale had 13 points and 16 rebounds.[7]

By December 6, two Big Ten teams had advanced to the top six in the nation, MSU at #4 and Michigan at #6. But, then Louisville upset the Big Ten applecart with an 86–84 win over Michigan. The Wolverines quickly rebounded to beat Dayton 66–61 on the Flyers' home court, with McGee scoring 27 and Hubbard 17. Michigan State had its own problems, barely edging Cal. State-Fullerton 92–89 in East Lansing, as Magic had just 5 points. Kelser saved them with 27.[8]

Indiana returned to winning ways with five straight victories, but then Bob Knight dropped three players from the team and put five others on probation. Put on indefinite probation but allowed to practice were Ray Tolbert, leading scorer, a sophomore center; Mike Woodson, junior forward; sophs Eric Kirchner and Phil Isenbarger; and a freshman, Landon Turner. Their scholarships would not be affected. No explanations were offered other than "team problems." In retrospect, it is now known that marijuana use was at the root of the dismissals.

This kind of disciplinary action had been taken before, and most of the time Knight's intensity was seen as the source. Rich Valavicius, who quit in 1977, said that Knight is "too intense a person." Derek Holcomb agreed and made a very prescient comment: "I think basketball will destroy him." Defenders of Knight like Scott May noted that it was not a personal thing, and Steve Risley, who was on the team and played from 1978 to 1981, said, "Sissies need to go back to mother if they can't take Bobby Knight."[9]

The dismissals brought the number of players who had left the team to ten since its 1976 NCAA championship.[10] *Chicago Tribune* columnist David Israel weighed in: "Knight's principles outrank victories.... [He is] one of the last honest men in an age of sporting hypocrisy."[11]

The massive alterations to his roster were instrumental in getting Bob Knight to hold his first press conference since 1976–77, following the Hoosier game against defending NCAA champion Kentucky in Bloomington, which

Mike Woodson, All-American (and later head coach) at Indiana. *(Courtesy of Indiana University Archives)*

Indiana won 68–67. Knight would only talk about the game, despite the obvious interest in the incident(s) that led to the disciplining of players. Knight used only seven players in the game, one for just five minutes, but the contest was finally won by the outstanding play of Woodson with 27 points and Tolbert with 21. Indiana was moving forward.[12]

Michigan State had its win streak stopped at three in Chapel Hill, where the Tar Heels edged MSU 70–69, despite 18 points each from Kelser and Johnson. Both Kelser and Terry Donnelly fouled out in the game where UNC had only 11 fouls to MSU's 20.[13] Roy Damer felt that the disparity in foul calls was disturbing and noted that it bothered Coach Heathcote enough that he pointed it out to the officials and received a technical for his "efforts." The technical came with 4:57 in the game when UNC had just two fouls. Mike O'Koren made both free throws on the technical to give the Tar Heels a nine-point edge, but MSU was able to cut the lead toward the end, although they fell just short.[14] Heathcote summarized the game: "They just outhustled us. . . . We were disorganized in this atmosphere."[15]

The Spartans took their revenge 63–52 against Cincinnati before 31,683 in the Pontiac Silverdome. It was the second-largest crowd to see a college basketball game up to that point, exceeded only by the legendary Houston-UCLA clash held in the Astrodome in January 1968, where Elvin Hayes and his Cougar teammates defeated Lew Alcindor and his Bruins 71–68 in the so-called game of the century.[16] Heathcote wasn't impressed by the win, noting that "as quick as we are, it would be hard for me to imagine any team slower than we were in the first half."[17]

The Holiday Season

Holiday classic games and tournaments dominated the next couple of weeks with a few major upsets gaining attention. The most surprising was Ohio State's defeat of #1 Duke 90–84 in overtime at the Holiday Festival in Madison Square Garden. Kelvin Ransey had 26, Herb Williams 23, and Carter Scott 19 for the Buckeyes; for Duke, Jim Spanarkel had 30, Mike Gminski had 27, and Gene Banks 12. In Portland, the Far West Classic found two Big Ten powers squaring off for the title, which Michigan State won 74–57 over Indiana. Again, only seven Hoosiers played, with Woodson (23) and Tolbert (13) leading the scoring for them. MSU, surprisingly, only played eight players, with Johnson's 20 points topping Spartan scoring.[18] In Alaska, Illinois won the Glacier Classic, keeping the team undefeated (12–0) and helping them remain among the top teams nationally at #3. MSU, with a 7–1 mark, was ranked #1, and Michigan, 5–2, was at #12, as the teams prepared to start conference play.

Besides the holiday tournaments, a most interesting series on college basketball recruiting was run in the *Chicago Tribune* by Fred Rothenberg, who later became a well-known NBC Sports producer. In part one of the series, Rothenberg noted that the freshman eligibility rule (now allowing them to play in their first year) and the NCAA's then-limit of fifteen basketball scholarships for any four-year period had all but ended the possibility of another UCLA dynasty, since players couldn't be "stockpiled"; however, he foresaw a "revolving door" for freshman players. Quoting a former recruit, Rothenberg summarized the issue clearly: "You have to win, and cheating just helps." The reason for the unprecedented growth in the game was television, money associated with television, and the greater national interest as a result of more television exposure. (Sounds like a theme!)[19]

In the second part of the series, Rothenberg noted a number of coaches as simply lying about their recruitment practices. Rick Pitino, an assistant coach at the University of Hawaii, had been implicated in a number of recruiting violations but claimed no knowledge of such practices, which the former head coach, Bruce O'Neil, called "a bunch of crap."[20] Alumni and local boosters were seen as complicit in the illegal recruitment, but NCAA officials said that "only" 15–20 percent of schools did this. In the final part of the series, Rothenberg concluded that NCAA enforcement is ineffective when schools flout the rules, a statement that resonates as much today as it did then.[21]

Big Ten Conference Play Opens

The Big Ten had compiled a nonconference record of 70–27 (.727 percentage), had captured six holiday tournaments (Illinois won the Kentucky and Glacier Bowl; MSU the Far West Classic; Purdue, the Rainbow Classic; Iowa, the Cabrillo Classic; and Minnesota the Pillsbury Classic), and only one team was under .500 (Northwestern). The Big Ten was as strong, it seemed, as it had been the prior season, making it one of the two best conferences in the nation from top to bottom.

Opening night saw some surprises, if not downright upsets. The most significant was Illinois's defeat of Indiana in Bloomington, 65–61. Indiana had three players score most of their points—Tolbert (18), Risley (17), and Woodson (15)—while Illinois had better balance. Meanwhile Ohio State beat Purdue in Columbus 75–71, led by Kelvin Ransey's 33 and Herb Williams's 23.[22] Michigan won their opener against Minnesota 88–75, but Roy Damer felt that Phil Hubbard was not the same, and his observation was seconded by Michigan coach Johnny Orr, who said that Hubbard's "quickness has disappeared."[23]

Purdue suffered its second loss in two conference games when they traveled to Bloomington, where Indiana won 63–54. Woodson (20) and Carter (13) led the Hoosiers in scoring, while Carroll (18) and Sichting (10) were the leaders of a meager Purdue offense. In referring to that poor performance, Jerry Sichting noted, "After we won the Rainbow Classic we were forced to stay in Honolulu three extra days because of a blizzard that hit the Midwest. A lot of planes were grounded and we flew to Columbus on a connecting flight, getting there the night before the game. Then after we lost the OSU game [Coach] Rose tried to get us back on the right time zone by getting us up early and going back to the gym. Then we got on the bus to Bloomington. We went to their gym and shot and went through things and then played IU at noon the next day! Our legs were rubber. That blizzard probably cost us the outright title."

Michigan State had its hands full at home with Minnesota, winning 69–62. Down by 7 at the half and by 13 with 17 minutes to go, the Spartans rallied to win after switching from a zone to man-to-man defense at halftime. "The man-to-man defense got us going," said Heathcote.[24]

Despite it being the first week of the season, Illinois fans were excited about the visit of Michigan State to Champaign on January 11 to meet the undefeated (14–0) Illini. The game would be broadcast on fourteen radio stations and WGN television with over a hundred press personnel expected for the first sellout game in three years. MSU was ranked #1 in the nation, and Illinois held the #3 or #4 slot (depending on the poll). Lou Henson said that Illinois would have to slow the game down to beat the Spartans, who were shooting 54 percent from the floor as a team.[25] Despite a massive snowstorm that hit central Illinois that day, a record crowd of 16,209, including Governor Jim Thompson, packed Assembly Hall.[26] The game itself was everything Illinois had hoped for, as the Illini edged Michigan State 57–55 on a shot with three seconds to go. Magic Johnson graciously called it "a beautiful game; but this game doesn't make their season or ours. We've got a long way to go." In retrospect, free-throw shooting certainly made a difference in the game, as MSU went 1 for 7 and Illinois 7 for 10. The Illini also outrebounded the Spartans 50–22—it made one wonder how the overall score had been so close.[27]

That same evening, Michigan lost at Purdue 77–67, and Minnesota defeated Indiana in Indianapolis 80–63. Michigan's problems stemmed from being outrebounded 35–22 and foul trouble, losing Phil Hubbard with five with 9:52 left in the game. Indiana was simply outplayed by the Gophers, led by McHale with 26 and supported by Mark Hall with 19 and Trent Tucker with 16. Tolbert (16) and Woodson (13) topped Hoosier scoring.[28]

The undefeated Illini had the Illinois media and fans dreaming big. Bill Jauss speculated that the team could be ranked #1 in the nation if they beat Ohio State on January 13, but they would need to stop the Big Ten's leading scorer (Kelvin Ransey) and leading rebounder (Herb Williams) to accomplish this task. Jauss compared Derek Holcomb to Bill Russell (a bit of a stretch) for his role on the Illini team—blocking shots, supplying a last line of defense, and rebounding. Alas, the dreams ended as OSU defeated the Illini in overtime 69–66. Illinois was plagued by mental errors and missed key shots. The Illini missed ten consecutive shots toward the end of the game and in the first 4:46 of the overtime period. They also had 30 fouls to OSU's 16, leading to an enormous free-throw advantage. OSU was 25 of 38 and Illinois 4 of 8 from the line. Ransey was held to 11, but Williams had 28 for the Buckeyes, while Smith led Illinois with 28 and Bresnahan scored just 10.[29]

The Illinois loss was balanced, somewhat, by the losses of both Michigan State and Michigan that same night. The Spartans fell at Purdue 52–50 on a 25-foot buzzer-beating heave, while the Wolverines lost in Madison to the Badgers 77–66. MSU got just 9 points and 6 assists from Magic Johnson. Heathcote noted, "He's not playing very well right now," but no one else on the team was either. Michigan State was outscored in the first twelve minutes of the second half, 31–4, and never recovered.[30]

The Midwest had record snowfall of 29 inches and –19 degree temperatures on January 15 and, in a tale that characterized the hazards of Big Ten travel in that famous winter, Northwestern spent two days waiting at Chicago's O'Hare Airport to fly to Minnesota to meet the Gophers. The Wildcats arrived too late for the shootaround but somehow led by 11 points (52–41) with nine minutes to go. At that point their legs seemed to give out, and the Gophers went on a run, winning 60–58 on Leo Rautins's tip-in with two seconds to go. Northwestern remained winless in the conference, while Minnesota went to 2–2.[31]

The national rankings now had three Big Ten teams listed: Illinois (#2 UPI, #4 AP), MSU (#6 in both polls), and Ohio State (#16 UPI, #11 AP), with Notre Dame at the top of both polls.

Ohio State stayed undefeated in the conference with a 5–0 mark after topping Minnesota 83–80 in Columbus, while MSU and Iowa were both right behind after wins over Indiana and Purdue, respectively.[32] Early key games kept appearing. Ohio State stayed undefeated by beating rival Michigan in Ann Arbor 78–69 behind Ransey's 25 points. Michigan hurt itself by shooting just 18 of 29 second-half free throws, with three of the misses being the front end of one-and-ones.[33] Purdue handed Illinois its second loss with a 69–57 victory in Champaign, where Joe Barry Carroll had 24 points and 10 rebounds. "Carroll," said Jerry Sichting, "was a great player—smart, strong and skilled, but Lee Rose made him a greater player." Michigan State edged Iowa in overtime 83–72, as Magic put on one of his dazzling shows with 25 points, 8 rebounds, and 9 assists. But the Spartans needed sub Mike Brkovich to make two free throws with three seconds left to tie the game and send it into overtime. "That one-and-one that Brkovich hit against Iowa is the most pressure-packed feat I've ever seen a college kid execute," Lynn Henning, a *Lansing State Journal* sports columnist, said. "Without that, they probably don't even make the (NCAA) tournament."[34] One-third of the way through the conference season, OSU was 6–0, with three teams, Iowa, Michigan State, and Illinois, all two games behind at 4–2.[35]

Michigan was a disappointing 2–4 but then reasserted itself with a slow-down 49–48 win over Michigan State in Ann Arbor. Jud Heathcote said that the Spartans got "lackadaisical" after gaining an eleven-point lead three different times in the first half. This was MSU's fourth loss; they had lost to UNC, Illinois, Purdue, and Michigan by a combined total of six points. Clearly, MSU had the talent to win any game, but they needed to keep their focus throughout the contest to do so in such a tough conference. Ohio State had no such problem as they remained undefeated in the league with a 73–61 win over winless Northwestern.[36]

Then, in what was certainly the upset of the year in the Big Ten, North-western routed Michigan State 83–65 in Evanston. Magic Johnson did his part with 26 points, 10 rebounds, and 10 assists, but he was the only Spartan in double figures. Magic was clearly upset in his postgame statements, saying that the losses were "killing him" and that his "stomach was turning." Jud Heathcote called his team "stagnant." Coach Rich Falk of Northwestern had considered a delay game, but when his team's back door cuts worked, he decided to push the ball after all.[37]

A team that was not stagnant and actually surprising was Ohio State. The Buckeyes defeated Indiana in what the *Chicago Tribune* called "routine overtime," 66–63. With 2:12 to go in the game, IU led 55–46, but OSU tied the game at 55, as Indiana could not make free throws down the stretch (they finished at 11 for 21), and the Buckeyes eked out the win in Columbus.[38]

Halfway through the Conference Schedule

The victory kept OSU undefeated in the Big Ten at 8–0. Almost as surprising was the second-place squad, Iowa, which was 6–2 after toppling Minnesota 81–64, behind 25 points from Ronnie Lester and 18 from William Mayfield. Purdue was third at 5–3 and three teams were 4–4, Illinois, Michigan, and Michigan State. This was quite a reversal for the Spartans. Roy Damer of the *Chicago Tribune* observed, "Just a couple weeks ago Michigan State was rated No.1 in the nation, but the Spartans now are .500 in the Big 10, tied for fourth and their title hopes are barely flickering. They are four games behind Ohio State (8–0) and need a winning streak to qualify for the NCAA tournament."[39]

Things were desperate for Michigan State as they faced Ohio State in East Lansing, but then they got worse, as Magic Johnson sprained his ankle with 2:23 left in the first half. His ankle was put in a pressure boot, but after Johnson begged to be reinserted in the game, he did return midway into the second half when Ohio State had taken the lead. The game went into overtime, before MSU won 84–79, as Magic scored 9 in the overtime and 23 in the game.[40]

The crushing defeat to MSU carried over to the next Ohio State game as the Buckeyes lost to Indiana two nights later in Bloomington 70–62. Iowa took advantage of the OSU loss to leap into first in the conference with a 97–71 defeat of Minnesota in Minneapolis. Michigan State rolled over Northwestern 83–65, with Magic Johnson playing just the last three minutes to test his ankle and settle his team.[41]

So it was a race again, and Michigan State was back in it. MSU briefly stepped out of conference to destroy Kansas 85–61, with Magic's playing resembling his normal with 12 points, 11 assists, and 10 rebounds. Then the Spartans whacked Iowa 60–57 in Iowa City. The key was MSU's defense, which held Big Ten scoring leader, Ronnie Lester, to just 5 points as he played only twenty-three minutes, fouling out with 11:34 left. Even so, Iowa could have won if they would have made their free throws. Iowa went just 9 of 21 from the line, while MSU was 20 of 27.[42]

The latest national polls had five Big Ten teams ranked in the top twenty nationally, led by MSU and followed by Iowa, Purdue, Illinois, and Ohio State. Noticeably absent were the Hoosiers of Indiana: this prompted David Israel to focus on Bob Knight, once again, and his behavior. Indiana was 5–5 in the conference, but Knight was still seeking what he termed "the perfect game." In just three years, five players had quit his squad, three were kicked off for what was determined to be marijuana usage, and Knight was battling a nagging image problem. Things seemed to have gotten worse for him with freshman eligibility letting them consider transferring to play three years somewhere else and players' concomitant "swelled heads" (i.e., thinking they could start and star right away) from wooing during the recruitment process. It was noted, however, that in the previous eight years he had sent more players to the pro ranks than anyone else and that eighteen of the nineteen players that stayed in school for four years had graduated.[43]

Things were starting to shake out in the conference race. Purdue defeated Illinois for the sixth Boilermaker win in a row, and Ohio State got back on the winning track, defeating Michigan 63–60 in Ann Arbor. OSU was still atop the standings at 9–2, but Purdue and Iowa were at 8–3, just a game back, with MSU lurking at 7–4. Michigan State shook up things a bit with a 73–55 defeat of OSU in Columbus. It was MSU's first conference road win, and Heathcote was pleased: "We are still a long way from the top, but we think we can win it."[44]

Iowa pushed Purdue out of a tie for first with a 75–72 win in Iowa City, despite 36 points from Joe Barry Carroll of the Boilermakers. Ohio State kept up with a 74–68 win at Minnesota. Michigan State also stayed in the picture by stopping Indiana in Bloomington 59–47, which was the Spartans' sixth win in a row. It was the third Spartan win over Indiana in the season: this time aided significantly by the disparity in free throws (IU was 1 for 1; MSU 17 for 20).[45]

Down the Stretch

The Big Ten title was still up for grabs, as were the two possible NCAA tourney slots for the Big Ten, with the NCAA field now up to 40 teams and seeding 24. OSU and Iowa were at 11–3 and MSU and Purdue were at 10–4 in league play. Nationally, Indiana State was still undefeated and had ascended to #1 in the polls along with MSU, the highest-ranked Big Ten team at #8. Purdue was at #13, Iowa at #14, and OSU at #17 with two weeks to go in the regular season.

The NCAA tourney would now be hosting forty teams and seeding twenty-four. Teams from the same conference could be in the same regional, and it was possible to seed a conference winner below another conference team, especially with more conferences using a tourney to determine the NCAA representative and generate more interest and income for the league.[46]

The first to crack under this pressure was Iowa, who dropped a 64–62 contest in Bloomington. Indiana slowed down the game, took good shots, and made 13 of 17 in the second half. Mike Woodson had half the Hoosier points with 31. Ohio State remained on top of the league with a 73–55 win over Illinois. Michigan State eked out a 73–67 victory over Purdue to move a game ahead of the Boilermakers and remain one behind OSU and Iowa. After the game, Heathcote quelled rumors that he might take the head coaching position at USC, saying that he would be back but doubted that Magic Johnson would be.[47]

The Big Ten now had a three-way tie at the top, with OSU, MSU, and Iowa all having 12–4 records in conference play and Purdue just a game behind at

11–5 with two games left for each team. MSU did its part and maintained the lead with a 78–63 win over Minnesota, but both Iowa and Ohio State lost, the former to Michigan 61–53 and the latter to Wisconsin 76–63. Purdue topped Indiana 55–48 to remain a game behind the sole leader, MSU.[48] Despite the victory, Heathcote noted that "our team was tight and the coach was tight."[49]

Then two nights later, Wisconsin surprised Michigan State 83–81, despite Magic's 26 points, 13 rebounds, and 8 assists. MSU was now 8–6 on the road but 12–0 at home. Purdue knocked off Ohio State to advance into a three-way tie for first and send OSU into fourth. Iowa pounded Northwestern to be co-leader in the conference, all with records of 13–5.[50]

The three-way tie was broken by MSU's superior overall record of 21–6. Iowa was 23–7. Michigan State, ranked #4 in the nation and winner of all four games against Iowa and Ohio State, and Iowa, #11, would be the Big Ten NCAA representatives. With that decided, the NIT invited Purdue (#14), Ohio State, and Indiana to join the field for that tournament. Clearly, the Big Ten had shown itself to be the most powerful conference in the nation from top to bottom, but that balance also hurt individual teams being ranked higher because of the difficult conference games, night in and night out.

The NIT

First up for the Big Ten was OSU, which overcame St. Joseph's University, in Columbus 80–66 behind Kelvin Ransey (18 points) and Herb Williams (16). The next night Purdue stomped Central Michigan 97–80 at home. Indiana also had no trouble with Texas Tech, defeating the Red Raiders 78–59 in Bloomington.[51]

On March 12, OSU, Purdue, and Indiana all continued their NIT title pursuit with home games. Indiana had the most trouble, winning 73–69 over Alcorn A&M, while Purdue eased past Dayton 84–70 and Ohio State topped Maryland 79–72.[52] All three continued the Big Ten surge, Purdue defeating Old Dominion 67–59 behind 30 points from Joe Barry Carroll. Ohio State and Indiana received byes to the semifinals.[53]

The NIT semifinals were played on March 19. The result was an all-Indiana NIT championship game, as Purdue beat Alabama 87–68, while Indiana beat Ohio State 64–55 in the rubber match of their three contests that season. Joe Barry Carroll had 42 points on 16 of 19 field-goal shooting, and Purdue shot 61 percent overall to overwhelm the Crimson Tide.[54]

On March 21, Indiana edged Purdue 53–52 for the NIT championship. Butch Carter and Ray Tolbert had 12 points each and were named co-MVPs. Carroll had 14 and Hallman 12 for Purdue. Knight was thrilled to win the

NIT: during his years at Army, the tourney had always been a big deal. He said, "I was more victory-dazed that night than any of the three NCAA championship nights."[1] Alabama prevented a Big Ten sweep by defeating Ohio State in the battle for third, 96–86.

The NCAA Tournament

On March 10, in its NCAA opener in Indianapolis, Iowa was unexpectedly beaten by Toledo 74–72 on a buzzer-beating shot. The Hawkeyes had led 41–29 at the half and extended the lead to 14 before going cold from the floor and the free-throw line. Iowa, the best free-throw shooting team in the Big Ten, made only 14 of 27 for the game and missed the front end of five one-and-ones to allow Toledo, which made 28 of 41 free throws, back into the game.[55]

The following night, Michigan State, with a #2 tournament seed, had no trouble with Lamar, winning 95–64 in Murfreesboro, Tennessee. Johnson had 13 points, 17 rebounds, and 16 assists (many of them to Greg Kelser, who scored 31 points). One concern was that Jay Vincent injured his foot late in the first half and left the arena on crutches.[56] Michigan State played its second NCAA game on March 16 against the LSU Tigers in Indianapolis's Market Square Arena and sent the Tigers home with an 87–71 loss. Johnson had 24 points and 12 assists, while Ron Charles, playing in place of the injured Jay Vincent (who had a stress fracture in his foot), had 18 points and 14 rebounds.[57]

The win over LSU set up Michigan State against Notre Dame for the Mideast regional championship and a trip to Salt Lake City. The game would be nationally televised on NBC and would be a very physical contest for both squads.[58] Surprisingly, Michigan State put away the Irish 80–68. Kelser had 34 points, while Johnson had 19 (and 13 assists). Heathcote called the game "a tribute to a great bunch who made a superb comeback this season" and noted that "we were able to control the tempo; we're a very good tempo club."[59] The team was ready to head to Salt Lake City, where they would meet Penn, the first Ivy League team to make it to the Final Four since Princeton in 1965.[60] In the other semifinal, West regional champion DePaul would play Midwest regional champion Indiana State.

On March 24, the NCAA semifinals were played on the University of Utah campus. In game two, Indiana State defeated DePaul 76–74 as Larry Bird scored 35 points and the Sycamores remained undefeated. In game one, Michigan State destroyed the Penn Quakers, 101–67. The Spartans led 51–17 at the half by shooting 63 percent from the floor and holding Penn to 17 percent shooting. Magic Johnson had 29 points, 10 rebounds, and 10 assists.

Heathcote said, "I was surprised to win so easily."[61] DePaul's coach Ray Meyer declared that MSU would be "just too much for Bird" and predicted victory for the Spartans.[62]

Meyer was right. But it was great MSU defense as well as their offense that carried them to victory 75–64 in the final game. Bird only made 7 of 21 shots against the matchup MSU zone. Anticipating that Johnson would be double-teamed most of the time, Heathcote decided that Terry Donnelly was likely to be open for jump shots when Magic drove—and he was. Taking open shots, he went 5 for 5 in field goal shooting plus hit 5 of 6 free throws for 15 total points. Johnson had 24 points and 5 assists, while Kelser had 19 points and 7 assists. Bird had 19 points and 13 rebounds but just 2 assists. Indiana State shot poorly from the free-throw line (10 of 22, 45 percent) and was not great from the floor either (27 of 64, 42 percent), while MSU shot very well from the field (26 of 43, 60 percent) and well enough from the line, considering they had many more attempts than Indiana State (22 of 33, 67 percent).[63] Heathcote's summation: "Unless other teams have played you and scouted you, it's hard to adjust to what Earvin Johnson does and what Greg Kelser does."[64]

This NCAA finals game has since become legendary, and a number of myths have been attached to it, such as the fine shooting by both teams (which was clearly not the case) and the quality of play by the two top stars, Johnson and Bird. Certainly, Johnson as Most Outstanding Player had an excellent game, but Bird's poor shooting and six turnovers were not characteristic of the future NBA Hall of Fame player.

What was not mythical were the enormous television ratings for the game—the highest up until that time—that were the impetus for later conference television packages and the unprecedented amount ($48 million for three years) that CBS paid to outbid NBC for the television rights when CBS's contract ran out in 1981. In addition, ESPN, which began in 1979, also joined the bidding, and this both upped the ante and made college basketball more visible nationally in future seasons.[65]

With the win, Michigan State and the Big Ten capped a fabulous season, and all indications pointed to things being almost as formidable for 1979–80. One NCAA champion, two NIT finalists, and one other team (Iowa) a co-Big Ten champ: the results and prospects were impressive. Of the fifty starters for Big Ten teams, only eight were seniors, and only Johnson was expected to leave school early to join the NBA. Half the squads would have all five starters returning, and two would have four starters returning. Roy Damer declared Ohio State, Indiana, and Purdue as favorites for the next season with only Purdue losing a starter (Jerry Sichting).[66] Johnson was the winner of the Silver Basketball, denoting the Most Valuable Player in the conference, with Carroll coming in second.

There was still some question about whether the top high school player in the Midwest, Isiah Thomas (from Chicago), would be playing for a Big Ten team the next year. His choices had been narrowed to DePaul, Indiana, and Iowa. On April 9, he announced for Indiana, but Thomas's mother had some concerns, as did certain members of the media, about how Thomas would fit with Knight's coaching style. At that time Knight noted that "our program is not for everyone. It takes a certain type of personality to play for Indiana." In addition, there was a concern that Knight would not even be in Bloomington the next season. But on April 17, he rejected an offer from the Boston Celtics, stating that he wanted to continue coaching at the college level, but if he ever wanted to coach at the professional level, he would "consider it an honor to coach the Celtics."[67]

The future was extremely bright for the best basketball conference in the country. How that would play out with or without Magic Johnson remained to be seen.

CHAPTER 6

INTO THE 1980s
The Big Ten Remains Assertive

When the Big Ten basketball season was previewed in mid-November, a number of writers predicted no repeat title for Michigan State. This was because MSU would lose their two top players: Earvin "Magic" Johnson, who went to the NBA under the "hardship" rule in place at that time, and Greg Kelser, who had been a senior. The Spartans returned four of their six top players but were "virtually ignored in preseason polls," noted Bill Halls of the *Detroit News*, who went on to assert that "there was little question that the Big Ten is the toughest basketball conference in the nation" with thirty-nine of fifty starters returning for the ten conference teams.[1]

At least one noted basketball annual (*Street & Smith's*) reflected this feeling, picking Michigan State for fifth in the conference behind Ohio State, Indiana, Purdue, and Iowa. Also consonant with Halls's views on conference strength was a comment by Illinois coach Lou Henson, who said, "Looking up and down the league, it's hard to believe but it's going to be stronger than it was last year."[2] Robert Markus agreed, selecting Indiana and Ohio State as the top two teams in the conference and calling the Big Ten "the strongest league in the country." Markus also noted that Joe Barry Carroll would be "the most dominant player in the country." Purdue's only problem would be replacing the graduated Jerry Sichting.[3]

An indication of the player quality of the Big Ten was that four of the top ten preseason All-America players as selected by *Street & Smith* were from the Big Ten: Joe Barry Carroll, Ronnie Lester of Iowa, Kevin McHale of Minnesota, and Mike Woodson of Indiana. Clark Kellogg of Ohio State was named as "High Honorable Mention" before even playing a college game.[4]

In mid-November, Indiana entertained the Soviet national team (which had won the bronze medal at the 1976 Olympics in Montreal) and sent them packing after a 78–50 Indiana victory. The Hoosiers would be a force to be reckoned with in the Big Ten chase.[5] Indiana followed up their triumph over the Soviets with an official season opener against Miami of Ohio, defeating the Redskins (changed to RedHawks in 1997) 80–52. In assessing his team, Knight, not known for excessive praise said, "We were awfully good."[6]

On that same night, four other Big Ten teams played early games with three (Ohio State, Michigan, and Iowa) romping to victories at home against overmatched opponents, but Michigan State lost in New York to St. John's at the Joe Lapchick Tournament. Jay Vincent had 30 points for the Spartans and was named tourney MVP, but it was not enough to prevent an 88–73 defeat. The Big Ten was 11–1 in early season contests, indicating another good year for the conference.[7]

The Big Ten continued to defeat respected but weaker opponents.[8] Tex Winter, who had coached Northwestern for five seasons before moving on to Long Beach State in 1978, proclaimed Big Ten basketball the best in the nation: "[The] players are so much bigger and physical—and there's more of them." At this point the Big Ten had five unbeaten teams, and all of them had limited their opponents to fifty-five points or fewer in each game.[9]

Indiana continued to look powerful as they defeated highly ranked Georgetown in Bloomington 76–69, behind 19 points from Isiah Thomas and 23 from Mike Woodson. Georgetown started the game making 22 of 32 shots, but the Hoosiers hung in until the Hoyas cooled off—then Indiana pulled away. Four days later, however, Indiana was beaten in Rupp Arena by Kentucky 69–58 before 23,789 Wildcat rooters. In that contest, Isiah Thomas fouled out with fourteen points but, more importantly, was forced to sit for two seven-minute periods in the game, and that was the biggest key to the Kentucky win.[10] The next day the UPI poll reflected the IU loss, as Indiana dropped to #4 behind Duke, Ohio State, and Kentucky. Purdue was #7 in this poll and Iowa #13.

An even bigger loss was suffered by Indiana when Mike Woodson went down with a bad back on December 20. He would be out for at least two weeks. Coach Knight took the occasion to call Woodson "the best player in history to not even get honorable mention All-America honors."[11]

The Big Ten was further bruised by Indiana's 61–57 loss in Bloomington to North Carolina. The Hoosiers had lost both Woodson and Randy Wittman to injuries, so much more pressure was on Isiah Thomas, who rose to the occasion with 18 points, 7 assists, and 2 steals while playing all forty minutes. UNC spread the floor and, as Thomas noted, "We couldn't help out on defense," especially missing Woodson. Dean Smith noted that, with Woodson out, "We played more zone than we normally do." The loss dropped the Hoosiers to 5–2, while UNC went to 5–1 for the season.[12]

Isiah Thomas, All-American at Indiana. *(Courtesy of Indiana University Archives)*

Ohio State asserted itself against Tennessee, a top SEC team, with a 91–65 walloping in Columbus, as four Bucks scored in double figures topped by Herb Williams with 28. Minnesota surprised unbeaten Kansas State in Minneapolis 78–61, as McHale scored 23 and took 11 rebounds. The big surprise, literally, was seven-foot-two freshman Randy Breuer who scored 18 off the bench and helped the Gophers up their record to 4–2.

Holiday Tourney Time

In Las Vegas, at the Holiday Classic, Weber State edged Michigan State 63–61, despite 17 points from Jay Vincent and 16 from Ron Charles. Illinois won its opener 75–48 over Army in Hawaii at the Rainbow Classic, while Michigan was upset by Mississippi 71–66 at the Sugar Bowl Classic in New Orleans.

Indiana won the Cabrillo Classic 61–52 over Brown. Isiah Thomas was the tourney MVP and had 11 points, 6 rebounds, and 5 assists in the final game. Ray Tolbert scored 15 points. Minnesota won its Pillsbury Classic 69–63 over Texas A&M, led by tournament MVP Kevin McHale's 21 points. Michigan took third-place in the Sugar Bowl Classic (Mike McGee had 29 points) with a 72–71 win over Tulane, and Wisconsin took consolation honors at the Rainbow Classic with a 78–54 Army win.

The 1980 Big Ten Season Opens

At this point, Iowa was 9–0, while Ohio State and Purdue were both 7–1. Illinois was 9–2, Indiana 8–2, and Minnesota 7–2. Northwestern was 5–4, so every team was at .500 or better as the conference season opened.

In a tight contest in Columbus, OSU topped Indiana 59–58 on two free throws by freshman Clark Kellogg with seven seconds remaining. Isiah Thomas had 15 points and 6 assists in the loss, impressing OSU coach Eldon Miller enough for him to call Thomas "the best first-year backcourt man I've ever seen." The loss dropped Bob Knight's team to a record of 13–5 against alma mater OSU, with all five losses in Columbus. Don Pierson of the *Chicago Tribune* saw Kellogg as the key to Ohio State success in balancing Kelvin Ransey and Herb Williams, adding another scorer and rebounder, both of which Kellogg did well.[13]

In what seemed to be a significant early season meeting, Ohio State was able to stay undefeated in the league by topping Purdue 67–58 in Columbus. Purdue had a 9–0 lead early on and held a 45–37 halftime lead; but once OSU took the lead, they went into a four corners offense with just under three minutes to play. OSU used the clock up and made free throws, led by four players in double figures. Slow, deliberate play was the story in Wisconsin where the

Badgers upset Indiana 52–50. Bob Knight, who had brought this tactic to the Big Ten, was hit with a technical for his continued referee haranguing. The Big Ten was playing rougher and more slowly, and the referees were accused of being inconsistent with their calls. *Inconsistent* would be a watchword for the season, with many coaches complaining about refereeing even more than usual.[14]

The conference returned to conference play when all the schools resumed following a break for semester exams. The leaders held serve with Purdue topping Northwestern in a surprisingly close game in Mackey Arena 68–63, Ohio State easing past Minnesota in Columbus 75–70, and Indiana beating Iowa decisively in Bloomington 80–69. In the latter game Isiah Thomas played what Roy Damer called his "best game" with 14 points, 13 assists, 6 rebounds, and 4 steals. Bob Knight said, "He [Thomas] controlled the game and got involved in more things."[15]

Ohio State at 5–0 was the only undefeated team in the conference, a game ahead of Purdue (4–1) and two games ahead of Indiana and Minnesota (both 3–2). Ohio State kept its conference record perfect two days later with a struggle at Champaign before beating the Illini 79–76. Herb Williams had a fabulous game with 24 points and 7 blocks and was backed by 15 from Kelvin Ransey, who also had 8 assists.

Purdue continued to rely on Joe Barry Carroll, and opponents continued to double team him or collapse three men in a zone on him when he received the ball, with the result being poor shooting by Carroll and losses for Purdue. The latest team to do this was Indiana, who held Carroll to 5 of 20 shooting in a 69–58 win at Bloomington.

Ohio State's grip on first was loosened when Michigan State, just 3–5 in the Big Ten, defeated the Buckeyes 74–54 in East Lansing. It was the Spartans' fourteenth victory in a row over OSU, seven of those under Eldon Miller. There was now a four-way tie for first in the Big Ten after Purdue and Indiana won at home and Minnesota at Northwestern. Two nights later, Ohio State continued its slump losing at Wisconsin 73–69 after blowing an 11-point lead with 7:20 to play. Minnesota also lost, at Iowa 73–63. Purdue moved into first, alone, after topping Indiana 56–51where 49 fouls were called.[16]

Ohio State ended its losing streak by defeating Michigan 66–63 in overtime. It was Michigan's fourth OT loss of the season, enraging Johnny Orr, who said, "Officials have decided three or four of our games this season." Purdue stayed tied at the top with a sloppy win at home over Minnesota 58–54, while Iowa managed to beat Michigan State 43–39 in overtime. The conference as a whole was playing more cautiously, and the slow-down games were boring the fans.[17]

Clark Kellogg, Big Ten MVP in 1982. *(Courtesy of Ohio State Athletics)*

Two-thirds of the way through the conference season, seven teams were still capable of winning the title. It may have been a question of parity or just a weaker year for the Big Ten, even though three teams were still ranked in the national polls with Ohio State at #9, Purdue at #15, and Indiana at #20.

Indiana joined Purdue, Ohio State, and Minnesota in a four-way tie for first (all at 8–5) by defeating Iowa 66–55 in Iowa City. The victory was doubly thrilling for the Hoosiers because of the return of the injured Mike Woodson after back surgery on December 27.[18] Ohio State, Indiana, and Purdue were now the three-way leaders, with Iowa and Minnesota a game behind with four games to go. Ohio State humbled Illinois 71–57, with freshman Clark Kellogg, the six-foot-eight forward, playing point guard and doing it well. Against the Illini, he had 11 points, 15 rebounds, 6 assists, and 2 blocks while guarding both Illinois centers.[19]

All three Big Ten leaders were still ranked in the national polls, but the next week started with the co-leaders down to two: Ohio State, who eased past Northwestern 68–59 in Columbus, and Indiana, who managed to defeat an inspired Michigan State squad 75–72 in East Lansing. Purdue collapsed in the second half in Ann Arbor. After building a seven-point lead at the half, the Boilermakers lost by 11, 75–64, as Michigan scored the first twenty points of the second half and never surrendered the lead.[20]

The excitement was building as both Ohio State and Indiana kept winning. The Buckeyes won at Purdue 64–60. In Bloomington, Indiana beat Wisconsin 61–52, with Isiah Thomas scoring 18 and Mike Woodson 16. It was a rugged game, with four Badger starters fouling out. The Badgers were called for 27 fouls to just 17 on the Hoosiers. After the game, Coach Cofield of Wisconsin picked Indiana to defeat the Buckeyes on the last day of the season and win the Big Ten title.[21]

On that last Saturday of the season, all three leaders won again to make their résumés even stronger. Purdue, with Carroll scoring 26 points and snaring 13 rebounds, won easily over Michigan State 91–73. Michigan State coach Jud Heathcote was impressed by the star center but cautioned, "If he goes through the motions, or gets in foul trouble, they're just an average team."[22]

The Big Ten title would come down to the last game, Ohio State at Indiana, which was pushed back to Sunday in order to provide a national television audience the pleasure of viewing the contest, which went to overtime before Indiana won 76–73. Both teams would receive byes in the NCAA tournament and play second-round NCAA games on March 9. Knight, commenting on the quality of the players in that game, later said, "Only thirteen players got into the game. Six of them became first-round NBA draft picks, three more played in the NBA, and a tenth, our Landon Turner, I believe would have been the first pick in the 1982 draft if not for the accident that ended his career in 1981."[23] Those players included Mike Woodson, Isiah Thomas, Herb Williams, Clark Kellogg, Kelvin Ransey, Randy Wittman, and Ray Tolbert.

Tournament Time

The NIT, with three Big Ten teams amid the sixteen teams invited, opened before the NCAA tourney. Minnesota began with a 64–50 win at home against Bowling Green. Illinois ran away from Loyola 105–87 in Champaign, as four players had 18 or more for the Illini. Michigan defeated Nebraska in Ann Arbor 76–69, led by Big Ten scoring leader Mike McGee's 25 points.[24]

With the new eligibility rules for the NCAA (a conference was no longer limited to two teams, plus there was seeding to try and make each region roughly equal in quality), four Big Ten teams were invited to the expanded forty-eight-team NCAA field: IU, OSU, Purdue, and Iowa. The latter two played first-round games: Purdue overpowered LaSalle 90–82 in West La-fayette, led by 33 points from Joe Barry Carroll. Iowa opened with an 86–72 victory over Virginia Commonwealth in Greensboro, North Carolina.[25]

The Hawkeyes followed with an impressive 77–64 win over North Caro-lina State in Greensboro, and Purdue also won, 87–72, over St. John's. Joe Barry Carroll was dominant with 36 points and 12 rebounds. The next night Indiana kept the conference win streak going with a 68–59 victory over Vir-ginia Tech in Lexington, Kentucky, while Ohio State, playing in the West region, defeated Arizona State 89–75 in Tempe.[26]

In the NIT, Illinois ended Illinois State's season with a 75–65 win in Champaign. Illinois surprised ISU by playing a zone defense that was de-scribed as rare as "members of Animal House use of a deodorant," by Rob-ert Markus of the *Chicago Tribune*. Michigan kept up its end of the Big Ten winning streak, toppling University of Texas-El Paso in Ann Arbor 74–65, as Mike McGee had 23 points in the win. Minnesota, too, won at home, beating Mississippi 58–56.[27]

Both #4 seed Ohio State and #2 seed Indiana were eliminated from NCAA play on March 13, the former losing to #8 seed UCLA 72–68 and the latter to #6 seed Purdue. Scott, Ransey, and Kellogg all fouled out for OSU. In the battle of Indiana, Purdue crushed Indiana and, at one point, led by 19 with 8 minutes to play. Indiana battled back to make it close but still lost 76–69. Bob Knight observed, "Purdue had better intensity and took it away from us at the beginning." Purdue coach Lee Rose said, "This certainly was a great win for our players. They played with a lot of commitment and heart."[28] Morris and Edmonson had 20 each, while Thomas led the Hoosiers with 30, but it was not enough. So the two top Big Ten teams were out.[29]

In the NIT, things were a bit better as Illinois defeated Murray State 65–63, and Minnesota pounded Southwestern Louisiana 94–73. Michigan was sent packing, however, by Virginia in Charlottesville 79–68, as a freshman,

Ralph Sampson, scored 26 points and snared 12 rebounds to lead the Cavs.[30] Two Big Ten teams would advance to the semis in Madison Square Garden, where they would meet each other while Virginia took on University of Nevada–Las Vegas. The Gophers edged the Illini 65–63, but Robert Markus felt that "it wasn't as close or exciting as the score indicated." Coach Lou Henson noted that "the stats say we should have lost by 15. The only thing we did right was show courage and guts. They just killed us. Man-to-man, they ate us up." It was Minnesota's eighth win in a row. The NIT final, however, went to Virginia 58–55, as Sampson scored 15 and took 15 rebounds.

Kevin McHale summed up Minnesota's end: "We just shot terribly twice in this tournament."[31] McHale's year was bittersweet. "I hoped that we would have gotten into the NCAAs that year, but we were just off probation, it was my only year eligible to go to a postseason tournament, and I was just happy to get into postseason play."[32]

In the NCAA tournament, both #5 Iowa and #6 Purdue managed to surprise higher seeded teams, Syracuse (#1), Georgetown (#3), and Duke (#4), respectively, to advance to the NCAA Final Four. Iowa beat the Orange 88–77 then defeated Georgetown 81–80 by shooting 71 percent and committing only one turnover in the second half. After the game, Lute Olson asserted, "The fact is the Big 10 is the toughest conference in post-season play, bar none."[33]

The Purdue win over Duke was keyed by Mideast region Most Outstanding Player Joe Barry Carroll's 26 points. Purdue also made 15 of 20 free throws in the last five minutes and 22 of 29 for the game; this from the team that finished last in the Big Ten in free throw percentage at .664.[34]

So the Big Ten had two teams in the NCAA Final Four and two of the four semifinalists of the NIT tourney. No league could compare. Bill Jauss tried to explain why. He cited gifted players; established, winning coaches who were brought together from around the country; and large new arenas. This latter point was vital as the NCAA selected such arenas for postseason play and at that time did not prohibit a team from playing NCAA tournament games at home. The result of this was a large league payoff, estimated at $1.23 million for NCAA and NIT participation. Each NCAA Final Four school received $320,000 because of increased television revenue. In the NIT, Illinois and Minnesota got $75,000 each, while Michigan received $40,000 for three rounds of play. Things would get better when NBC signed a two-year $18.5 million pact with the NCAA for future tourneys. As for Big Ten performance, the conference had gone 17–2, including the Purdue-over-Indiana and Minnesota-over-Illinois victories. Over the previous five years, the Big Ten had gone 27–6 in the NCAA tourney, and eight different Big Ten teams (all but Northwestern and Wisconsin) had made the Final Four of the NCAA or the NIT since 1976.[35]

The Final Four was played in Indianapolis. UCLA, now coached by Larry Brown, topped Purdue 67–62. Brown rotated four players to cover Joe Barry Carroll. Brown said, "You don't stop Carroll with just one man." Lee Rose, Purdue coach, observed, "It was a hard fought game. Very physical." Nevertheless, it was free throws that killed the Boilermakers as they went 12 of 27 to UCLA's 21 of 25. As Purdue forward Arnette Hallman noted, "This was a real team effort; we all played poorly."[36]

Iowa fell 80–72 to Louisville and Darrell Griffith's 34 points. Iowa was "throwing up bricks" but might have survived had Ronnie Lester not reinjured his knee with 7:57 left in the first half. Lester reinjured his knee when he collided with a Louisville player on a fast-break drive. Before the injury, he had racked up 10 points in ten minutes and had covered Griffith well.[37]

At that time a third-place game was still played, and Purdue defeated Iowa 75–58. Joe Barry Carroll had 35 and totaled 160 points in the tournament to lead in scoring. Louisville defeated UCLA for the championship 59–54.[38]

The Big Ten still had lots of postseason action. On March 28, the *Chicago Tribune* announced the winner of the Silver Basketball and Most Valuable Player in the Big Ten. Mike Woodson, who had come back from injury to play 14 games, averaged 19.3 points, and led IU to the Big Ten title, was the winner. There were also some dramatic coaching changes.

First, Johnny Orr jumped to Iowa State as the highest-paid college coach in America at an annual salary of $45,000. In addition, Orr would have a television show, two radio shows, a camp, cars, and a large insurance package. Apparently, his wife had wanted to retire, and this additional salary made it possible, as he left behind a salary of $33,500 at Michigan.[39]

Later that week, rumors were flying when Lee Rose, Purdue's coach, interviewed at the University of South Florida. The idea was mind-boggling. In two years, Rose had led Purdue to two Final Fours and a record of 50–18 in the best conference in the country. Why leave, then? For some reason, Rose had a bad relationship with Athletic Director George King, who had been the basketball coach from 1965 to 1972 and liked to interfere with Rose in his position. King called Rose's departure "bad timing." That same day, Bill Frieder was named coach at Michigan.[40]

A week later, Purdue signed a new coach, forty-three-year-old Gene Keady, who had gone 37–20 in his two years at Western Kentucky. Despite the big step up, Keady was confident, noting, "I thrive on pressure and I'm looking forward to coaching in the greatest basketball conference in the country."[41] He faced a daunting task because both Carroll and Hallman were departing, and no one had yet signed a letter of intent with Purdue. Trying to rectify that, Keady was already in pursuit of Chicago Manley High star Russell Cross.[42]

Looking to the 1980–81 Season

The Big Ten basketball season began with high expectations. Most of the teams started with exhibition games. Illinois played the South Korean National team in Champaign and won easily 97–73. With nine lettermen returning from a 22–13 team, Illini hopes were high, but coach Lou Henson noted after the game, "We're not a very good defensive team right now." Freshman Derek Harper looked like he would be a great addition to Illinois.[43]

At the Big Ten press conference for coaches, only Bob Knight was a no-show. His team was picked by the other coaches to win the Big Ten title, along with Ohio State and Iowa. The same three teams were seen by Lee Caryer in *Street & Smith's Basketball Yearbook* as the top Big Ten teams, followed by Minnesota, Michigan, Illinois, Purdue, Northwestern, Michigan State, and Wisconsin. Isiah Thomas and Herb Williams were seen as two of ten top All-America players.[44] Roy Damer considered Indiana the toughest team in the Big Ten and noted that in the previous season, six Big Ten teams had won at least twenty games, the league won 76 percent of its nonconference games, and thirty-four of fifty starters returned for the 1980–81 season. The Big Ten would still be the toughest kid on the block.[45]

Most of the early Big Ten games were against weak nonconference opponents, but a few were interesting. In a rugged contest where fifty-three fouls were called, #2 Kentucky defeated #9 Ohio State in Lexington 70–64. Bill Jauss called it "a rugby scrum disguised as a basketball game." Kentucky then defeated Indiana in Bloomington 68–66, despite 20 points from Isiah Thomas and 15 from Landon Turner. Notre Dame then defeated the Hoosiers in South Bend 68–64 behind 23 from Jim Paxson, who "wanted to get back at Bobby Knight" after being cut from the US Pan Am Games team by Knight the previous summer.[46]

After his Marquette squad lost to Illinois, Coach Hank Raymonds declared Illinois to be the "best Illini team ever."[47] At this point, Illinois was one of four unbeaten Big Ten teams, and the conference record against nonconference foes was 41–8. The UPI poll had Indiana at #7, Ohio State #10, Iowa #15, Illinois #16, and Michigan #17, all behind the top three of Kentucky, DePaul, and UCLA. Then the wheels started to come off for the Big Ten as South Alabama beat Ohio State in Columbus, BYU defeated Michigan State in Provo, Marquette topped Minnesota, and BYU continued their spoiler role with a win over formerly undefeated Illinois in a Tennessee tournament.[48]

During the holiday tournament season, Illinois rebounded from the loss to BYU to defeat Iona in a consolation victory. Arizona State, however, was an unkind host, topping Ohio State 71–58 in Tempe. In a nationally televised contest, Indiana fell to North Carolina 65–56 in Chapel Hill, despite 20 points from Isiah Thomas.[49] Minnesota beat national champion Louisville 62–56 on the road in what was called an "ugly game."[50] Purdue was crushed at Tulsa 90–76, and Indiana battled back to win at Kansas State 51–44. But by Christmas, the Big Ten had only one undefeated team: Michigan at 7–0.[51] Minnesota entered Big Ten play with a record of 8–1. In Hawaii, Indiana was upset by Clemson 58–57 and then by Pan American 66–60 at the Rainbow Classic. It would be the low point of the Hoosier season.[52]

Overall, the conference record was now 71–20. Favorites Indiana (7–5) and Ohio State (5–3) were disappointing, while Minnesota (9–1), Iowa (8–1), and Illinois (7–1) looked stronger than expected.

The start of the Big Ten season, however, would see a return to normality on the opening night of the season, when Purdue (8–2) handed Michigan its first loss with an 81–74 victory in West Lafayette. Freshman Russell Cross went 9 of 11 from the floor (21 points), and Keith Edmonson was 10 of 13 (20) as Purdue "shot the eyes out" at home with 37 of 49 field goals (76 percent), a Big Ten record. As Gene Keady said in an understatement, "The kids were really ready to play tonight."[53]

Indiana opened its conference season by seemingly awakening from a deep torpor and routing Illinois 78–61 in Bloomington. Ted Kitchel dropped 40 on the Illini by shooting 11 of 13 field goals and 18 of 18 free throws. Illinois, as a team, was 15 of 17 from the line. Purdue kept up its winning ways against Ohio State, 73–65, who fouled their way to the loss with 35 of them, leading to Purdue making 31–48 free throws. Herb Williams snared 27 rebounds for the Buckeyes, who "played a mediocre game," according to coach Eldon Miller.[54]

Purdue followed up its Ohio State win by losing badly to Illinois 87–65 in a running game that Coach Gene Keady said they never should have engaged in. "We tried to run with Illinois and caught 'slow foot road disease,'" he remembered.[55] Michigan battled Indiana in Ann Arbor and prevailed 55–52 in overtime. Mike McGee had 18, while Isiah Thomas had 18 points, and Ray Tolbert had 14 for the Hoosiers.[56] The league seemed to be a toss-up with no squad stepping forward to dominate.

Michigan followed its big win over Indiana by forgetting to show up for its game against Iowa in Ann Arbor. The Hawkeyes crushed them 73–56, and Coach Bill Frieder said, Iowa "just outhustled us in the first half."[57]

Indiana played in Columbus the next night on national television, and the Hoosiers were 67–60 winners, supported by 17 from Ray Tolbert and 16 from Isiah Thomas. After the game, Bob Knight commented on the successful academic record of his players. In ten years and with 36 recruits, he had 7 men transfer while the remaining 29 had all graduated. "The three things most important to me as a coach are one, play as hard as you can; two, be competitive; three, be smart." Spoiled by the likes of Scott May, Quinn Buckner, and Steve Green, Knight admitted that he was unable to lose "unemotionally; that's where I'm an abject failure."[58]

The next week Illinois hit a new low in scoring, while losing at home to Wisconsin 54–45. Lou Henson called it "the worst game we've ever played at Illinois. . . . I don't think I've had another team flatter." Michigan was unable to build on its big win over Illinois at home; they lost 69–63 in Columbus to an Ohio State team that moved into a tie for first. Michigan State surprised Purdue in West Lafayette 74–68; Russell Cross disappeared, scoring just 8 points and snaring 6 rebounds. Coach Gene Keady described it as a "typical freshman game." Ohio State grabbed a share of first by beating Michigan in Columbus 69–63 behind 23 from Herb Williams.[59]

The Buckeyes were not able to sustain their momentum. They lost at #1-ranked Virginia 89–73, as OSU just ran out of gas while Ralph Sampson dropped forty points on them. The Big Ten seemed to have no dominant team and the conference standings reflected that. Four teams were tied for first and three others were just one game behind as the conference race reached its halfway point. Coach Bill Frieder observed that "teams are mentally tougher these days." Eldon Miller said, "You have to play well day in and day out." It was a draining prospect.[60]

The next week, Ohio State stayed on top by edging Wisconsin in Madison 71–67. Iowa remained tied with OSU by running Purdue out of Carver-Hawkeye Arena 84–67, and Indiana also stayed tied for the top by edging Minnesota in overtime in Minneapolis 56–53. The Hoosiers came back from a 30–18 deficit to tie the game at 43 before winning. Tolbert (17) and Thomas (13) were leading scorers, while Breuer led the Gophers with 21.[61] The mashed-up standings now had Iowa, OSU, and Indiana at 5–2 while Minnesota, Illinois, and Michigan stood at 4–3.

The tie at the top was broken when Illinois pounded Iowa 79–66 in Champaign; Indiana got by Purdue 69–61 in Bloomington, and Ohio State lost in East Lansing to MSU 60–54. In the first game there were 52 fouls called, 30 of which were on Iowa, allowing Illinois to make 33 of 42 free throws to Iowa's 16 of 25. The Indiana game had 53 fouls called, and Roy Damer said that the game "looked more like football." Gene Keady said "the officiating was horrible. . . . They wouldn't let you play basketball."[62]

Despite leading the Big Ten by one game, Bob Knight was still treading a fine line between intimidation and violation. He was warned by the conference to keep his hands off the referees, but he responded by saying that he was just trying to see around the third official for "the 50th time in my career."[63]

The next Thursday, OSU, Iowa, Indiana, and Purdue all won; so the standings, after 11 games, had Iowa and Indiana tied at 8–3, with Michigan, OSU, Purdue, and Illinois all at 7–4. This showed the league's parity but hurt in national rankings with no Big Ten team in the top ten. The back and forth continued as Minnesota and Michigan State topped favored Purdue and Michigan, respectively. It was becoming a free-for-all.

In a showdown in Iowa, the Hawkeyes pounded the Hoosiers 78–65, "lowlighted" by Isiah Thomas's ejection with 39 seconds left after he hit Steve Krafcisin, who led Iowa with 18 points.[64]

The mess continued two nights later. Illinois topped Michigan State to tie Indiana, who defeated Minnesota, for second place, while Iowa won at Purdue, 67–62, to take over first place. This game was won at the free-throw line as Iowa went 21 of 33, while Purdue was just 6 of 12.[65]

This put Iowa at 11–3, with Illinois and Indiana at 10–4, while Purdue fell to 8–6 and three teams to 7–7. There were just two more weeks left in the regular season. February ended with Illinois being toppled at Minnesota 75–59 and Iowa scraping by at home against Michigan and Mike McGee's 29 points. Indiana crushed Ohio State 74–58 as OSU blew apart with 25 turnovers to just 11 assists.[66]

It all would come down to the last day of the conference season with Iowa and Indiana tied for the top. The Hoosiers won easily at Michigan State 69–48. Tolbert had 17 points, and Thomas had 14. But it was free throws and overall defense that made the difference. Bob Knight acknowledged that "our defense was very good and it was different," switching from man-to-man to match-up zones. Indiana was 21 of 29 from the line to just 6 of 10 for MSU.[67]

Iowa could not keep the tie as they lost at Ohio State 78–70. Coach Lute Olson called it "a horrible effort from some people." The result was Indiana winning the Big Ten with a 14–4 record, Iowa finishing second at 13–5, and Illinois third at 12–6.

The expectation in the league was that at least three teams (Indiana, Iowa, Illinois) would get NCAA bids and maybe more. But in the end, it was only those three that got bids despite the record that the league had compiled over the previous five years. Gene Keady said, "The record speaks for itself." Both the ACC and the SEC got four teams into the tournament and the Big

Eight had three. The Big Ten coaches considered it a slap in the face to the conference. Bill Frieder said that "Wayne Duke [chair of the NCAA selection committee and current Big Ten commissioner] should be ashamed of himself." Judd Heathcote said, "Based on our record in the tournament I think we proved that we're the strongest league and until that is disproved, I think we deserve more representation."[68] Marquette coach Al McGuire blamed the NCAA's interest in full conference representation, rather than getting the best forty-eight teams in the tournament. He thought that the automatic bids for twenty-three conference champions and three ECAC winners diluted the field. He would have taken ten or eleven of those out and put them in the NIT.[69]

Purdue, Minnesota, and Michigan all received NIT bids. Despite Michigan's excellent overall record, Jim Dutcher of Minnesota thought the Wolverines had "backed in" to the NIT with a weak nonconference record and having lost seven of their last eight contests.[70] These issues would all have to be played out, literally, in the two tourneys.

Sam Vincent of MSU led the conference in scoring with 433 points (24.1 ppg) with Mike McGee of Michigan second with 428 (23.8 ppg). Vincent was also named UPI's Big Ten Player of the Year with Isiah Thomas second. The AP selected Vincent, McGee, Isiah Thomas, Kevin Boyle (Iowa), and Eddie Johnson (Illinois) as their All-Big Ten team.[71]

The Tournaments

The NIT would open first. Minnesota hosted Drake with the Gophers winning easily, 90–77. Purdue had no trouble winning at home 84–58 against Rhode Island, outrebounding their smaller foes 49–27 and shooting 56 percent from the floor to URI's 35 percent. Michigan, led by twenty-six points from McGee, won 74–58 in their opener, defeating Duquesne.

Michigan, Purdue, and Minnesota all won in their next NIT contests, but Purdue just squeaked by. Michigan easily beat Toledo 80–68, and Minnesota had no trouble against Connecticut, 84–66. Purdue seemed asleep, defeating Toledo, 50–46, and it took two technical fouls on coach Gene Keady, apparently, to rouse the Boilermakers to defeat Dayton, 50–46. Keady said "Eastern refs don't know me. . . . This was one of our worst performances of the year."[72]

Minnesota could not keep up the Big Ten winning streak in the Gophers' next NIT contest, losing 80–69 to West Virginia. Michigan followed suit, losing badly at Syracuse 91–76. The Orangemen put the game away early in the second half by hitting sixteen field goals in a row. This left only Purdue to represent the Big Ten in the NIT.[73]

Purdue rolled on with an 81–69 win over Duke. The game was decided at the line as the Boilermakers were 17 of 24 and Duke just 5 of 7. Gene Keady was excited over the win but also glad to just be there, noting that he had never even seen a game in Madison Square Garden. He obviously needed to get out more.[74]

Alas, three nights later the magic ended for Keady and his squad in the semifinals with a 70–63 loss to Syracuse. Overall the Boilermakers shot poorly and weren't quick enough for the Orangemen, who ended up losing in overtime 86–84 to Tulsa in the NIT finals two nights later. The Boilers did salvage third place with a 75–72 overtime win over West Virginia.[75]

The NCAA Tourney

The NCAA tournament opened on March 12, but all three Big Ten teams had opening round byes because of their seeding. The Illini looked good in their first game, defeating Wyoming 67–65 in Los Angeles behind Eddie Johnson's nineteen points.[76] Indiana followed suit in their opener that same day, crushing Maryland 99–64 in Dayton. Isiah Thomas dominated the game with 19 points (on 9 for 11 field goals), 14 assists, and no turnovers. Despite that success, Thomas saw room for improvement; the goal last year, he said, was to win the Big Ten; his goal this year was to win the NCAA. To do this, Thomas said, they would need to improve their consistency and cut down on errors. Knight was clearly reflected in Thomas's comments in the concern for consistency.[77]

Iowa could not continue the Big Ten winning trend, losing the next day to Wichita State 60–56. Iowa led by 15 points early, but Wichita scored 15 consecutive points to tie the game at 40. Still, Iowa led by four with seventeen seconds to go before calling a time-out when they had none. The technical and the subsequent return of the ball to Wichita made Iowa a loser.[78]

With Iowa eliminated, it was just Illinois and Indiana carrying the Big Ten banner. The Illini, a #4 seed, lost 57–52 to Kansas State, a #8 seed, in Salt Lake City to end the Illini season. Kansas State led the entire game but never by more than seven, and Illinois closed to 52–50 with a minute to play before free throws put away the victory for the Wildcats.[79]

As for #3 seed Indiana, the only Big Ten team left, they were picking up endorsements as well as wins. Al McGuire picked them to win the Mideast and *Tribune* columnist David Israel, a Northwestern alumnus (but a Knight admirer) also was for IU.[80]

In the Mideast regional semis, Indiana pounded Alabama-Birmingham 87–72, as Isiah Thomas scored 27 with 8 assists to lead the Hoosiers into the regional finals, where they would meet St. Joe's two nights later. It was no contest, as the Hoosiers hit 35 of 51 from the floor against the St. Joe's zone, winning 78–46.[81]

The Final Four would be a #3 seed, Indiana against a #1 seed from the Midwest, LSU; and it would be a #1 seed from the East, Virginia, against the #2 seed from the West, North Carolina.

Indiana crushed LSU 67–49. Isiah was in foul trouble, and LSU led 30–27 at the half. LSU slowed the game down without Isiah in for ten minutes and had a 6-point lead in the second half. With Jim Thomas in for Isiah, the Hoosiers outscored LSU 18–7. At game's end, Turner's 20 points and Isiah's 14 topped the Indiana scoring. The Hoosiers would meet UNC, a 78–65 winner over Virginia, in the NCAA Finals.[82]

Anticipation was great, and David Israel waxed enthusiastic about this game, calling it "the best and the brightest": it was the ACC versus the Big Ten, the proudest traditions, the best teams, and the brightest coaches. Indiana was now the fourth Big Ten team to reach the NCAA Finals in the last five years, counting the two teams in 1976.[83]

Indiana tipped off against UNC for the championship. Isiah Thomas got 23 points (19 in the second half) and was named Most Outstanding Player of the Final Four to lead the Hoosiers to a 63–50 victory. As Knight correctly predicted after the game, "That's the last we'll ever see of Isiah Thomas at Indiana."[84] Significant help in the championship game came from Jim Thomas off the bench, who had 8 assists, as Indiana outscored North Carolina 55–34 when he was in the game.

Indiana and the Big Ten were tops once again, but there was still news about and from the conference, including the Most Valuable Players. Ray Tolbert was named Big Ten MVP. He was the "landslide" winner after leading the team in rebounds (6.4 pg), shooting a school record field goal percentage (.588), second in team scoring (12.2 pg), led in blocks (38), third in steals, fourth in assists, and shot.626 from the field in Big Ten games, which led the conference.

Tolbert was the seventh Hoosier to receive this honor. The others were Don Schlundt, 1953; Archie Dees, 1957 and 1958; Steve Downing, 1973; Scott May, 1975 and 1976; Kent Benson, 1977; Mike Woodson, 1980.[85]

CHAPTER 7

THE BIG TEN

1981–83

After Indiana's championship in 1981, as well as the success of the Big Ten with three teams in the final thirty-two in the NCAA tournament, there was no one team or conference seen as dominant as the 1981–82 season began. The Big Ten, clearly the strongest conference over the previous five years, loomed large, although no one team seemed to stand out nationally as in prior years. The AP poll of mid-November had UNC, UCLA, Kentucky, and Louisville as the top four schools, with three Big Ten teams ranked in the top twenty—Iowa (#9), Minnesota (#10), and Indiana (#12). Indiana and Iowa had ended the prior season both ranked in the top twenty; Indiana, of course, won the NCAA tourney, defeating North Carolina in the championship game. Indiana's "engine," Isiah Thomas, a first-team All-America player, had chosen to leave school early and went to the Detroit Pistons in the NBA draft as the #2 overall selection. Still, Indiana had a lot of talent returning, and *Street & Smith's* picked the Hoosiers as #11 in the preseason ranking.[1]

Purdue was hurt early by an injury to Russell Cross in preseason practices. His knee was ailing: strained knee ligaments were suspected, which might lead to surgery. The lack of advanced diagnostic tools available today was an obvious drawback, and only time would tell how his knee would respond in both the long and short run.[2]

Other teams had their own hopes to go along with injuries. Iowa was hopeful that freshman Michael Payne would be able to help lift the Hawkeyes, who had "probably the league's strongest recruiting year from top to bottom." Indiana was significantly damaged by the loss of Landon Turner, who had been paralyzed in a car accident in July. Michigan, too, was weakened by the loss of Tim McCormick for the year after surgery on both knees.[3]

Early season games were often inconclusive because of the quality of the opponents. In a rugged game, Purdue, with Russell Cross back and Keith Edmonson both scoring 36 points, looked impressive against Tennessee. Michigan State was defeated by Western Michigan, despite 30 points from Derek

Perry of the Spartans. Indiana struggled against Miami of Ohio before winning 71–64. Illinois went to overtime against Loyola before winning 87–83.[4]

Roy Damer of the *Chicago Tribune* provided his early insights into the conference. He saw Minnesota, led by Randy Breuer, as the favorite, even though the Gophers had lost Mark Hall to academic problems. Purdue was a "solid club," while Indiana and Iowa would battle for the top spot. Michigan State would be exciting to watch. Coach Heathcote said, "We're a young and immature team. I think we'll be decent by the middle of the year." With Tim McCormick out, Michigan would be small, but freshman Eric Turner would be a great complement to Thad Garner, a "terrific player," according to his coach, Bill Frieder. Ohio State would be led by Clark Kellogg, who had averaged 17.3 points and 12 rebounds a game the previous season. Coach Bill Cofield of Wisconsin was not optimistic. "We may have the kiss of death in the Big 10 because we'll start three freshmen."[5]

Purdue was buoyed by the return to action and strength of Russell Cross, who had gained twenty pounds and was now playing as a six-foot-seven, 240-pound forward. As the Big Ten Freshman of the Year the previous season, he had scored 475 points (16.9 pg) (a Purdue freshman record) and led the team in rebounding (6.3 pg) and blocks (60). It looked like he was fully recovered from his knee ailments and was ready for the Big Ten season. Then DePaul surprised the Boilermakers in the Horizon in Chicago, topping them 73–67, despite Cross's thirty points. Purdue was sloppy with twenty turnovers, six by Cross.[6] In another significant contest, Purdue lost at home to Louisville 73–71, before over fourteen thousand rooters. Both teams shot over 55 percent, but Louisville's 33 of 52 for 63.5 percent was amazing. Purdue went on to Norman and lost again, this time to Oklahoma 80–77, despite twenty-four points from Russell Cross. The Boilermakers were whistled for thirty-two fouls, which was a big factor in the loss.[7]

It was still unclear who was the top team in the conference and how strong the Big Ten really was for 1981–82. Just after Christmas, the conference announced that, beginning in the 1983–84 season, Big Ten teams would not take long trips during the nonconference season in order to minimize missed classes and to keep teams fresh for conference play. In addition, teams would not play more than two games in a row on the road during the league season.[8]

The last week of 1981 brought a number of surprises, mostly unwelcome ones. Indiana lost to both Villanova (63–59) and to Kansas (71–61) in Madison Square Garden on consecutive nights. Purdue lost to Houston 59–58 then to Wake Forest 76–68 in New Orleans at the Sugar Bowl Classic. Ohio

State, led by Clark Kellogg's 20 points and 13 rebounds, topped Washington State 63–54 at that same tourney.[9]

Minnesota had mostly good news. After topping Arizona 91–62 at their own Pillsbury Classic, the Gophers beat Long Beach State 75–67 at home. Guard Mark Hall was deemed eligible after a judicial ruling. At about the same time, the 1976–77 Gophers team was stripped of its 24–3 record (it became 0–27 officially) because of playing Mychal Thompson, "Flip" Saunders, and Dave Winey in defiance of the NCAA order not to do so under Coach Jim Dutcher.[10] The next day, Dutcher said that he wouldn't play Hall for ten days because he (Hall) had not been allowed to practice while the case was being reviewed. In an interesting comment, the judge who made the ruling said that Hall "was recruited to play basketball, rather than as a scholar," something no one had actually ever questioned.[11]

There was fallout from the other coaches who felt that Judge Lord's ruling cut into Big Ten rules designed to prevent hiding athletes in easy, so-called Mickey Mouse courses and to keep them progressing toward degrees. Coaches also thought the ruling unfair because of Lord's blanket indictment of other schools' programs when he conceded that Hall was recruited as a basketball player, not a scholar. Gene Keady of Purdue wondered, "What does a judge know about Big 10 or school rules?" Both Rich Falk and Lute Olson spoke on the record in defense of Big Ten rules and standards.[12]

The 1982 Big Ten Season Begins

There were surprises to open the season, with Minnesota's loss to Ohio State in Columbus and Indiana's loss to Michigan State.[13] Iowa humiliated Purdue in Iowa City, not just by winning 62–40 but by clamping down on defense and forcing Purdue into 4 of 21 field goal shooting in the second half, turning a 26–26 halftime score into a rout.[14]

The shockers continued two nights later as Northwestern defeated Indiana 75–61, the first Northwestern win against the Hoosiers since 1970. It was not a pretty game as IU had 30 turnovers and piled up 39 fouls (to Northwestern's 20) with six Hoosiers fouling out. Northwestern was 31 of 44 from the line and Indiana 15 for 19. The Wildcats also outrebounded Indiana 34–27. It was surely the low point of the season for IU and, ultimately, the high point for Northwestern.[15]

The Indiana loss was its fourth straight and illustrated that what Knight had brought into the league—a great emphasis on defense—had come back to bite him. Coach Rich Falk noted that there were now "more zones and match-up zones," making it difficult to work an offense: "Knight brought great defensive thinking when he came into the Big 10. Now everyone accentuates tough defense." It was a trend that would go national.[16]

The next week saw Illinois allow Ohio State to eke out a 51–50 win in Champaign and Indiana stop its losing streak with a vengeance, defeating Michigan 81–51 in Bloomington as five Hoosiers scored in double figures. Michigan extended its losing streak to eight straight. Purdue defeated Michigan State, 53–47, which wasn't a big surprise, but the way it happened spoke to the plodding that was beginning to characterize Big Ten basketball. Gene Keady said, "Our primary goal was to get a lead so they couldn't use the four corners." Because Purdue did get a lead and kept it, MSU was forced to foul, making the game a contest of free throws, with Purdue going 27 of 36 and MSU only 7 of 11.[17]

The consistent slowing of the game was bothering coaches, players, and fans alike. Illinois defeated Michigan State in Champaign 55–51, but after the game both coaches agreed that stalls were hurting college basketball and suggested a 25-, 30-, or 35-second shot clock. Also eliciting more ire from coaches was the inconsistent refereeing. After Indiana stopped the nine-game Ohio State win streak with a 66–61 win in Bloomington, Knight railed against the unpredictable officiating.[18]

The weather was certainly a factor when Iowa defeated Michigan 56–38 to take over first place in the conference at 5–1. The Wolverines had to bus from Chicago's O'Hare Airport, where they had flown into, to Iowa City, a distance of 220 miles. Besides the weather, strange calls by referees returned. In Northwestern's defeat of Ohio State, Rich Falk was given a technical foul for talking to his players, and the Wildcats were called for a five-second violation where there was no defensive pressure.[19]

Over the next week, Iowa was the only consistent winner, with its closest rivals knocking each other off. By the beginning of February, the Big Ten standings showed only three losing conference teams. Iowa was 7–1; Minnesota 6–2; Illinois, Purdue, and Indiana 5–3; Ohio State and Michigan State were both 4–4; Northwestern sat at 2–6; and Michigan and Wisconsin were both 1–7.

Down the Stretch

Indiana defeated Iowa 73–58 at Assembly Hall and Illinois 73–60, also in Bloomington. In the latter contest, Indiana's Ted Kitchel showed why he was the best shooter in the conference. He scored 34 points on 14 of 17 field goals, plus he snared 9 rebounds. Kitchel had been held in check by tough man-to-man defense, but as the Illini tired, they dropped into a zone and hard picks by Uwe Blab sprung Kitchel open for jumpers, which he canned. In the Iowa

Trent Tucker, All-American at Minnesota. *(Courtesy of University of Minnesota)*

game, Kitchel had 33 points on 13 of 22 field goals and 7 of 7 free throws. He earned accolades from Bob Knight who said, "He's smart and has an excellent touch." Lute Olson thought his team played "hard but ridiculous basketball. Our shot selection wasn't very good."[20]

Minnesota got back on the winning track with a tough 53–52 win at Purdue, leaving the Gophers (9–3), a game behind Iowa (10–2) in the race and a game up on Indiana (8–4), with Illinois and Ohio State a game behind IU. Bob Logan felt that the NCAA tournament was likely to include at least three and maybe all five of these teams.[21]

The slowdown games in the Big Ten (and the rest of the nation) had many coaches concerned about the direction and appeal of their game. In 1970 Iowa averaged 103 points per game. In 1981, no team even averaged 70, with Minnesota tops at 69.9 ppg. Overall, the average per game (both teams combined) was 135.8 ppg total scoring, the lowest since 1952. The shot clock solution was not agreeable to all, and even those that supported it did not agree on the length of the time needed to shoot.[22]

Iowa, Minnesota, Indiana, and Ohio State kept up the winning the next week, but no Big Ten team seemed to be able to attain and keep the lead in the conference race. Minnesota was upset by Illinois 77–65, when Craig Tucker had a field day against his cousin, Trent, getting 32 points on 11 of 15 field goals and 10 of 10 free throws.[23]

Minnesota was hurt by the continuing Mark Hall saga. This time he quit the team after being denied eligibility, both because of $800 worth of unaccounted-for telephone calls and his failure to be enrolled in a degree-bearing program. Nevertheless, the Gophers kept winning, beating Michigan in Ann Arbor and then overtaking Iowa in triple overtime in Iowa City 57–55, ending Iowa's eighteen-game home win streak.[24] The latest national poll had Minnesota as the highest-ranked Big Ten team at #7, with Iowa at #11.

As the season wound down, Big Ten leaders were Ted Kitchel in scoring (20.6), Clark Kellogg in rebounds (11.2), Derek Harper in assists (5.3), and Kitchel in field goal percentage (57 percent) and free-throw percentage (88 percent). Kellogg was third in scoring (17.2). So it seemed likely to be Kellogg or Kitchel as Big Ten Player of the Year. Ultimately, Keith Edmonson edged Kitchel for the scoring title, 20.5 to 20.1.

It came down to the last week when Minnesota edged Michigan State 54– 51, despite the Gophers shooting just 23 percent from the floor. Then Minnesota pounded Ohio State 87–75 to clinch the conference title. Breuer (32 points) and Tucker (23) led the Gopher attack, while Kellogg (20) and

Campbell (17) topped Buckeye scoring.[25] Minnesota ended at 14–4, with Iowa, Ohio State, and Indiana all at 12–6.

Iowa, Ohio State, and Indiana joined Minnesota at the NCAA tournament, and Illinois and Purdue would be invited to the NIT. Two ranked teams not in the NCAA tourney were UCLA and Wichita State, both of whom were on NCAA probation for recruiting violations. This was costly as each first-round team was guaranteed $121,000, with regional final four teams receiving $364,000 and national Final Four teams, $500,000.[26]

Tournament Time 1982: The NIT

Illinois opened at home where they crushed Long Island University (LIU) 126–78, setting both NIT and Illinois scoring records. Purdue defeated Western Kentucky, Gene Keady's former team, 72–65 in West Lafayette. Keady was not happy with the pairing and was disappointed that the NIT set up the brackets in this manner since he still had close ties to the Bowling Green, Kentucky community. His Boilermakers met a strong challenge from the Ohio Valley champion Hilltoppers, but Keith Edmonson's twenty-nine points were instrumental in the win.[27]

Five nights later in Champaign the Illini lost to Dayton 61–58, but Purdue kept going with an easy 98–65 victory at home against Rutgers.[28] Purdue's victory allowed them to play another home game, this one against Texas A&M, whom they defeated 86–68, causing Coach Gene Keady to concede, "That home court advantage really pays off." The victory would now send Purdue to New York City in the semifinals of the NIT to face Dominque Wilkins and Georgia, which had crushed Virginia Tech 90–73.[29]

Three nights later, the Boilermakers were able to edge the Bulldogs in a back-and-forth contest 61–60, holding Wilkins to just 15 points while Edmonson and Cross scored 25 each. Keady was pleased with the season and saw an NIT title as "more than just consolation." He noted that "we were dead in January (they were 9–12) and came back to life" (they were now 18–13).[30]

Alas, in the finals, Bradley defeated the Boilermakers 67–58, who were led by Cross (18 points) and Mac Scearce (16) in their last contest of the season. Coach Gene Keady said, "Bradley played better. Their rebounding hurt us, along with our missed free throws in the first half."[31]

The NCAA Tournament and After

Ohio State, Iowa, and Indiana all played first-round games, but only the latter two won, as Ohio State was beaten in Charlotte 55–48 by James Madison, after the Buckeyes scored just nineteen points in the second half. Eldon Miller said, "It was as bad a half as I've seen us play." Indiana romped in their opener in Nashville, defeating Robert Morris 94–62, and shooting 66 percent from the floor. In Pullman, Washington, Bob Hansen's 19 points and Ken Arnold's 14 led the Hawkeyes to a 70–63 win over Northeast Louisiana.[32]

Indiana and Iowa were both eliminated in the second round, ending a disappointing year for Big Ten basketball and leaving only Minnesota in the tournament. The Hoosiers were dumped 80–70 by Alabama-Birmingham. Ted Kitchel led with 24, but he shot just 3 of 14 in the second half as the Hoosiers failed to overcome an early 19-point deficit. Iowa's loss was more painful as Idaho won in overtime 69–67. Free throws and fouls were the difference as Idaho shot 29 of 35, while Iowa was just 11 of 19.[33]

So it was left to Minnesota alone to carry the Big Ten banner. The Gophers began with a second-round win after their #2 seeding allowed them a first-round bye. The Gophers slipped by Tennessee-Chattanooga 62–61 in Indianapolis, but the thrill didn't last as the Gophers were edged 67–61 by #3-seeded Louisville in Birmingham. Suddenly, the Big Ten was out of the tournament.[34]

There was still Big Ten news of interest, however. Jim Dutcher was named conference coach of the year. Off the court, the Big Ten agreed to a better television package with Metro Sports: games would be on Wednesday nights rather than Thursday, and the packager would put together a network of stations in the Midwest to carry these contests.[35]

The winner of the Silver Basketball and MVP of the Big Ten, was announced on April 1. The honor went to Clark Kellogg of Ohio State.[36]

Wisconsin was still in search of a coach, and a number of prospects were pursued. The coach at University of Wisconsin–Eau Claire, Ken Anderson, signed a five-year deal on April 9 to take the Wisconsin position and retained one assistant coach, Bo Ryan. Four days later, Anderson resigned, deciding to remain at Eau Claire.[37] A week after that, Wisconsin nabbed Steve Yoder, head coach of Ball State, as its new head coach. He retained Bo Ryan as an assistant.

1982–83 Preseason

Was the relatively poor Big Ten showing in 1981–82 an aberration? Jud Heathcote summed it up, "We were a really poor league six years ago and we were really down last year, but in between we were awesome." Lou Henson agreed, "We've been a very strong league. Until last year."[38]

The Big Ten's weak showing in the NIT and the NCAA tournaments was compounded by a 54–40 record (57 percent) in nonconference games in

1981–82, a significant decline from the previous three seasons when the conference had a winning percentage of more than 75 percent. The league's scoring was also shockingly low, at 123.1 collective points per game in conference competition, the lowest scoring output in the conference in thirty-one years. A lot of this reflected the youth of the league: top seniors and early departers were replaced by young or inexperienced players. Minnesota, with the most senior starters, won the conference. Jim Dutcher said, "That's probably why we won it down the stretch."[39]

Things looked to be different for 1982–83. Thirty-five of fifty starters were expected to return, including ten sophomores. Indiana returned all its starters for the new season, two of them fifth-year seniors (Ted Kitchel and Randy Wittman). Ohio State had four returners, but the one who left early was Big Ten MVP Clark Kellogg, who had led the Buckeyes in scoring and rebounding. Noting this, Jud Heathcote summed it up this way, "You won't see a complete return to power this year. But there will be an escalation in overall strength. And next year will be even better."[40]

The Nonconference Results

The Soviet Union's national team made a tour through the United States in early November, so teams were allowed to play the Soviets in exhibitions before the official start of the NCAA basketball season. The Soviets made two stops in the Midwest to play the Illini and the Purdue Boilermakers. In the former game, the Soviets came back to beat the Illini 77–70, but Illinois fans were thrilled to see freshman Efrem Winters, a six-foot-nine center from Chicago, score 16 points. Derek Harper led the scoring with 23. Two nights later, Purdue topped the Soviets, 66–63, led by 15 from Russell Cross.[41]

The next week, official contests began, and the Big Ten had one new wrinkle to its game: the three-point shot would be used on an experimental basis, with an evaluation at the end of the year to decide whether it would be continued. Other leagues had already done this, with the NCAA's approval, but the distance varied from league to league. The Big Ten would use a twenty-one-foot distance. Big Ten coaches commented on which Big Ten players seemed capable of hitting this shot with any consistency. Bob Knight thought that there were only three players in the conference who could do so, and he felt that he had two of them (Kitchel and Wittman). Lute Olson of Iowa thought his guard Steve Carfino and Eric Turner of Michigan would be tops at this distance.[42]

As far as the coaches were concerned, the top teams in the Big Ten were Iowa, Indiana, Illinois, and Purdue. Minnesota was seen as middle of the pack, having lost six seniors, but the Gophers returned Randy Breuer. Michigan, Michigan State, Ohio State, Northwestern, and Wisconsin were expected to follow.[43]

The Big Ten conference started the season at a collective 32–3 in their nonconference games. There was optimism for the holiday and conference seasons. Purdue won its fifth in a row, 71–58 over Miami of Ohio, with Russell Cross (20 points) and Jim Rowinski (11) the top scorers. Indiana and Iowa also kept their records solid with wins, the former over Notre Dame in South Bend 68–52 and the latter in Iowa City over Marquette, 87–66.[44]

Illinois won the Illini Classic with victories over Southern Illinois 79–61 and Illinois State 67–60. Derek Harper and Anthony Welch were the leaders with the latter capturing the tourney MVP award.[45] Indiana was still undefeated (7–0) and ranked #5 nationally after topping Kansas State 48–46 in Manhattan, but Iowa dropped its first game of the season 75–66 to #4 UCLA in Pauley Pavilion. Iowa's terrible first-half shooting (12 of 34) doomed them, even though they outscored UCLA in the second half.[46]

The most exciting holiday tournament clash was in Bloomington, where #5 Indiana topped #2 Kentucky 62–59. With 3:52 to go and Indiana clinging to a 56–55 lead, the Hoosiers went into a stall until Kentucky fouled with 1:02 left. IU hit both free tosses to lead 58–55 and seal the win. After the game Joe B. Hall, Kentucky coach, was very clear in saying he favored some kind of shot clock.[47] Indiana's victory vaulted them into the top spot in the country.

Big Ten Season

The nonconference records of Big Ten teams were impressive. Indiana was 10–0; Michigan, Purdue, and Northwestern were all 9–1; Iowa and Minnesota were 7–1; Ohio State and Michigan State were both 7–2; Illinois was 9–3; and Wisconsin was 5–3. In the latest national poll, Indiana was #1, Iowa #8, and Purdue #20. The nonconference record of 83–17 was the best for the Big Ten in sixty-eight years and included exemplary wins like Indiana over Kentucky and Purdue over Louisville.[48]

Opening night started with upsets. Michigan State edged Iowa 61–59 in Iowa City, and Northwestern defeated Michigan 69–64 in Evanston. Kevin Willis and Sam Vincent each had 18 points for MSU as they spoiled the opening night in Carver-Hawkeye Arena. The Northwestern defense held Michigan to 24–74 shooting (.324); Wolverine star Eric Turner shot 8 of 22 and had four turnovers.[49] Just two nights later Ohio State defeated Indiana in Columbus 70–67. Indiana outrebounded the Buckeyes 35–18, but OSU went 22 of 25 from the line, while Indiana was just 13 of 18.[50]

In Evanston, Northwestern claimed first place (at least for a little while) after defeating Michigan State 62–51 behind 17 points from Jim Stack and 16 from Art Aaron. Almost as surprising was the 54–48 Minnesota victory over Purdue. It was not so much the win itself but the fact that Curt Clawson and Steve Reid put up thirteen three-point shots and made eight of them, causing Minnesota coach, Jim Dutcher to declare "I don't think you're ever going to see more 3-point baskets in a game."[51]

Northwestern's time at the top did not last long, as Iowa defeated them 66–57 after shooting 64 percent from the floor in the second half. Two other games had interesting aspects. In West Lafayette, Purdue hit 29 of 35 free throws, while Ohio State was just 10 of 16 to edge the Buckeyes 64–57. In Champaign, Indiana defeated Illinois 69–55, led by Wittman's 27 points, (including two for two on 3-pointers) and Kitchel's 20 (also two for two on 3-pointers). After the game Bob Knight nonetheless claimed that he "despises the three-point rule."[52]

As initially predicted, Indiana looked like the class of the conference, beating Purdue in West Lafayette, 81–78. Kitchel had 23 and Wittman (now a grad student in the School of Business) had 22. Indiana was 30 of 35 on free throws to complement its 24 of 38 performance (63 percent) from the floor.[53] Indiana's win helped them to a #2 national ranking behind UCLA.

Bob Knight pulled a fast one, literally, on Michigan in a 93–76 victory in Bloomington. Facing the best rebounding team in the country, Knight went small, going with four guards and either Uwe Blab or Steve Bouchie at center. The Hoosiers burst out to a 22–4 lead and then coasted. Indiana also snared 37 rebounds, the same number as the Wolverines. The victory left IU on top of the conference at 4–1; Minnesota, Iowa, Purdue, and Ohio State all had two losses, but the season was not even a third over.[54]

Halfway through the Big Ten season, Indiana still held first at 7–2, but Purdue, Minnesota, and Illinois were all 6–3, with Ohio State the only other squad above.500 at 5–4. Indiana met Minnesota's challenge in Bloomington and sent the Gophers back to their dens, 76–51. Jim Dutcher described the game: "It was like putting a Band Aid on an ax wound and we had openings all over."[55] Indiana stretched its lead with a win in Minneapolis 63–59, while Iowa defeated Purdue in Iowa City 55–46. In the former contest, Minnesota dominated the boards 40–26 but shot themselves out of the game, going 28 of 67 from the floor (.416) and 3 of 10 from the free-throw line. Randy Breuer got nearly half their points (28), plus 14 rebounds.[56]

Indiana continued to win, crushing Wisconsin 75–56, but Iowa lost to Illinois 68–66. Northwestern surprised Purdue 66–55, and Ohio State beat

Bruce Douglas, All-American at Illinois. *(Courtesy of University of Illinois Athletics)*

Minnesota 74–69. The new standings had Indiana at 9–2 with Ohio State at 7–4. Another game back were Purdue, Iowa, Minnesota, and Illinois, all at 6–5. Nationally, Indiana was back at #2 in the AP poll and #1 in the UPI, swapping places with UNLV. Indiana seemed to have the Big Ten title well in hand.

On February 19, Derek Harper highlighted the week by making 11 of 11 field goals, three of them 3-pointers, while scoring 27 points in Illinois's 69–61 win over Michigan State. Jud Heathcote was ebullient in his praise of Harper: "If Harper's not the premier guard in the conference, then I don't know anything about basketball." Harper had hit his last seven shots in the Illini's prior win over Michigan, so he was on a streak of 18 straight shots made from the floor.[57]

In a contest that both teams really needed to win, Purdue defeated Illinois in Champaign 56–54 in a game that Coach Lou Henson would surely replay in his mind for a long time. Illinois blew a twenty-point lead, going scoreless for the last 9:28 of the game, while playing against Russell Cross and four second teamers for Purdue. Cross and Illini Bruce Douglas were top scorers with thirteen points each. After the game Henson's frustrations showed: "I think our inexperience showed. We just didn't play like a veteran team, like you have to, down the stretch. We didn't play with poise."[58]

The next night, however, things continued their topsy-turvy ways. Ohio State lost at Michigan State 101–94 in triple overtime, and Indiana was defeated in Ann Arbor 69–56. In the former game, Scott Skiles with 35 points and Sam Vincent with 23 led the Spartan scoring, while Campbell had 29 for OSU.[59]

Illinois complicated the conference title picture by edging Ohio State in overtime at Columbus, 74–73. Bruce Douglas (22) and Derek Harper (21) keyed the Illini win. Indiana battled back to soundly defeat Purdue 64–41, leading Gene Keady to truncate his postgame press comments: "When you get your butt kicked like that, there's nothing to say."[60]

In the last week of the conference season, Indiana continued to rise to the occasion, defeating Illinois 67–55 and Ohio State 81–60 to win the conference with a record of 13–5.[61] So now the battle was not only for second place but also to determine which teams would be invited to the NCAA tournament; there was also a fight for good seeding in that tourney as well. Ohio State, Illinois, and Purdue all finished at 11–7 and, overall, with 19, 20, and 21 wins, respectively. Iowa also won 19 games and finished 10–8 in conference. They were all selected for the NCAA tournament. Minnesota, Michigan State, and Northwestern were NIT selections.

Tournament Time

The NCAA tourney had two Big Ten teams in the Mideast regional and one in each of the other three regionals. Fifty-two teams were now in the field, with eight of those playing preliminary games to even the field at forty-eight. No Big Ten team was in that preliminary group; each of the Big Ten teams was seeded much better: Iowa and Illinois were both at #7, Purdue at a #5, Ohio State at #3, and Indiana at #2 in the Mideast.[62]

The NIT opened a day earlier than the NCAA. Minnesota dropped its opener to DePaul, in Chicago 76–73, despite 26 points and nine rebounds from Randy Breuer and 17 points from Marc Wilson. The next night Northwestern won its first postseason game ever, defeating Notre Dame 71–57 behind 24 points from Art Aaron. Then in an exciting all-Chicago game, DePaul topped Northwestern 65– 63 to end the Wildcat season at 17–13. Michigan State edged Bowling Green 72– 71 in East Lansing, led by Kevin Willis with 16 points and 12 rebounds. The Spartans dropped their second-round game to eventual NIT champion Fresno State 72–58 to end Big Ten play in the tournament.[63] It was not a good showing for the conference.

Meanwhile Illinois opened its NCAA title pursuit with an early exit, losing to Utah 52–49 in Boise. It was a slow-paced game with Winters, Harper, and Welch all scoring 11 points, but the Illini were disappointing overall. Purdue held on to win over Robert Morris in Tampa. Steve Reid, the shortest player on the court at five-foot-nine, was 9 of 11 from the floor, scoring 20 points, while Russell Cross had 14 inside. Purdue could not sustain their winning ways, however, dropping a 78–68 contest to Arkansas two nights later. Gene Keady saw no shame in the loss, noting, "It was disappointing . . . but they probably should have beaten us, because they had better players than we did."[64]

The next night, Iowa defeated Utah State in Louisville 64–59, despite shooting only 36 percent from the floor. Two nights later, the Hawks continued rolling, defeating Missouri 77–63. The big difference was free throws. Iowa went 25–33 and Missouri just 5 of 11.[65] Ohio State struggled to beat Syracuse in Hartford 79–74 then met #2 seed North Carolina five days later, losing 64–51 despite holding Michael Jordan to 5 of 15 shooting. In Kansas City, Iowa lost 55–54 to Villanova, the #3 seed.[66]

Indiana opened in Evansville against Oklahoma and Wayman Tisdale, defeating the Sooners, 63–49 and holding Oklahoma to 19 of 49 field goal shooting, while Indiana hit 25 of 49. The Hoosiers next met a traditional rival, #3 seed Kentucky in Knoxville four nights later and were defeated by the Wildcats 64–59, after holding a 59–57 lead with 2:49 to play. The game was characterized by good shooting, with IU going 25–50 and Kentucky doing even better with 27 of 43 from the floor. The Big Ten was out of the tournament with no conference squad reaching the regional finals.[67]

After the Season

It was a disappointing showing for the Big Ten. Many teams made the two tournaments, but the Big Ten had no dominant team that could go far in those tournaments. Still, there were exciting things going on in the league. One of these was the increased revenues derived from television packages for the various teams in the conference, as well as a Big Ten deal with CBS and NBC for the next two seasons. The league contract would be for $3 million and would guarantee twelve national appearances, bringing $150,000 to each conference school. In addition, there was a separate $12 million three-year pact with Metro Sports that would provide another $550,000 for each of the Big Ten universities. Metro Sports noted in a press release that the Big Ten was "a great product with great markets," with 22–24 percent of the nation's population in the seven-state "Big Ten area," not to mention the alumni all over the country.[68]

As for the packages involving independent stations, Ohio State was renegotiating the $15,000 per game it had received for 1982–83, Indiana was in the second year of a similar pact, and Purdue was in the second year of a three-year deal at $200,000 per year. Illinois was in the second year of a local pact that brought in $13,500 per game in 1982–83 and was renegotiating with WGN in Chicago, which had paid $10,000 per game in 1982–83. Iowa was in the final year of a three-year $255,000 per year agreement and Michigan State in the second year of a $50,000 per year deal. Northwestern was in the second year of a more complex agreement that could bring up to $1.4 million, if all options were picked up for the third year. It was a three-year option package to include radio, football, a coaches' show, and radio and television for basketball. Michigan, Minnesota, and Wisconsin were all negotiating pacts that would be similar to those of their conference brethren.[69]

In other news, Lute Olson decided to forsake the Hawkeyes for a most attractive offer from Arizona. He would get a base salary of $58,500 annually, but various fringes could bring the total package to $150,000 per year. Iowa announced almost immediately that the new coach would be Washington State head coach George Raveling.[70]

Despite lots of speculation and pressure, the NCAA announced that there would be no shot clock or three-point shot nationally for 1983–84. Conferences could decide on their own to adopt either rule for their league games (and use them in home nonconference games if visitors agreed).[71] The Big

Brad Sellers, All-Big Ten at both Wisconsin and Ohio State.
(Courtesy of University of Wisconsin Athletics)

Ten coaches and athletic directors then decided to drop the three-point shot as well as to not implement a forty-five-second shot clock for 1983–84.[72]

Brad Sellers, who had averaged 17.6 ppg at Wisconsin, disclosed that he would be transferring to Ohio State. Sellers did not like playing center, as he had been doing in Steve Yoder's offense, and he apparently also didn't like playing for Yoder period. As an Ohio native, this was a logical move for him, and both he and Ohio State would reap benefits in the future.[73]

The announcement of the Big Ten's Most Valuable Player and winner of the Silver Basketball, was announced on April 21, 1983. The winner was Randy Wittman of conference champion Indiana.[74]

Overall, 1982–83 was not a great year for the Big Ten, but with the great freshmen who had stepped into starting and, in some cases, starring roles, as well as the relatively few top stars who were seniors, prospects for 1983–84 were quite bright. The stage was set for what would to be another top year in 1983–84 in Big Ten basketball.

CHAPTER 8

RULES AND REFEREES

This chapter takes a different turn, in that it contextualizes the most important issues in college and professional basketball in the 1980s, specifically in relation to the Big Ten conference (representing the NCAA) and the National Basketball Association. These issues were not unique to the period; in fact, some issues, like referee incompetence, could be traced back to the 1920s, before the job of refereeing was professionalized. Rule changes, of course, are vital to keeping a sport dynamic and to prevent it from stagnating under outdated regimentation: that is, the rules had to be tailored to the skill levels of the players and to the coaches that were now in the game and to the fans' changing views of college basketball as entertainment.

The most vital rule-related concerns had to do with a time clock for offensive possessions and the question of the three-point shot. The alternative possessions rule was also implemented.

The Three-Point Shot

The most dynamic and long-standing issue was the proposed three-point shot, a question debated within the Big Ten and other conferences but also the NCAA at large. The impetus was largely related to concerns over sloweddown and lower-scoring games (which had become much more zone-oriented) and worries about overly physical inside play. In addition, a greater emphasis on tighter and rougher defense was limiting what the offense could do, especially on individual moves; teams were regularly doubling down on post players, exposing a long-range game that wasn't nearly as effective as it is today.

Discussions regarding the use of a three-point shot had begun as early as the 1930s. There was even an exhibition game played in February 1945 between Columbia and Fordham that used the shot, but it remained unused in real contests until 1961 when the American Basketball League (ABL), which was just formed as a professional conference, announced that the league would use the shot in their games. The ABL three-point distance was twenty-five feet, measured from the backboard outward.

Although the ABL folded after two years, its employment of the three-point shot provided a source of excitement and discussion. Tony Jackson, a former St. John's All-America who had been indicted in the point-shaving scandals of the 1960s and banned from the NBA, found a home in the ABL. He made 141 three-pointers in seventy-two games in 1961–62, with a high of 12 in one game. He shot 37 percent from the twenty-five-foot distance. Only one other player (Bucky Bolyard) made more than a hundred three-point shots that season. The ABL folded at the end of December 1962.

Since the fans enjoyed the three-point shot, the American Basketball Association (ABA) made the three-pointer part of that league's rules when it formed in 1967. The shot was exciting, but teams did not utilize it as part of their regular set offense. Players mostly tried threes as the ABA's thirty-second shot clock wound down or when a team was down by a wide margin late in the game.

In 1970–71 George Lehman of the Carolina Cougars had a three-point percentage of.403 to lead the league and also made 154 three-pointers, which led the ABA. After that no player in the ABA would make more than one hundred three-pointers in a season.[1]

In 1976 the ABA collapsed, with four teams entering the NBA and the remainder ceasing play. In 1979 the NBA reintroduced the three-point shot, from a distance of 23 feet, 9 inches, on a trial basis. On the opening night of the 1979–80 season six players made three-point shots, with Chris Ford of the Boston Celtics credited with making the first in league history. No player made more than ninety three-pointers for the season. Most teams hardly used the shot, with Boston leading in three-point attempts with 5.1 per game. The next most attempted by a team in the season was 2.2 per game. By comparison, the NBA three-point shots leader in the 2020–21 season was Stephen Curry of the Golden State Warriors, who made 5.3 per game and attempted 12.7 per game. By 2022, many NBA teams shot more three pointers in a game than two-point shots.

The NBA tried to increase the amount of three-pointers shot per game by shortening the distance to 22 feet for the 1994–95 season. The result was an enormous increase in the number of three pointers taken and made; two players (Steve Kerr and Detlef Schrempf) actually shot over 50 percent from beyond the arc. This pattern continued the next year, and in 1996–97 at least three players made over two hundred three-pointers, and the NBA decided to revert to the prior distance of 23 feet, 9 inches for the 1997–98 season, and that distance has remained in place since that time.

Despite the league rollback to the greater distance, Ray Allen broke the three-point mark in 2005–6 with 269 three-point shots, since broken by Stephen Curry with 402 in 2015–16. Allen was also the career leader with over 2,900, a mark also broken by Curry with over 3,100 as of 2022.

In 1986 the NBA inaugurated a three-point shooting contest as part of the NBA All-Star Game festivities. The first winner was Larry Bird, who won two more times in a row. Meanwhile FIBA (the International Federation of Basketball Associations) began using a three-point line of 6.25 meters (20 feet, 5 inches) for all their federation games beginning in 1984. This would have little impact on American teams, except in international tournaments like the Olympics and the Pan American Games.

The shot's popularity caused the NCAA to consider adopting its use, and in 1980, the NCAA allowed for a three-point shot to be used in games, with the distances ranging from 17 feet, 9 inches to 22 feet, the determination of which would be left up to the individual conferences. It caused confusion when teams from different conferences met, as well as for tournaments at the end of the season; however, in general the move met with approval.

For the 1982–83 season, the Big Ten coaches and athletic directors decided to experiment with the three-point shot at a distance of 21 feet. The coaches and athletic directors approved its use for that season. Bob Knight voted to utilize the three-pointer because he felt that there were only three players in the league who could hit the shot consistently and he had two of them: Ted Kitchel and Randy Wittman.

Other conferences were also experimenting with the shot. The ACC was using a nineteen-foot distance and combining that with a forty-second shot clock, which would be turned off for the last four minutes of play. Both the Missouri Valley and the Atlantic Ten would use a 19-foot distance, but the Atlantic Ten would combine that with a forty-second shot clock, turned off for the last five minutes of play. The Southeastern and the Southwest conferences would not be using the three-point shot, but would be utilizing a forty-five-second shot clock. The NCAA wanted data kept on all these experiments in order to decide what direction the game would take over the next few seasons.

The 1982–83 season began with nonconference contests, in which the three-pointer would be used on the home courts of those conference teams that had agreed to experiment with it. The distance would be decided by the home team. Initially, the shot was not employed very often nor did it affect outcomes.

In the conference season, the three-point shot was being utilized judiciously for the most part; Indiana and Minnesota had the best three-point shooting percentages with IU at .643 and Minnesota at .483. By the end of the season, the leaders were the same, but the shot was not critical to Indiana's conference title, which was won by two games. In 2002 Knight noted, "Kitchel's three-point percentage that year, .656, is still the best ever in the Big Ten, and Wittman wasn't bad at .444. All those coaches who were so in favor of the experiment voted it out the next year, over my vote for it. We didn't have to look at three-point shots again until it became a national rule in 1986–87."[2] The three-pointer would not be a part of the NCAA tournament at that point. About a week after the NCAA tournament ended, the NCAA announced that there would be no shot clock or three-point shot nationally for 1983–84, the experiment having not been conclusive enough to warrant altering rules. There was simply no strong consensus from the faculty reps. Conferences were free, however, to utilize either in the upcoming season if they chose to do so.

For the 1986–87 season, the NCAA adopted the three-point shot from 19 feet, 9 inches for all contests, and the complexion of the game changed dramatically. During the recruitment process, long-range shooters were now in higher demand. The "inside out" game would be a much greater part of most offenses.

Some coaches and fans called the three-point shot the "Steve Alford rule." Alford himself noted that Bob Knight continued to dislike the shot. In the preseason, Alford said he "wasn't even sure that he [Knight] was going to let us shoot it."[3] About two-thirds of the way through the 1986–87 season, coaches were still questioning the value of the three-point shot, although players and fans seemed to love it. Many of those in favor were still concerned with the distance of 19 feet, 9 inches, feeling it was too short.

When the members of the National Association of Basketball Coaches (NABC) met during the 1986 Final Four, a survey was taken indicating that 84 percent of the 2,422 coaches, referees, administrators, and media personnel surveyed by the NCAA Rules Committee wanted to retain the three-point shot. The preferred distance, however, varied. Thirty-nine percent wanted the distance at 21 feet. 9 inches (the Olympic distance); 35 percent wanted the 19 feet, 9 inches distance retained; and 26 percent wanted the distance longer (or they did not respond to the question).[4] Within a week the Rules Committee said that the three-point shot would stay but that conferences could experiment with a 20 feet, 6 inches distance, as long as they petitioned the NCAA before August 15 in order to implement such a change for the upcoming season.[5] Today the NBA retains the 23 feet, 9 inches distance, while the NCAA adopted a distance of 22 feet, 1 ¾ inches, the same as the international distance.

The Shot Clock

At that same 1986 meeting the Big Ten coaches also voted against a forty-five-second shot clock. The votes on the three-point shot and the shot clock would now go to their respective athletic directors who were expected to formally change conference policy at their May 10 meeting. That, indeed, took place, as the coaches and athletic directors decided to stick to the rules used in the NCAA tournament at that time.[6]

The NBA had adopted a twenty-four-second clock in 1954 after a series of games where teams held the ball for at least five minutes with a lead. One game involved six overtimes with only one shot taken in each of those periods. The advent of the shot clock in the NBA increased scoring dramatically, distinguished the pro game from the college game, brought back fans, and received generally universal praise from journalists who covered the NBA. The ABL utilized a thirty-second clock in its two years of existence (1961–63), and the ABA also used a thirty-second clock in its ten-year life. Still, college basketball chose to resist both the clock and the three-point shot.

In the NBA the shot clock only resets when a basket is made and possession changes or when the ball is knocked out of bounds by the defensive team, and it resets to the time on the clock when a foul takes place or a jump ball happens and the offense retains possession. In those cases, the shot clock is set to fourteen seconds.

In college, discussions continued into the 1980s, and there were arguments for and against the clock. Ray Meyer, the Hall of Fame DePaul coach, agreed with Lou Henson of Illinois who felt that the lack of a clock made the game boring. Digger Phelps of Notre Dame and Rich Falk of Northwestern thought the clock reduced upsets and were therefore against it. The key concerning clock adoption centered on the length of time. Bob Knight felt that twenty seconds would be best.

At the end of the 1983–84 season, the NIT invited Michigan and Ohio State to join their tourney but with a caveat: the NIT would be using the forty-five-second clock, something that the Big Ten had eschewed that year. So the two teams would have to prepare themselves accordingly for postseason play, defensively and offensively.

The day after Michigan won the NIT, the results of a survey conducted by the NABC were released and a majority (53 percent) of college coaches voted to approve a forty-five-second clock. Now it was up to the NCAA to respond to that. The NCAA Rules Committee, however, in a meeting a few days later, disagreed, saying that it was not time for the forty-five-second clock.

For the time being, the conferences were still free to make their own decisions on the clock and the three-point shot; a few weeks later, the Big Ten
announced that the conference would be using a forty-five-second clock on
an experimental one-year basis starting with league contests in January 1985.
The clock would be in use for the whole game.[7]

As many predicted, the NCAA revisited the three-point shot at the
NCAA meetings in spring 1986 and voted to adopt the three-pointer, at a
distance of 19 feet, 9 inches for all NCAA games, beginning with the 1986–87
season. The forty-five-second clock utilized in most conferences the prior
year would also be in effect, as well as the use of instant replay to correct timing or scoring errors. Passage of the three-point shot surprised some coaches,
but research indicated that coaches favored it by about a 2–1 margin and generally agreed on the 19 feet, 9 inches distance.[8]

Other Rule Changes and Referee Issues

The roughness issue, however, became even more of a problem in the 1980s,
as players got bigger and stronger and referees became less consistent in their
calls, especially regarding defensive holding moves like the "waistband grab"
or "the arm lock." Certainly, these tactics had been around for a while, but
they were becoming increasingly consequential in game play, and coaches
were quite disturbed over the lackluster officiating. The overall competence of some of the refereeing was also brought into question by some of
the coaches, who risked fines for such criticism. As early as 1977, Johnny Orr
of Michigan risked being sanctioned when he went ballistic in a win over
Wisconsin when referees missed a dunk call (dunks were not allowed at that
time) on Wisconsin, but called rim-hanging against Michigan's Joel Thompson. "That's the most incompetent thing I've ever seen in officiating. (It)
changed the whole tempo of the game," said Orr.[9]

Before the beginning of the 1990–91 season, the NBA determined that
an especially hard foul (as determined by the referee) would constitute a
flagrant foul and the injured player (or a teammate—if that player was too
badly injured to shoot) would be awarded two shots and the ball. The fouler
would not necessarily be ejected.

Finally, starting in the 2003–4 season, the NBA began to address hand-
checking more fully. This allowed for more scoring because of the swiftness
of many players, mostly guards. This became a challenge for referees in deciding to call a hand check or an arm bar by an offensive player. There had
been great inconsistency in these situations, which more often than not has
resulted in "play on" no calls. This has become a more difficult issue in the

college ranks as players get bigger stronger and more "subtle" in the ways they foul.

In the college ranks there were concerns about the new structure of Big Ten refereeing that involved three (rather than two) referees, an arrangement that the NBA adopted in the 1988–89 season (after a brief trial in 1979).[10] Rich Falk, Northwestern coach, thought that keeping three referees allowed the game to get too physical. Ohio State coach Fred Taylor was in agreement. He felt that not enough fouls were being called and that, when asked, referees often responded "it's not my call" because there was not enough clarity as to which part of the court each of the three referees was responsible for.[11]

The next season, the complaining reached a new peak. In a tight battle between Iowa and Purdue, played in Mackey Arena, the Boilermakers prevailed 66–65, dropping the Hawks into a tie for second with Ohio State and Illinois in the final conference standings. All this did not sit well with Iowa coach Lute Olson, who said, "Jim Bain and his crew deserve to be in jail, not officiating . . . I will personally lead a campaign to make severe changes in the whole system of referee supervision in our conference."[12]

The Big Ten administrators responded by saying that they would review Olson's complaint and view game films. Big Ten Commissioner Wayne Duke said that a review of officiating practices had begun before Olson called for one. In response to this announcement, both Rich Falk and Bob Knight said that the officiating suffered from "inconsistency."[13]

In April 1982, after the Iowa-Purdue game had roused coach Lute Olson's ire, referee Jim Bain admitted that he had called the wrong foul in that contest, which resulted in a free throw for Purdue that gave them a 66–65 win. As a result, Bain was banned from officiating Iowa games for the upcoming season. It seemed that there was more than just the usual coaches' whining after a tough loss.[14]

The dissatisfaction with the referees in the Big Ten conference seemed to dissipate the next season, but there were still grumblings. Those were sometimes voiced by "outsider" coaches like Ray Meyer. In December of 1984, Northwestern hosted the University of Chicago, a D-III school, and soundly defeated them, 74–49. Chicago coach John Argelis said, "This officiating was terrible. I get better reffing on the road in my league (the Midwest Conference) than I got here." Bill Jauss observed, "Nearly everybody is ripping Big 10 referees these days."[15]

This unhappiness with the referees was most often expressed by Bob Knight. An infamous incident occurred in February of 1985 in an Indiana loss to Purdue in Assembly Hall. Angered at a foul call on Steve Alford, Knight protested vehemently and was assessed a technical foul. Later in the game he was angered by another call and drew a technical for language that was offensive to the referees. He then threw a chair across the floor, drawing a third technical.[16] Knight's temper and demands for perfection on the part of the referees were rubbing against what many of the coaches saw as poor refereeing in terms of positioning, knowledge, and temperament. Knight, however, was not afraid to call the referees out on a regular basis. Only adding to his volatility was that this squad of referees was particularly inconsistent as he saw it. The day after the game, Knight apologized for his conduct, noting that "the officiating has frustrated me the past couple years" and that he had met earlier in the season with Bob Burson, supervisor of Big Ten officials, but came away feeling that his concerns were not being addressed. He found it all a "hopeless situation."[17]

The next week, the Big Ten announced that Knight would be suspended for one game for having violated three rules in the conference handbook on sportsmanlike conduct. Subsequent misbehavior, it was noted, would lead to suspensions of at least two games.[18]

The issue with Knight may have seemed resolved, for he remained calm as the Hoosiers played much better at the end of the season and were invited to the NIT, despite a losing record in the conference (7–11) but a winning record overall (15–13). But after his team won a double overtime contest to get Indiana into the NIT Final Four, Knight made another subtle dig at the Big Ten referees: "I think that of the five best officiated games we've had this season, three of them have come in the NIT."[19] (The tournament did not have a Big Ten team of officials.)

The issue of questionable refereeing did not diminish in the next season (1985–86). Early in the Big Ten season, Indiana won a close game against Ohio State in Bloomington, ending a seven-game home losing streak in the Big Ten. After the game, Knight praised the officials—George Solomon, Darwin Brown, and Gil Haggart—but then went on to lament the continued pattern of poor officiating in the Big Ten. "The officiating has almost ruined basketball in this league. It's sickened me on basketball in this league." Eldon Miller of Ohio State was asked about officiating after a loss to Indiana and was silent for twenty-five seconds before remarking, "That's what I have to say about it."[20]

Just over a month later, George Raveling was revisiting the topic of referee competence after the Hoosiers defeated Iowa in Bloomington, 80–73. Commenting on the referee team of George Solomon, Gil Haggart, and Darwin Brown, Raveling said, "Something has to be done or we're going to ruin a good league. The Big 10 deserves a better quality of officiating. It's gonna affect our teams in the NCAA tournament."[21]

The concerns over referee competence were finally addressed in April of 1986. The Big Ten fired six officials after "increasing criticism from the coaches about the caliber of officiating," said Bob Wortman, supervisor of Big Ten officiating. He predicted improvement right away and noted that "some of these guys have been working on their laurels."[22] Wortman went on to note that officials would now receive $300 per game, plus expenses. The Big Ten would reorganize the revamped staff into three-man crews as soon as possible. "We were one of the last to make assignments; we should be one of the first," he noted. The conference also would be limited in its search for good replacements. Wortman stressed that he was a great believer in "preventive officiating" but that his remarks "weren't aimed only at Bob Knight."[23]

Was this the end of the issue? Hardly. Knight continued to hammer at who he called incompetent, tired, or indifferent officials. At the beginning of the 1986–87 season, when Knight was asked about his toughest opponent, he replied, "Our most difficult opponent will be the officials."[24]

Later that season, Knight had some critical commentary about the officiating in a postgame conference following a victory over Purdue in which no fewer than five players fouled out. He said, "There's no reason you should have so many fouls. That can be eliminated in the first five minutes of the game if the referees take charge and let the kids know how they are going to call the game."[25] In February of 1989, there was a rare retort from Bob Wortman. His response to his officials regarding complaints of the greater physicality being seen in the paint was that they should call the game more closely in that area. Little seemed to change, however.[26]

Ugly commentary on referee competence continued. Within a week in February of 1991, three coaches had less-than-complimentary comments about referees. After a one-point loss to second-ranked Ohio State in Minnesota, coach Clem Haskins said that the officials "put the big-time screws to us at the end." And after a very ugly Indiana victory in East Lansing, both Bob Knight and Jud Heathcote found the officiating wanting and said so.[27]

Rule Changes in the 2020s

In 2002 Knight noted the lack of regulation on the number of games the officials could work. As independent contractors, some were working as many as five or six games a week around the country with no regulation. He said, "There's no way a guy over thirty can just physically work six games a week well, and here we're talking about guys who are over forty and fifty." He also wondered about the mental state of officials going into different games, whether they were big games between two powerful programs or between two lesser teams. Regarding Indiana games, he concluded by asserting, that "a lot of games were worked by tired officials."[28] This was also true of NBA officials, especially in the playoffs, where they often worked four games in a week and traveled hundreds of miles between games. They were simply tired.

Perhaps in response to all this, the Big Ten looked into stiffer penalties for coaches who abused Big Ten referees, noting that other conferences had stiffer penalties for such behavior, especially for the first offense.[29] It would be nice to say that the concerns with referees were beginning to fade. As recently as the 2019 NCAA tournament, there was considerable concern about the quality of referees throughout the country and the abuse directed at them. The Big Ten was no exception in that regard, but the hope remains that these concerns will continue to be addressed and that some human error will be seen as normal and expected, given the limits of human competence and training.

Adding to all this was the use of replays, which got more and more precise with increasing use of multiple cameras. NBA and NCAA coaches were given a certain number of challenges per half, and referees were required to examine these via replay at the end of a half or a game, leading to possible technical foul calls if an extra challenge proved unsupported by video evidence. There was also the possibility of having a referee's call overturned by an "eye in the sky" ref in New York City, where a referee supervisor could examine the call using a number of camera angles. This was done either on appeal or if the referees were uncertain about a call.

It should be noted in passing that a few other rules affecting college basketball (but not on-the-court play) have been implemented since 2020, and one in particular was still unsettled as of 2022. The first was college athletes being granted an extra year of eligibility because of losing a year to COVID-19 restrictions, meaning some players could stay eligible for up to six seasons. That rule would no longer be applicable once COVID-affected players had left school.

Another new rule allowed players to receive compensation for commercial use of their "name, image, [and] likeness" (the NIL rule) as long as boosters, coaches, or schools were not providing this compensation. As of 2022, the details of this rule were still being negotiated.

Two rule changes of note that would have little bearing on game outcomes, except in unusual circumstances, were in regard to coaches and ball possession. First was the NCAA's adoption in 2017 of the thirty-eight-foot coaching box, keeping the coach basically in front of his bench and unable, for example, to invade the opposing team's bench space or chase a referee down the floor while addressing a call. There had been times in the past where coaches were unable to restrain themselves and, after fair warning, suffered a two-shot technical foul. If there were instances where this altered the outcome of a game, they were not apparent.

The second rule of note was the elimination of the jump ball after a tie-up on the floor; instead the "alternate possession" rule (i.e., teams would alternate getting the ball, rather than a jump ball) came into effect, as of the 1982–83 season.[30] This was a response to two shortcomings perceived to plague some referees. First was the inability of the referees to make a good toss on a regular basis. Second and more important, the new rule made the game a bit less rough as players no longer piled onto one another while scrambling for a loose ball. It also sped up the game, which everyone (players, coaches, fans) appreciated. During the 1981–82 season, the new rule was tested in the Southwest and Atlantic Coast conferences and seemed to appease those who were irate over inconsistent tosses.[31] (The NBA continues to use the jump ball after tie-ups.)

The rules of basketball continue to evolve to keep the game interesting and maintain equal advantage to both teams before the ball is even thrown for the initial tap. Referees in tip-top physical shape are in greater demand as the game continues to get faster and faster. Both the players and the fans demand that.

CHAPTER 9

THE BIG TEN IN THE MID-1980s
Penn State Enters the Picture

In a surprise announcement on December 14, 1989, Penn State was invited to join the Big Ten at a meeting of the Council of Big Ten Presidents.[1] There was no apparent consultation or agreement with the Big Ten's athletic directors or their faculty athletic representatives, and many of them were disturbed by both the announcement and their ostensible lack of input. (The last Big Ten expansion in 1949, adding Michigan State for the 1950–51 basketball season and 1953 for the football season, had also been met with resistance.[2])

The next day sportswriter Ed Sherman noted that Penn State football and basketball would not be part of the Big Ten's schedules until the mid-1990s with basketball conference play beginning in 1995–96 at the earliest. Sherman also observed that the Big Ten presidents and athletic directors didn't talk much and reemphasized that the Penn State entry was a presidential-level decision. The decision also set off speculation on other possible conference realignments, especially for the Big Ten with Pittsburgh and Rutgers seen as possible future members of the conference.[3]

(Just as an aside, Penn State was threatened with the consequences of exiting the Atlantic Ten, a conference that had started in 1975 as the Eastern Collegiate Basketball League [ECBL] but changed to the Atlantic Ten in 1982 after some realignments and additions. Penn State, a founding member of the conference, was now threatened with expulsion after the university announced the potential alignment with the Big Ten. The Atlantic Ten members did not like "lame ducks" apparently.[4])

It seemed that the agreement was a fait accompli, but all was not as it seemed. The flirtation between the Big Ten and Penn State had been going on, intermittently, since the 1970s. Former Penn State president John Oswald and faculty athletic representative John Coyle had, in fact, traveled to Ann Arbor in the late 1970s to discuss the possibilities of such a jointure with Big Ten leaders, but nothing came of it.[5] Talks continued, at least unofficially, until 1980 when Oswald put in an inquiry to Big Ten Commissioner Wayne

Duke whether the Big Ten might be interested in Penn State as a conference member. Joining would help relieve pressure on the football program's funds, which were supporting twenty-eight other PSU sports at that time. It also would help a rather weak basketball program and apply pressure to build a new basketball arena to replace the outdated 1929 Recreation Building.[6] Penn State needed more basketball revenue, as it had been crippled by the looming presence of the Big East.[7]

Little came of the earlier discussions, but just before Wayne Duke retired in the spring of 1989, Penn State athletic director, Jim Tarman, asked about possible membership, and Duke said that "Tarman should pursue it." To Bryce Jordan, who had succeeded Oswald as Penn State president in 1983, the academic considerations, which were more vital to his thinking, made sense, and being in a top conference made sense in light of the new demands of Title IX and women's athletics, which Penn State already had. Penn State had embraced women's athletics early on and was already prominent in many women's sports, so joining the Big Ten seemed consonant with this action.[8]

The decision by the presidents to invite Penn State to join the Big Ten was partly a result of the fact that the conference had incorporated in 1987: "The 1987 Big Ten incorporation mandated that the Council of Presidents have final authority over all conference matters." This superseded the authority of faculty athletic representatives who had generally run the conference (and kept close contact with their respective athletic directors) since its origins in 1895–96.[9]

Nevertheless, there was a lot of complaint from prominent coaches about the decision to invite Penn State and the secretive manner in which it was done. Some of the important behind-the-scenes work was done between John Oswald and Stanley Ikenberry, the president of the University of Illinois and former senior vice president for administration at Penn State. Ikenberry was a champion for Penn State's entry into the Big Ten, noted John Coyle, since Ikenberry was then serving as chair of the Council of Presidents of the Big Ten.[10]

Following the announcement in December of 1989, there were various signs of dissatisfaction among Big Ten members. The chair of Ohio State's Athletic Council "responded to all the presidents that the presidents had 'violated the spirit of faculty governance on which the conference was founded.'"[11] Bo Schembechler, the head football coach at Michigan, remarked that "this confirms the worst fear I have of presidents getting too much control in athletics." And Bob Knight complained as well, calling Penn State a "camping trip for visitors." Rick Bay, the Minnesota athletic director said what the presidents did was "bassackwards." All worked to get their presidents to rescind their votes for Penn State's entry.[12]

In January of 1990 the Council of Presidents announced that Penn State had been only "invited in principle" and that there were still answers to questions that needed to be provided. The presidents then held another meeting, this time including the faculty athletic representatives and the athletic directors, and agreed to gather further data before taking another vote by the presidents in late spring of 1990.[13] Data on academic standards, facilities (Penn State did, ultimately build a new arena for basketball, as agreed upon), and potential television revenue were all gathered. University of Wisconsin's chancellor, Donna Shalala, viewed the impact of Penn State's joining the conference as "making us more powerful as a conference, particularly as we try to add constituencies as we try to work within the NCAA."[14]

Still, there was a lot of pushback within the Big Ten to rescind the Penn State invitation. Rick Bay at Minnesota continued to foment opposition, and other unnamed people at Michigan, Indiana, and Purdue spoke against it. Commissioner Jim Delany said that the two-step process had the invitation as step one and the formal entrance as step two, and that the latter was still "under the process of review."[15]

Three days before the vote, the preliminary views made the passage problematic. President Thomas Ehrlich of Indiana said that he'd vote against the admission of Penn State to the Big Ten if the IU Athletic Commission did not support it.[16] President Jordan wrote a statement regarding Penn State's denial of admission to the Big Ten, which he was prepared to release were the vote to enter the conference not favorable. But in the end, the vote on June 4, 1990, was positive, "possibly seven to three, although the exact vote may never be revealed."[17]

"In retrospect," President Jordan wrote to his friend Stanley Ikenberry at Illinois, "the whole thing seems to have been more difficult than one would have thought."[18] Penn State would now join the Big Ten and be competing in the conference basketball race as soon as 1995 if the speculation was accurate.

After a very disappointing showing for the Big Ten in the 1982–83 season, personnel moves roiled the conference in the off-season. Iowa's coach, Lute Olsen, left for Arizona. Brad Sellers transferred to Ohio State, and Jimmy Collins came to Illinois as Lou Henson's top recruiting assistant coach. In addition, the three-point experiment of 1982–83 would not be in effect for the 1983–84 season. The Big Ten national television schedule would begin December 3 with CBS broadcasting Indiana against Kentucky, and the overall conference schedule would start on January 4 with conference contests packaged and shown via Metrosports. There would be two to three games per week for the conference, shown nationally, with three committed to CBS in February and March and three on NBC those same months.[19]

The Preseason

Only two Big Ten squads made the UPI's top-twenty rankings: Iowa at #6 and Michigan State at #14.[20] In the AP, three Big Ten teams were ranked—Iowa at #7, Michigan State at #12, and Indiana at #18.[21] Four days later, the Big Ten coaches expressed their views and were most impressed with Iowa and Michigan State. George Raveling, who had come from Washington State to be the new Iowa coach (replacing the departed Lute Olson), said that he was "shocked, amazed and amused" by the predictions of his peers, considering he had not coached a game in the Big Ten yet.[22] Rich Falk of Northwestern commented that "come league time, the Hoosiers will always be ready."[23]

Nonconference play, which began in November, was rarely exciting since most top teams play at home and schedule games with weaker teams. There were exceptions, of course, and one was the Illinois performance against Utah in the Tribune Charities Classic (also referred to as the "Crush Classic"), played at the Horizon Center (now called the Allstate Arena) in suburban Rosemont, Illinois. The Illini had lost 52–49 to Utah in the NCAA tournament the previous season, and the Illinois squad clearly had payback on their collective minds. The final score was 99–65 after a 50–40 Illinois halftime lead. In the second half, Illinois shot 67 percent to Utah's 27 percent. The Illini placed five players in double figures, led by Bruce Douglas with 15 and both Scott Meents and Efrem Winters with 14. The Illini continued that surge in the championship game, topping Loyola 70–53 behind Winters's 21 and George Montgomery's 19.[24]

Indiana was startled 63–57 by Miami of Ohio in the home opener for the Hoosiers, with missed free throws leading to the defeat. After the game, Bob Knight expressed admiration for how Miami played, but Steve Alford recalled that "we were the first Knight-coached Indiana team ever to lose its home opener."[25]

Indiana's loss did not encourage opposing coaches with title hopes. Bill Frieder of Michigan said, "He could lose them all and he'd still be in there. Anybody who doesn't think that way is nuts."[26]

Illinois's high hopes were brought down quickly because of early season injuries. Coach Lou Henson said that Illinois "would struggle in December, but be okay in January."[27] That wasn't exactly right, since Anthony Welch's injury was worse than suspected, and the next day he was declared out of the Illini plans for the season.[28]

Purdue upset #6 Louisville in West Lafayette 90–83, in overtime, to insert the Boilermakers into the Big Ten title conversation.[29] In a significant contest, preseason #1 Kentucky edged Indiana 59–54 in Lexington before 23,864 Wildcat fans.[30] Michigan also beat #16 ranked Georgia 76–70 in Atlanta, keeping the Wolverines undefeated for the season. Tim McCormick had 25 points and 13 rebounds to pace Michigan.[31]

Holiday Tournaments

It was again time for the start of holiday basketball tournaments, and Big Ten teams were playing all around the Midwest. Some teams, like Indiana, sponsored their own tournaments, but most were being played on neutral sites. Indiana won its Indiana Classic against mediocre competition (Utah State, Texas A&M, Illinois State), as well as its Hoosier Classic against Ball State, Iowa State, and Boston College. Michigan was upset by both UTEP and Texas Tech in the Sun Bowl Classic in El Paso.[32]

Purdue had its best start in forty-six years at 7–0, but the excitement didn't last long, as the Boilermakers lost at Evansville. Coach Gene Keady said, "We had no intensity. You win if you play hard. We didn't."[33]

On Christmas Eve, Kentucky topped Illinois in Champaign, 56–54 as the Illini played only six players. More noteworthy was the fact that the weather left the referees scheduled to work the game stranded on an icy highway somewhere in central Illinois, and the game was officiated by three local high school referees who were either in the audience or nearby.[34] Kentucky followed up this victory with a crushing win over Purdue in Louisville 86–67.[35]

Big Ten Conference Play

The Big Ten had not exactly shined in the tournaments, and the hope was that teams would get themselves into shape with the start of the conference season on January 5, 1984. Heading into that, Illinois had the best nonconference record at 9–1 with Minnesota at 8–1, and Michigan at 8–2. It was hard to discern where the power in the conference was, but there did seem to be some degree of parity.

In the opening game Michigan State edged Iowa in East Lansing, 73–72, led by Scott Skiles with 19 points and seven assists.[36] The next night, Illinois, Purdue and Michigan all won their openers easily over Minnesota, Wisconsin and Northwestern respectively.[37] Two nights later, Illinois was fortunate to squeeze past Wisconsin in overtime in Madison, 63–62. Lou Henson made a most prescient comment after the game: "They beat us in every phase of the game, but the final score. . . . This is a good example of what can happen on the road in the Big 10."[38] Also on the road that night was Northwestern in East Lansing, but they were apparently very ready to play and upset the Spartans 76–69, snapping an eighteen-game Big Ten road losing streak.[39]

There were injuries and academic issues making it difficult for certain teams. Indiana was down to eight scholarship players and was still 2–0 in conference. But that would soon end when they faced 3–0 Purdue in Bloomington. Purdue scored the last five points of the first half and the first seventeen of the second to lead 47–35. No visiting team had ever scored twenty-two straight points at Assembly Hall, and Gene Keady called this his "biggest win since it's Indiana." The Hoosiers "stank" according to Steve Alford.[40] Bob Knight decided that the freshmen would have to be more prominent in his season plans. The next week, he started four of them: Steve Alford, Daryl Thomas, Marty Simmons, and Todd Meier—against Michigan State in a 70–62 overtime win in East Lansing. The four frosh scored 52 of the 70 points.[41]

The Big Ten was an unpredictable mess. At the end of January, Purdue and Illinois were tied at 6–1 with Indiana at 5–2 and OSU at 4–3. No one else was above .500, and Michigan State was last at 1–7. It was not looking like a memorable year for the Big Ten, either inside or outside the conference. The games were often slow, and subject to long periods of holding the ball on offense.

The conference race was coming down to three teams, Purdue (10–1), Illinois (9–1), and Indiana (8–2). Late in February, both Big Ten leaders lost on the same night, Purdue at MSU, 63–53, and Illinois at Michigan, 62–60. Indiana, playing in Bob Knight's new deliberate style, edged Iowa, 49–45 in Iowa City. The conference was not doing well nationally, and locally was not very entertaining.[42]

Down the Stretch

At the end of February three teams were still in the running for the Big Ten title. Indiana had been coming on, until a loss at home to Michigan State, which Bob Knight called his "biggest disappointment since he began coaching IU," where he was now in his thirteenth season as head coach. Indiana was 11–4, a half game behind Illinois (11–3) and a game and a half behind Purdue, with a clash between the two Indiana schools set for Purdue on February 29.[43] Despite the anticipation, the game was not close, as Indiana handed Purdue its worst defeat at Mackey Arena since 1972, snapping an eighteen-game home win streak. The score was 78–59.[44]

The stage was set for an Illinois vs. Indiana clash in Champaign, but Indiana forgot to show up, and Illinois stomped on the Hoosiers, 70–53. Bob Knight was succinct in his summary of the game. We "flat out got our butts kicked.... They just took it away from us right from the start."[45]

The final standings had Illinois and Purdue at 15–3 and Indiana two back at 13–5 and these three teams were invited to the NCAA tournament of 53 teams. Two others were invited to the NIT's field of thirty-two: Michigan and Ohio State.

The UPI Player of the Year for the Big Ten was shared by Jim Rowinski of Purdue and Bruce Douglas of Illinois. In a vote of the coaches, Gene Keady was voted Coach of the Year, Tommy Davis was voted MVP, and Steve Alford was voted Big Ten Freshman of the Year. The USBWA named Keady as its national Coach of the Year.[46]

Tournament Time

The NIT opened first for the Big Ten on March 15 with Michigan defeating Wichita State 94–70 in Ann Arbor, while Ohio State lost 60–57 to Xavier in Cincinnati.[47] Michigan got by Marquette, Xavier, and Virginia Tech to reach the championship game against Notre Dame. There the Wolverines crushed the Irish 83–61. Two nights later, Tim McCormick was named MVP of the tourney after he had 28 points and 14 rebounds in the final game. That game was played with a forty-five-second clock, exciting Coach Bill Frieder with the possibilities of such a clock in the Big Ten in the future. He noted that he'd "vote for that clock in a minute."[48]

Frieder's comments preceded by a day the release of a poll by the National Association of Basketball Coaches of college coaches, wherein 53 percent voted to approve a forty-five-second clock. The NCAA was not convinced of its utility, however, and the Rules Committee announced three days later that they had rejected the use of a clock for the 1984–85 season but would bring up the issue again the next year. The vote was not disclosed.[49]

The opening of NCAA play on March 17 had Purdue at Memphis State, where the Boilermakers absorbed a 66–48 hiding. The Boilermakers could not find the basket, shooting just 28 percent from the floor (19 of 68). On that same night Indiana defeated Richmond 75–67 in Charlotte, North Carolina.[50] Illinois, the third Big Ten rep in the NCAA, played Villanova in Milwaukee the next night and won 64–56.[51]

In East regional play in Atlanta, Indiana, seeded #4, defeated the #1 seed, North Carolina, in a major upset, 73–68. Steve Alford had 27 points. UNC scoring was topped by Sam Perkins with 26, while Michael Jordan had just 13 and fouled out.[52]

In the Mideast, Illinois edged Maryland in Lexington, Kentucky, but lost 54–51 against Kentucky (when teams could play on their home court in the regionals), leaving only Indiana to represent the Big Ten in the NCAA tournament. Indiana, seeded #4, lost to #7-seeded Virginia in the East finals in Atlanta 50–48.[53] The Big Ten had no teams in the NCAA Final Four.

Between Seasons

The rest of April and May brought lots of news regarding Big Ten basketball action. Bob Knight had been named Olympic basketball head coach for the Games of the XXII Olympiad in Los Angeles that summer, and he and assistant coaches George Raveling and Don Donoher (Dayton) put together one of the most impressive squads of the preprofessional era, led by Michael Jordan, Patrick Ewing, Chris Mullen, and one Big Ten player, Steve Alford, whom Knight later called "our best player."[54] In April, the Big Ten voted to use a forty-five-second clock on an experimental one-year basis for 1985 conference contests. The clock would be in effect for the entire game.[55]

Jim Rowinski was voted Big Ten MVP and winner of the *Chicago Tribune* Silver Basketball.[56] It was unusual in that Rowinski and Rickey Hall, the Big Ten Defensive Player of the Year, had been voted co-MVPs by their teammates and this was the first time a team's co-MVP had been named sole conference MVP. Rowinski nosed out Bruce Douglas of Illinois.

1984–85, Hoping for More

Just before fall practice opened in mid-October 1985 the conference was shaken by a heart attack suffered by Jud Heathcote, which would keep him out until December. The outlook was deemed "excellent" for the fifty-seven-year-old and, ultimately that proved to be the case, as he came back and remained coach until retiring after the 1994–95 season. He lived to age ninety, before passing away in 2017.[57] Mike Conklin saw the upcoming season as a big year for the conference. Besides Illinois, he noted that Indiana had more than five starters returning from their freshmen-laden 22–9 club that had been plagued by injuries. Gene Keady said, "I think we have more pure talent than last year, but we'll have to work even harder to even be close to the same kind of success!"[58]

In what was becoming a pattern, Bob Knight skipped the Big Ten coaches meeting. There the Minnesota coach, Jim Dutcher, saw Ohio State as "overlooked" and predicted a good season for that squad. The coaches hoped for seven teams to be in the expanded sixty-four-team NCAA field, and almost all of the coaches said that they liked the forty-five-second clock, which would now be used.[59]

As the month of December progressed Big Ten teams showed their inconsistency, with the hope that this "habit" would be altered as the holiday tournament season loomed. One notable contest was Indiana's easy victory over Kentucky in Bloomington 81–68, led by Steve Alford's 24 points, 7 assists, and 6 rebounds. Referring to the game, Alford said, "This is what the team has been looking for, especially out of me." The victory was also the four hundredth for Bob Knight, making him, at forty-three, the youngest coach to achieve this milestone.[60]

Indiana's success was matched more generally by the conference, which had a record of 41–9 with five unbeaten squads by mid-December. The teams began playing holiday tourneys. Indiana won their Indiana Classic tournament, as usual, but the biggest stories seemed to be the two teams from the state of Michigan. By Christmas, both the Wolverines and the Spartans were undefeated at 8–0.

Michigan State's streak was ended by Boston College 82–78 in San Diego at the Cabrillo Classic, and Michigan's ended the next night when they lost at Tennessee, 81–77. Indiana managed to win the Hoosier Classic, despite bumbling against Miami of Ohio 77–74, then crushing Florida 80–63 in the title game. After the former contest, Knight was nearly apoplectic, noting, "Miami should have won the game. We had absolutely no awareness of what was going on. We got no guard play. Alford played poorly." The next night, Alford had 24.[61]

Big Ten Play Begins

The Big Ten season began. Indiana traveled to Ann Arbor, where it was really no contest as IU embarrassed the Wolverines 87–62. Illinois could not match the Indiana win, losing their opener to Minnesota 60–58.[62] Despite the loss, the Big Ten looked terrific, again, with five teams having just one loss and only Northwestern having more than three. The conference record was 41–9, 80 percent, as league play heated up. Iowa toppled Illinois, in Iowa City 64–60, handing the Illini their third straight loss, the first time that had happened since 1979.[63]

Two interesting contests on the same night saw Minnesota top Michigan State in East Lansing and Purdue edge Wisconsin in Madison. Wisconsin coach Steve Yoder noted that "we have to be smarter. Purdue wins because they use the entire 45-second clock and we come down and only use 10 seconds."[64] Michigan State beat Indiana, 68–61, making the Big Ten more egalitarian but messier.

Illinois won its eighteenth straight game in Assembly Hall by crushing Ohio State 84–46. Eldon Miller summed up his team's effort as a "defensive breakdown and probably one of our worst shooting efforts [37 percent]." The next night Purdue overcame an eight-point deficit to Indiana with twelve minutes to go and won by ten, 62–52.[65] The blown-lead loss to Purdue affected Knight apparently because the next Hoosier game saw Uwe Blab and four freshmen start the contest. Steve Alford was on the bench the whole game, as were Marty Simmons, Todd Meier, Stew Robinson, and Dan Dakich. Mike Giomi and Winston Morgan did not even make the trip to Champaign, a 52–41 loss to the Illini. Knight offered no explanation, and IU fans were irate. Knight commented more than ten years later on the line-up, noting, "I didn't think we had been getting the kind of effort that we had to get."[66] Giomi, the team's leading rebounder through fifteen games, was dismissed from the team the next day.[67] Indiana responded by dropping its fourth game in a row for the first time since 1971–72, Knight's first season, 72–59, to Iowa, in Bloomington. In a most telling statistic, the Hoosiers were outrebounded, 39–22.[68]

Illinois also ran into problems that week. They were humbled by Purdue 54–34 in West Lafayette. Illinois shot just 36 percent from the floor, but Purdue didn't do much better at 37 percent. Lou Henson, clearly exasperated, said, "In my 30 years of coaching, I've never seen such inept playing."[69] The final month of the regular season, Indiana came out of its funk after Knight's tirades and machinations and destroyed Minnesota 89–66 in Bloomington. Indiana then lost two in a row, 66–50, at Illinois and 72–63, at home to Purdue, the latter loss highlighted by Knight's ejection for his now infamous chair-throwing incident, which led to a one-game suspension by the Big Ten. Iowa was shocked by losing two games to the bottom dwellers in the conference 54–53 at Wisconsin and 78–58 in Evanston to Northwestern.[70] Michigan finally ended the suspense of a murky Big Ten season. The Wolverines clinched the title in a romp against Wisconsin on the last day of February.

The Post Season Tournaments

A record six Big Ten teams were invited to the NCAA tourney. The sixty-four included thirty automatic qualifying conferences—a number that was capped for five years.[71] Indiana was the only Big Ten team selected for the NIT. The final Big Ten records for 1984–85 had Michigan at 16–2, Illinois at 12–6, with Purdue and Ohio State at 11–7.

In the NIT Indiana, was the sole Big 10 team and defeated Butler 79–57 in Bloomington. Continuing in Bloomington, the Hoosiers defeated Richmond 75–53. In the quarterfinals, again in Bloomington, Indiana topped Marquette in two overtimes 94–82 to send themselves to Madison Square Garden for the NIT semifinals. There they topped Tennessee 74–67 behind

Bob Knight throwing a chair at Northwestern, February 24, 1985.
(Courtesy of Indiana University Archives)

Doug Altenberger, All-Big Ten at Illinois. *(Courtesy of University of Illinois Athletics)*

Uwe Blab (24 points, 10 rebounds) and Alford (23 points). In the finals, the Hoosiers were brought down 65–62 by another great power a bit down on its luck: UCLA.[72]

In the NCAA, the six Big Ten teams started tournament play with #8 seed Iowa losing to #9 Arkansas 63–54 in Salt Lake City and #6-seed Purdue losing 59–58 to #11 Auburn at Notre Dame.[73] In Tulsa, the conference got a small boost from Ohio State's 75–64 win over Iowa State and former Michigan coach Johnny Orr. Illinois and Michigan also won opening round games: the #3 Illini 76–57 over #14 Northeastern in Atlanta and the #1 Wolverines 59–55 over #16 Fairleigh Dickinson in Dayton.[74]

Michigan State, a #10 seed, dropped the Big Ten's opening record to 3–3 with a 70–68 loss to #7 Alabama-Birmingham in Houston.[75] Fourth-seeded Ohio State lost to #5-seed Louisiana Tech 79–67 in Tulsa, then Michigan was shocked in Dayton 59–55 by #8-seed Villanova, who played slow, ball-control basketball. Bill Frieder lamented, "I'd hoped that we could get ahead and speed up the tempo. But we couldn't sustain it and they were perfect at countering almost everything we tried the rest of the way."[76]

The Illini, the Big Ten's last hope, went into the final sixteen with a 74–58 win over #6 Georgia in Atlanta.[77] The Illini "high" did not last as they were dumped by #2-seeded Georgia Tech in Providence 61–53. Doug Altenberger had nearly half the Illinois points (24), but Bruce Douglas was outplayed by Mark Price, who had 20 points and harassed Douglas into 9 turnovers and just a single field goal. There would be no Big Ten teams in the Final Eight.[78]

The Postseason

Despite having six teams in the tournament, the conference went just 4–6. It was a better record than the previous season, but a big disappointment. One small solace was that Bill Frieder was voted national Coach of the Year, edging Lou Carnesecca of St. John's and John Thompson of Georgetown.

There was room for growth and alterations in the Big Ten. Rich Falk was contemplating his future at Northwestern and decided to hang on, but he retired after the next season. Exciting news for "run and gun" squads was that the NCAA had voted to adopt the forty-five-second clock for all games as well as to award two shots and possession of the ball for intentional fouls.[79]

Roy Tarpley of Michigan was named the first league-sponsored Big Ten Men's Player of the Year, and also received the *Chicago Tribune* Silver Basketball as Big Ten Player of the Year, while Bruce Douglas was awarded Defensive Player of the Year. Tarpley led Michigan with 19 points and 10.4 rebounds per game. Shon Morris called him the most talented player that he had faced in college, and compared him to a younger version of Kevin Durant, who would have been one of the fifty greatest NBA players ever if not for his substance abuse.[80]

The exodus from Indiana continued as Marty Simmons transferred to Evansville to play for a former Hoosier, Jim Crews, who had taken the head coaching job there. Five Big Ten teams (Michigan, Purdue, Iowa, Minnesota, and Ohio State) announced they would be routinely testing football and basketball players for drugs.

1985–86

After three years of relative unimportance on the national scene, the Big Ten wanted to return to prominence in 1985–86, especially after the poor results from the NCAA tournament. The predicted conference order was Michigan, Illinois, Iowa, Purdue, Indiana, Minnesota, Ohio State, Wisconsin, Michigan State, and Northwestern. Of the thirteen players listed by *Street & Smith's* as likely All-America players, two were from the Big Ten, Roy Tarpley (picked as Player of the Year) and Steve Alford.[81]

In mid-November, Michigan State reinstated Scott Skiles after he had been suspended pending his court plea on marijuana charges. This would pay dividends, of course, for the Spartans. In reviewing the Big Ten teams, Bob Logan saw the conference with a "big 5" and a "little 5," with Michigan and Illinois the leading squads. Bob Knight expressed disdain at the tempo of the league, noting that "our league has fallen into a very slow pace recently. I'd like to see us play against that pace."[82] After that comment, it was no surprise that Knight did not show up for the Big Ten media day where the big news from Commissioner Wayne Duke was that the conference had signed an agreement with CBS, in which they would broadcast thirty-one Big Ten games over the next three years.[83]

The Games Begin

In the Hawaii Aloha Classic, Illinois was stunned by Oklahoma 59–57, but this was the only surprise of the Hawaii contests. Purdue and Minnesota were playing in Alaska and Michigan State hosted the Spartan Classic. There were no unexpected results.[84]

In the "official" opening contest of the college season, played at Springfield as the Hall of Fame Classic, Michigan defeated Georgia Tech 49–44 in a very ugly game. Antoine Joubert led Michigan with 21 and called the game "very physical." His coach, Bill Frieder, commented, "That's the way you play in the Big 10." The Wolverines came home to rout Tennessee 87–52 two nights later.[85] They went on to go undefeated in the nonconference schedule.

In Indiana the big story was again off the court, as the #19 Hoosiers lost Steve Alford for a game because his photo was used in a charity calendar. This decision, by the NCAA Eligibility Committee, on December 6, meant that Alford would miss the Kentucky contest the next day in Lexington. Indiana led Kentucky most of the game, only to fall, 63–58. Bob Knight faulted the NCAA's strict interpretation of the rule regarding "professionalism" (not the rule itself) in lamenting Alford's penalty.[86] Meanwhile the rest of the Big Ten was beating up on almost everyone: the conference had a record of 51–7 for the season against their nonconference foes. That dominance was upset by two big losses on December 10: Iowa got a pounding in Ames from Iowa State 74–61 and Illinois suffered a disappointing loss to Tennessee in Knoxville 54–51. Still, the Big Ten on December 17 had their top three teams (Michigan #3, Illinois # 13, and Indiana #16) still in the top twenty of the UPI. Directly after that, Louisville entertained the Hoosiers and edged them 65–63, despite twenty-seven points from Alford.[87]

Holiday Tournaments

Indiana once again won the Hoosier Classic, routing Idaho 87–57 and then Mississippi 74–43, with Calloway, Alford, and Daryl Thomas leading the way in scoring. Indiana also won the Indiana Classic, with Daryl Thomas being named MVP. In New Mexico, Michigan State defeated Massachusetts 93–45 and then won the tourney with a 76–61 win over host New Mexico State. Scott Skiles had twenty-five points in each game to garner MVP honors for the tournament.[88] Purdue defeated Lamar 67–56 in the Cable Car Classic in Santa Clara and then defeated the hosts 84–56 behind tourney MVP Troy Lewis's twenty-four points.[89]

The Big Ten Season Opens

The results of the preconference schedule were reflected in the relatively low rankings of Big Ten teams as the conference season began. Michigan was still #2, nationally, but only Illinois at #14 and Indiana at #15 were listed in the top twenty. The conference had been 89–22, the best in Big Ten history against nonconference opponents, but many of those wins were against decidedly weaker teams.

On opening night two of the top teams squared off when Michigan invaded Bloomington and came away with a 78–69 win. The difference in the game was at the free- throw line, where Michigan was 26 of 35, while Indiana was just 5 of 10. Illinois kept pace with a 76–57 rout of Minnesota in Champaign. Illinois outshot the Gophers (57 percent to 44 percent), outrebounded them 35–22, and led from start to finish.[90]

Michigan continued winning: they were victorious in Columbus 78–68, against Ohio State, and against Illinois 61–59 in Ann Arbor but were upended at Minnesota 73–63, breaking the Wolverine thirty-two-game regular season and nineteen-win Big Ten streak. The Wolverines were not sharp, and Minnesota committed only twelve fouls in the game.[91]

Illinois dropped three in a row before finally winning in Wisconsin 73–54. Indiana lost its second straight in the conference 74–69 to Michigan and 77–74 to Michigan State. Indiana then lost Delray Brooks, who decided to transfer, becoming the third key player (Mike Giomi and Marty Simmons) to leave the program in two years. The games were played without Daryl Thomas, who had sprained an ankle in practice. Bob Knight saw that as the reason that his IU team was not co-champions of the Big Ten that year. Larry Polec of the Spartans said, "I don't know if it's because we're playing Indiana or at Assembly Hall or coach Bobby Knight. We all seem to get up for the game."[92]

With a third of the conference season complete, Michigan stood at 5–1, Purdue 5–2, and five teams had three losses, with only Michigan State, Wisconsin, and Northwestern under .500 in conference play. One of those with three losses was Minnesota, a team with their own unique problems.

Minnesota in Trouble

Three Minnesota players, Mitchell Lee, Kevin Smith, and George Williams were ousted from the team in January after they were arrested on sexual assault charges, leading to the resignation of Coach Jim Dutcher and the naming of Jimmy Williams as interim head coach. He would be the third African American to be named a Big Ten basketball coach. Lee had just been acquitted in January of his last rape charge, and these new charges devastated not only the Gopher team but the entire university and the state of Minnesota as well.[93]

In retrospect, Dutcher said that he quit because he was embarrassed and that "Jimmy Williams, the assistant coach who has taken over the team, was to check that all players were in their rooms, normal responsibilities for the traveling assistant. Williams, however, was sick with a cold, took some medicine, and went to bed early." The players had been told to be in by midnight since they had a 5 a.m. call. Dutcher never checked rooms, always leaving that to his assistants.[94] Minnesota would play out the season after adding five football players to fill out their roster, but the problems weren't over yet. Two more players, Todd Alexander and Terrence Woods, were suspended: Alexander was out for the rest of the season and Woods indefinitely, both for unspecified violations of team rules. Then Mark Anderson withdrew from the university, leaving five players plus the late joiners for the next game against Ohio State. Surprisingly, the Gophers defeated OSU 70–65 in Minneapolis. The five starters played thirty-six minutes each.[95] After a 13–7 start, the Golden Gophers went 2–9 under Jimmy Williams with a depleted roster and were essentially done for the season.

The whole controversy caused many to scrutinize more closely the entire Minnesota athletics program, and the findings were not impressive. From 1973–83 Minnesota had the worst graduation rate in the Big Ten for male scholarship athletes, with basketball being the worst. Of twenty-three freshmen on scholarship during that period, only two graduated, a rate of 9 percent. (The next lowest in the Big Ten was 30 percent.) Richard Heydinger, senior vice president, asserted that Minnesota would recruit first and foremost on academic merit from that point forward.[96]

With the league still reeling from Dutcher's resignation, Ohio State's Eldon Miller was out of a job after resigning on February 3, effective at the end of the season. Miller contended that he had actually been fired and blamed many of his problems on Ohio State's practice of having just one-year contracts. He said that this hurt recruiting, which was "the life blood of the program."[97] Ohio State athletic director, Rick Bay, was quoted by the *Cleveland Plain-Dealer* as refusing to give Miller a long-term deal, based on Miller's "unpopularity with fans" and OSU's tradition of one-year contracts to coaches and administrators.[98] The rumor that Bob Knight would be offered the position at his alma mater was denied by Knight on February 12. Knight noted that he intended to stay at Indiana for the rest of his career. The one-year contract situation at OSU might have been a factor, but more than that was his success and popularity in Bloomington, despite his occasional curmudgeonly antics.[99]

Back to Basketball

The drama on the court was exciting and inconclusive in determining the top team. Despite his legal difficulties, Skiles was having an amazing year, averaging twenty-nine points per game in conference play and helping Michigan State to lead the Big Ten in team field goal shooting (55 percent) and team free-throw shooting (79 percent).[100]

Michigan looked to be on its way to a second consecutive title after edging Purdue 80–79 on February 7 in West Lafayette, sending the Boilermakers to a fourth consecutive loss (the first time that had happened since 1982). Purdue shot 31 of 60 from the floor, but Michigan was even better with 31 of 48 (65 percent).[101] Illinois upset the Wolverines in Champaign 83–79 in overtime to delay any premature celebration and, after Indiana defeated Northwestern, there was a tie at the top between the Wolverines and the Hoosiers, both with 8–3 records. Michigan then defeated Iowa in Ann Arbor 82–66 on national television, eliciting the following comment from Iowa coach George Raveling regarding the Wolverines: "This is a Final Four team."[102]

Despite Raveling's encomium, Michigan fell to Michigan State in Ann Arbor 74–59, as Indiana defeated Illinois in Champaign 61–60. Purdue's 85–79 win over Ohio State tightened the race: it looked as though five or six Big Ten teams would eventually head to the NCAA tournament. At this point, IU was 10–3, Michigan 10–4, MSU and Purdue both 9–5, and Illinois was 9–6. Purdue muddied title possibilities even more by defeating Indiana 85–68 in West Lafayette.

The last day of the season saw the two leaders, Michigan and Indiana, both with records of 13–4, meeting at Michigan. It was no contest. The Wolverines were much better, winning 80–52 and outrebounding IU 47–29. Tarpley had 21 points and 11 rebounds. Alford led Indiana with 15. "We were totally dominated,"[103] said Alford after the game.

Postseason Platitudes

A number of announcements and decisions now came forth. First, was the award of Player of the Year to MSU's Scott Skiles by the Big Ten coaches as well as by the *Chicago Tribune*. For his senior season, Skiles endured taunts from the crowds in many arenas because of his DUI and marijuana possession convictions but still managed to shoot 55 percent from the floor and 90 percent from the line in Big Ten games.[104] Indiana's Ricky Calloway was selected as Big Ten Freshman of the Year after averaging 14 points per game and 4.8 rebounds. Another issue was the continued uncertainty of Rich Falk's position at Northwestern. Ultimately, Falk was fired, despite being the second-winningest coach in Northwestern history, prompting Dean Smith to remark, "Northwestern should admit some academic risks who have a chance to graduate, like Duke and Carolina do, or they should get out of the Big 10." Reflecting on his time at Northwestern, Big Ten Network sportscaster Shon Morris expressed his gratitude to Falk for spotting something in him that others did not and providing the opportunity to play Big Ten basketball.[105] The next month, Bruce Douglas was named Big Ten Defensive Player of the Year by the Big Ten radio broadcasters for the second straight year after leading the conference in steals and assists.[106]

The Tournaments

In NIT action, Ohio State, playing for lame-duck coach Eldon Miller, chalked up wins against Ohio University, Texas, and BYU to face Wyoming in the NIT championship at Madison Square Garden. During that run, Ohio State named Gary Williams of Boston College as their new coach (with a $75,000 per year, five-year contract, the first OSU multiyear contract in any sport). But that did not deter the Bucks as they rallied to win the championship for Miller 73–63 behind Brad Sellers, who was named NIT MVP. Miller was named coach at Northern Iowa just before the victory.[107]

Six Big Ten teams were selected for the NCAA tourney. In the East, Indiana was a #3 seed. In the Southeast, Illinois was a #4 seed with Purdue a

#6 seed. In the Midwest, Michigan was #2, Michigan State #5, and Iowa #11. Purdue coach Gene Keady expressed his concern over his team's first-round matchup against #11 LSU on their home floor in Baton Rouge. His worries proved to be well founded.[108] Purdue was upset by LSU 94–87 in double overtime. The Boilermakers were weakened significantly when their third-leading scorer, freshman Melvin McCants, left the game with a leg injury late in the first half and was unable to return.[109]

Other Big Ten teams were also surprised: Indiana lost to Cleveland State 83–79 in Syracuse, and Iowa fell to North Carolina State 66–64 in Minneapolis. Michigan State, behind thirty-one from Skiles, edged Washington, 72–70 in Dayton. Illinois had an easier time against Fairfield, winning 75–51 in Charlotte. Michigan was sluggish in a 70–64 win against Akron in Minneapolis.[110]

Michigan State upset #4 Georgetown 80–68 in Dayton behind Skiles's 24 points and 5 assists. Larry Polec, who had 16 points and 10 rebounds, praised Skiles to the skies after the game, "In order to win, you have to spill your guts out on the floor. We count on Scott to do that every game. He rubs off on us."[111]

The Spartans were the last Big Ten team left after both Illinois and Michigan were upset, the former to Alabama 58–56 in Charlotte and the latter to Iowa State and former Michigan coach Johnny Orr 72–69 in Minneapolis. Illinois lost on a disputed last-second shot, which prompted Lou Henson to note that "refs make mistakes, but they didn't lose it." The Illini shot no free throws, while Alabama was six of nine in a game where the refs clearly let them play. Roy Tarpley, commenting on the Michigan loss, said that he and his teammates had a "lack of concentration once we got on the floor. We made too many turnovers (15) and missed too many free throws (6)."[112]

MSU lost in overtime,96–86, to #1 seed Kansas in Kansas City, partly due to a malfunctioning clock that allowed Kansas to tie the game in the last minute of regulation. Scott Skiles had 20, and Danny Manning had 17 for Kansas.[113]

The action in the Big Ten was still not over. Northwestern hired Bill Foster from the University of South Carolina as coach after Jim Calhoun of Northeastern rejected the position, noting, "I don't do miracles." Calhoun had reportedly been offered $80,000, but after consulting with Bob Knight, Gene Keady, and Johnny Orr, refused the offer and went, instead, to Connecticut as coach.[114] George Raveling joined the Big Ten coaching caravan, leaving Iowa for the University of Southern California. As a former coach at Washington State, Raveling had Pac Ten roots, and USC pursued him hard. The next week, Clem Haskins accepted the head coaching position at Minnesota. Just ten days after Raveling announced his departure, Iowa hired Stanford's head coach, Tom Davis, signing him to a five-year contract at $75,000 per year.[115]

As if there hadn't been enough coaching turmoil for this past season, one last issue arose in late April. Coach Steve Yoder of Wisconsin was reprimanded and nearly fired for failing to reveal that he knew of guard Cory Blackwell's acceptance in 1982 of a loan from a Badger booster and then lying about it to a special investigator and the university's Athletic Compliance Board in February 1986. Yoder would have his salary frozen for 1986–87. Wisconsin would have to forfeit twenty-two games wins during Blackwell's three seasons, 1981–82, 1982–83, and 1983–84.[116]

This last action was in keeping with what had been one of the worst seasons in Big Ten basketball history. Sam Smith of the *Chicago Tribune* called it "the weakest Big Ten in several years."[117]

CHAPTER 10

ENDING THE 1980s
The Big Ten Renewal

The end of the 1985–86 season did not mean the end of active basketball news in the Big Ten. Of particular importance to the conference and conference coffers were the television dealings. ESPN contracted with the conference to air nine night games during 1986–87 and ten for each of the following seasons. ABC would be airing conference games on Saturday and Sunday. The Big Ten already had a CBS deal for eleven games and one with NBC for seven games in the upcoming season. This was more than about money, however; it was also a significant recruiting tool. All this stimulated more discussion on a postseason tournament, depending upon if such an event could attract a good sponsor, a good venue, and a good network to broadcast it.[1]

Off-season personnel moves involved both coaches and players. Eldon Miller, who had been fired from his Ohio State coaching job, was off to Cedar Falls, Iowa, as the new coach of the University of Northern Iowa.[2] As noted earlier, Bill Foster was named in April 1986 to replace Rich Falk as Northwestern coach. Shon Morris, his top player at NU, said that Foster was very impactful on his life. The two remained in close contact from 1988 until Foster's death in 2016.[3]

And there were the rule changes. The NCAA, and thus the Big Ten, would be using a 19 feet, 9 inches three-point shot in all games, plus a forty-five-second clock, tried in the previous season. There would also be the use of instant replay to correct timing or scoring errors.

Meanwhile, Kenny Battle, a star at Northern Illinois and from Aurora, Illinois, announced his intention to transfer after the coach who recruited him for NIU was fired, and he finally wound up choosing the Illini. He would sit out a year and have two years of eligibility beginning with the 1987–88 season.[4] Illinois was also buoyed by the announcement that Marcus Liberty from Chicago's King High School, described as "the best high school player in the U.S.," would also be enrolling at Illinois for the 1987–88 season.[5]

Rickey Calloway, Big Ten Freshman of the Year, 1985–86.
(*Courtesy of Indiana University Archives*)

It was one of those years when the Soviet basketball team made a tour through the United States before the start of the college basketball season. The Soviets came to Bloomington on November 15, where Indiana edged them 97–95, behind 25 points from Rickey Calloway and 24 points by Darryl Thomas, who was back in Bob Knight's good graces after being suspended by the coach for missing classes.[6] Knight had a very clear rule: you miss class, you don't play.[7] The Soviets next went on to Iowa City where they edged the Hawkeyes 95–93, behind twenty-four points from Sarunas Marciulionis.[8] Both Indiana and Iowa would field top squads for the upcoming season.

In the preseason coaches meeting with the press, there was interest in a postseason conference tourney by both Steve Yoder, Wisconsin coach, and

Bill Foster from Northwestern. (Bob Knight had not expressed any views because he did not attend the meeting, as usual.) In a formal vote, the coaches supported the postseason tournament idea by a vote of 8–1: that is, if the regular conference schedule were to be reduced to fourteen conference games.[9]

Preconference Games

In the preseason NIT, Michigan opened in Ann Arbor with a running contest in defeating Bradley, 115–107. Two nights later, Memphis State brought the Wolverines down to earth with an 82–76 victory in Memphis. Gary Grant had 32 and Glen Rice 19.[10]

The BYU-Hawaii tournament title was won by Illinois, beating Duke, 69–62, in what Mike Krzyzewski called "one of the most physical games we've ever played." Ken Norman, the tournament's MVP, had twenty-two for Illinois.[11]

Most of the other preconference contests were easy victories for the Big Ten squads, usually at home. One big surprise was Michigan State traveling to Maine and losing 84–81 as Maine dropped fourteen three-pointers on the Spartans.[12] The three-point shot was now a national rule that had been adopted by the NCAA at a distance of 19 feet, 9 inches. Bob Hammel said, "Around the nation, it quickly took on the tag of 'the Steve Alford rule.'"[13]

Indiana continued its impressive start with a 71–66 win over Kentucky and freshman sensation Rex Chapman, who scored twenty-six in the loss in Bloomington.[14] Other Big Ten wins that night included Illinois defeating Pitt in Pittsburgh 99–97, as Doug Altenberger hit six 3-pointers for 18 of his 26 points. After the game, Altenberger said, "I don't think an Einstein thought up the [three-point] rule, but if they're going to give me three points for the same shot I've been shooting for two points all my life, I'll take it." Despite that, Altenberger's coach, Lou Henson, was still opposed to the rule![15]

Two nights later, Vanderbilt shocked Indiana in Nashville with a 79–75 win over the Hoosiers, despite 28 points from Alford and 21 from Darryl Thomas. The Hoosiers had just been moved to #2 in the UPI poll behind UNLV. That same night, Iowa (#3 in the nation) blasted BYU in Iowa City 86–75 behind Jeff Moe's 28 points on 8 of 13 field goal shooting. B. J. Armstrong observed that Moe "had a super game. I was looking for him all night on the left wing and he shot the heck out of the ball."[16]

Michigan was surprised at home by Western Michigan, who defeated the Wolverines, 62–59, ending their streak of thirty-six wins in a row at home. That same night Purdue pounded Wichita State in West Lafayette 77–61, eliciting this comment from Wichita coach Ed Fogler: "I vote on the UPI board and I'll vote Purdue No.1 next week."[17]

Illinois dropped its first game of the season to North Carolina 90–77 in Chapel Hill. The Tar Heels held Illinois to 43 percent field goal shooting after the Illini entered the game shooting 55 percent for the year. Illinois, now ninth in the nation, lost to Loyola 83–82. Coach Lou Henson was fit to be tied by the officiating.[18]

North Carolina continued to break the hearts of Big Ten fans by topping Purdue in the Dallas Morning News Classic 94–81. Coach Gene Keady said, "North Carolina came out to play and they outhustled us." This, on the same day that both the AP and UPI polls had Purdue as #2, nationally behind UNLV.[19]

The Big Ten Conference Season Begins

It was a good opener for Illinois as they defeated Michigan in Champaign 95–84 on January 3. Ken Norman had 29 points, 9 rebounds, and 5 blocks. Minnesota won its opener for new coach Clem Haskins 69–67 over Wisconsin in Minneapolis.[20] Purdue had little trouble with Michigan State 87–72, and Iowa crushed Northwestern 80–44 in Iowa City.[21] Indiana opened in Columbus and defeated OSU 92–80.[22] In its next game, Illinois struggled at home, but defeated Michigan State 79–72.

The next week, Alford pushed Indiana to victory over Michigan 85–84 in Ann Arbor, as he scored twenty-three. Alford hit a ten-footer at the buzzer to win it.[23] Iowa surprised Illinois the next night with a 91–88 win in overtime in Champaign. Down twenty-two points early in the second half, the Hawkeyes rallied behind Brad Lohaus, now playing at a strong forward (rather than center) who had twenty-three points.[24] Iowa responded well to its newly attained #1 status by dropping Purdue 70–67 in West Lafayette. Despite a snowstorm, 14,123 fans packed Mackey Arena but left despondent after the Purdue loss. The win, at one of the toughest courts in college basketball, was impressive to a number of Big Ten coaches.[25]

Besides Iowa's undefeated mark (17–0), Indiana was also unblemished (5–0) in the conference and 17–1 overall. This set up an early meaningful contest in Iowa, when Indiana came to town on January 22. It was a smashing Iowa victory 101–88, as the Hawks had six players in double figures and outrebounded the Hoosiers 46–19.[26] Despite the loss, Daryl Thomas saw the Iowa game as a real turning point for the Indiana squad: "Although we lost that game, I really felt that we had potential to be pretty good. . . . I really felt that we had a good team. But the key was we had to win every game and then play Iowa again." The game was also significant in that it was "the first time in 467 games that an opponent had scored at least 100 points against a Knight-coached team."[27]

Iowa's ascent to the top of the conference and the national polls was short-lived as they were upset at home 80–76 by Ohio State in their next game. The end of the month saw three teams bunched at the top of the league at 7–1: Iowa, Indiana, and Purdue.[28]

The new month brought swift alterations at the top as Indiana defeated Purdue 88–77, and Michigan ran past Iowa 100–92. In the former contest, Steve Alford scored 31 points on 8 of 18 field goals and 13 of 15 free throws. The latter contest saw Glen Rice dominate the Hawkeyes with his 33 points on 15 of 20 field goals, 10 rebounds, and 5 assists.[29]

Illinois needed to reassert itself against an opponent of quality and beating Ohio State, 82–65, in Columbus, accomplished that. Illinois turned around a 51–45 second-half deficit by hitting four quick three-pointers to lead 58–55, and they never trailed after that.[30]

It was clear that the Big Ten was experiencing a savage battle, and the league's coaches were almost unanimous in asserting that six Big Ten teams deserved to be in the sixty-four-team NCAA tournament field. Also noteworthy was the fact that six players were among the top ten in the league in both scoring and rebounding. These were Dennis Hopson (28.8 ppg, 8 rpg), Troy Lewis (23.1 ppg, 15.8 rpg), Ken Norman (20.4 ppg, 9.4 rpg), Glen Rice (16.7 ppg, 10.0 rpg), Shon Morris (16.0 ppg, 9.2 rpg), and Kevin Gamble (15.8 ppg, 6.2 rpg).[31]

Down the Stretch

Steve Alford scored forty-two points on February 4 to set a new Assembly Hall record and push Indiana past Michigan State 84–80. Iowa maintained its share of the conference lead with an easy 78–47 win over Minnesota in Iowa City, after leading at the half 51–27. The next night, Purdue also kept pace with a tougher-than-expected 70–62 win in West Lafayette over Wisconsin. Ohio State stayed in the tournament picture with a win over Michigan in a 95–87 game in Columbus.[32]

Back in Bloomington, Steve Alford had 30 points (including 4 of 5 three pointers) to move into fourth place in all-time Big Ten scoring behind Mike McGee of Michigan (1977–81), Rick Mount (1967–70) of Purdue, and Don Schlundt of Indiana (1951–55) as the Hoosiers ripped Michigan 83–67. Dennis Hopson, the leading scorer in the conference for the season and #2 in the country, had thirty-four points in a 90–72 Ohio State win over Michigan State. After the game Jud Heathcote linked the two scorers by noting, "Hopson is one of the best players in the Big 10 along with Steve Alford."[33]

Indiana and Alford were fortunate a couple days later when they edged Northwestern 77–75 in Evanston, as Alford went 4 for 13 from the floor. Bob

Knight was displeased: "I'm ashamed we won. Alford was horrendous. . . . We're not a good basketball team."[34] Indiana played another poor game, yet managed to win, defeating Wisconsin in three overtimes, 86–85, as Alford's shooting slump (4–19 from the floor) continued: he missed the winning shot in regulation as well as in each of the first two overtimes. The "winning slump" continued at Minnesota, where the Hoosiers won 72–70. Alford's poor shooting continued as he went 7 for 20 from the floor (3 of 9 three point-ers).[35]

With three games to go, Indiana had a one-game lead on Purdue and a three-game lead on Iowa. Purdue moved closer to Indiana on February 26 with a 75–64 victory over the Hoosiers at Mackey. That same night Iowa crushed Michigan State 93–64 in Iowa City, a school record twenty-fourth victory of the year. Jud Heathcote noted, "We seemed to be rooted to the floor."[36]

Purdue kept up its winning, defeating Ohio State 87–73, despite thirty-one points from Dennis Hopson. Illinois tightened the race even more by defeating Indiana in Bloomington 69–67 before an Assembly Hall crowd of 16,793.[37] The Boilermakers then clinched a tie for the Big Ten title with a 69–59 win in East Lansing, while Illinois routed Michigan in Ann Arbor 89–75. Bill Frieder called it "the worst loss in seven years at home. . . . They beat us every which way." Lou Henson said, "We did everything right and they were flat."[38]

With a title and a potential top seed in the NCAA tournament at stake, Purdue lost their focus and was embarrassed in Ann Arbor by Michigan 104–68. Michigan had 43 field goals on just 74 shots (55 percent) while Purdue was 24 of 61 (39 percent). Gene Keady summed it up: "We weren't ready coming out of the chute." Indiana took advantage of the Purdue loss by beating Ohio State 90–81 to tie with the Boilermakers for the Big Ten title at 15–3. Hopson's twenty-five topped the game's scoring. Knight referred to Hopson as "the best all-around player since Magic Johnson at Michigan State."[39]

The NCAA Tournament

Final Big Ten standings had Purdue and IU at 15–3, Iowa at 14–4, and Illinois 13–5, with each of those teams having at least twenty-three wins. Six teams would be invited to the NCAA tournament. In the Southeast, Illinois would be the #3 seed and Ohio State #9. In the East, Purdue would be #3 and Michigan #9. In the West, Iowa would have the #2 seed, and in the Midwest, Indiana would have the #1 seed. No Big Ten teams would be in the NIT since none of the four remaining teams had achieved a .500 record.[40]

Illinois opened play for the Big Ten, but the Illini were upset by #14-seed Austin Peay 68–67 in Birmingham, Alabama. Top-seeded Indiana would not be upset, crushing #16 Fairfield 92–58 in Indianapolis. That same evening Michigan allowed fifty points to David Robinson, but still won 97–82 over Navy in Charlotte.[41] The next night all three Big Ten squads won easily, OSU over Kentucky 91–77, Iowa topping Santa Clara 99–76, and Purdue defeating Northeastern 104–95.[42]

Michigan reduced the Big Ten to four teams remaining in the tourney with a 109–97 loss to North Carolina, while Indiana slammed Auburn before 34,183 in Indianapolis, 107–90. Keith Smart had 20 points plus 15 assists.[43] The Big Ten was disappointed the next night as both Purdue and Ohio State were beaten: the Boilermakers fell 85–66 to Florida in Syracuse and the Buckeyes 82–79 to Georgetown in Atlanta. Purdue star Troy Lewis said, "We dug ourselves a hole we really couldn't get out of."[44]

Big Ten hopes were buoyed somewhat by Iowa's 84–82 victory over Texas El-Paso (UTEP) in Tucson. Shortly after the victory, in a purely coincidental release, Iowa coach Tom Davis was named conference Coach of the Year by the Big Ten with Gene Keady second.[45]

Two Big Ten teams appeared in the regional semis, Iowa in the West and Indiana in the Midwest. Indiana made its way to the regional final with an 88–82 win over Duke; this was the first coaching meeting between Knight and one of his former players. (Mike Krzyzewski had captained the 1968–69 Army team under Knight.) After the win, Knight said, "I'm very happy for our players. But that was a tough ball game."[46] Iowa also won, in Seattle, defeating Oklahoma in overtime 93–91.[47]

Two nights later, Indiana was Midwest regional champion after topping LSU 77–76. The Hoosiers were down 75–66 with 4:38 to go but mounted a brilliant comeback to edge the Tigers in Cincinnati.[48] Iowa was not as fortunate, falling to #1 UNLV 84–81 after leading 58–42 at the half.[49]

It was Final Four time again, and Bob Knight and his team were able to edge #1 UNLV 97–93 as Alford scored thirty-three points in the first semifinal.[50] The Hoosiers would meet Syracuse, an easy 77–63 winner over Providence, in the championship game. The two semifinal contests drew 64,959, an NCAA record, to the New Orleans Superdome.[51]

On Monday, March 30, Indiana won the NCAA title when Keith Smart sank a sixteen-foot baseline jumper to give Indiana a 74–73 victory. As Steve Alford recalled, "Nobody remembers the game; everybody remembers The Shot."[52] Smart was named the tournament's Most Outstanding Player after making six of IU's final seven field goals and scoring twenty-one points in the final, but Steve Alford took game honors with twenty-three. After the victory, Bob Knight was candid and surprising in his assessment of his team and the tournament. He noted, "I'm not sure we're a good basketball team," noting that they "could have lost to either LSU or Syracuse."[53]

Indiana's win moved them into first place in all-time NCAA tournament won-lost percentage (.771, 37–11), past UCLA (.767, 56–17) for teams with at least ten NCAA tournament games. Tenth was Michigan State with a record of 12–6 (.667).[54] Alford's twenty-three points made him the highest-scoring player in IU history, with 2,438 points; he was also IU's all-time leading NCAA tournament scorer with 217 in ten games, although Don Schlundt had a better points per game average: 27.0 in six games.[55]

The next day Knight commented, "This wasn't a dominant team. . . . I didn't think we couldn't win it, but I didn't think we would win it." Jim Boeheim, the Syracuse coach, said, "That kid (Smart) made the kind of shot only the great players make under pressure." The Naismith Coach of the Year award went to Knight.[56]

At the end of the month, Steve Alford was awarded the *Chicago Tribune*'s Silver Basketball as Player of the Year in the conference, with Dennis Hopson second.[57] In a vote taken shortly before the NCAA tournament, Hopson had been named Big Ten Player of the Year by the UPI and the Big Ten conference. This was the third year that the Big Ten had awarded a Player of the Year trophy.[57]

The 1987–88 Season

With a national champion and six teams having competed in the NCAA tournament, the Big 10 was certainly viewed as one of the toughest conferences in the country for 1987–88. No fewer than five conference teams were ranked in the top twenty by at least one ranking service. Many Big Ten coaches saw the Big Ten as the best it had been since their various arrivals into the conference. Gene Keady of Purdue said, "The Big 10 is the toughest I've seen it since I've been here, eight years. I think it's the toughest from top to bottom. There's a lot of talent."[58]

The season opened with a preseason Big Apple NIT, and Purdue defeated Arkansas-Little Rock 102–88 in Mackey Arena.[59] Bob Knight's team began its exhibition play the next night against the touring Soviet team. Indiana had an unusual start, forfeiting to the Soviets when Knight picked up his third technical foul in the game with fifteen minutes to go with the score 66–43 in favor of the Soviet Union. Knight refused to leave without his team and the forfeit was called when the team left the floor with their coach.[60] The next

Gary Grant, Big Ten Player of the Year, 1988. *(Courtesy of Bentley Historical Library, University of Michigan)*

day Knight expressed contrition about his behavior and was subsequently reprimanded by Indiana University.

After its win against Arkansas-Little Rock, Purdue was surprised by Iowa State 104–96 in the Big Apple NIT semis, despite the game being played in West Lafayette. The Boilermakers blew a 93–90 lead with under four minutes to play. Seeking a positive spin, Gene Keady called the loss "an excellent learning tool in that it got our players' attention regarding shot selection." And they did seem to learn, since Purdue then racked up sixteen wins in a row.[61]

Over the next week, favored Big Ten teams beat weaker opponents, as expected, until a meaningful game on December 5 in Indianapolis, where #5 Kentucky defeated #3 Indiana, 82–76 in overtime.[62] In a romp over Western Michigan in Ann Arbor, Gary Grant had 16 points and 14 assists. That brought his total of assists at Michigan to 540, making him the all-time leader in school history in that category.[63]

In an interesting administrative "non-development," Big Ten presidents delayed a final decision on whether to hold an end-of-season basketball tournament. The presidents wanted more information on a site, potential loss of class time, and financial considerations. Moving with glacial speed, Big Ten leaders did not approve such a tournament until ten years later, after the 1997–98 season.[64]

Just before Christmas, after the first semester had ended, there were a number of games that were surprises or had significance. Eastern Michigan defeated Michigan State in Ypsilanti 84–80, which marked the beginning of a downward plunge that season for the Spartans, who ended up at 10–18 for the year. North Carolina came into Assembly Hall and knocked off the Illini 85–74 to end a twenty-two-game home winning streak against nonconference foes. Louisville upended Indiana in Louisville 81–69, with fouls/free throws being the difference. IU had 35 fouls to Louisville's 17, and the Cardinals shot 31 of 36 from the line, while IU was just 7 of 11.[65]

The day after Christmas, it was announced that the Big Ten would tighten its academic rules: junior college transfers would face stiffer standards, if they did not originally meet NCAA Proposition 48 requirements. Freshmen were already subject to these tough standards if they were not "qualifiers": they were not able to practice with their teams, let alone suit up for games.[66]

League Play Begins

Purdue seemed to have perfected some of those things Keady worked on after their loss to Iowa State as they dumped Illinois 81–68 in Champaign on their way to winning nine games in a row.[67] In West Lafayette, Purdue won

Shon Morris, All-Big Ten at Northwestern. *(Courtesy of Northwestern University Archives)*

its tenth in a row, 84–77, over the Buckeyes, but Coach Keady was not happy with the victory: "We aren't ready to beat anybody. All we wanted to do was shoot the ball quick. Do that in this league and you're going to get beat. We were lucky not to get beat tonight."[68]

Next, Purdue had another difficult victory over a much more formidable opponent: Iowa. Nevertheless, the Boilermakers managed to eke out an 80–79 win. Illinois, by contrast, had a much easier time with Michigan State, defeating them 77–62 in Champaign. The game was won at the foul line as the Illini were 23 of 37 while the Spartans were 5–5.[69]

In an early season surprise, Northwestern defeated Indiana in Evanston 66–64, in a game that also was decided by free throws. Northwestern was 25 of 28 and 21 of 21 in the second half. Bob Knight summed up the loss: "They just completely outplayed us."[70] Shon Morris, Northwesterrn's top player, recalling this game twenty-five years later, called it "memorable because of the atmosphere, the spotlight of national television, and the fact that we played them so close the year before when they ended up winning the national title."[71] A few nights later, three of the four games went as expected, but the exception was Michigan State's upset of Indiana 75–74 in East Lansing, which left both squads with 1–3 marks in the conference. This was not normal for a Bob Knight team.[72] The Hoosiers would have six days off to regroup before facing Michigan, but they did not respond well as they lost once again, this time in Bloomington 72–60 to put an end to their twenty-nine-game home court win streak.[73]

Michigan was coming off their own upset loss in Columbus 70–68 to OSU, which ended the thirteen-game win streak of the Wolverines. Before the game the AP/UPI national rankings had Michigan as #7. It was still early, of course, and things would surely change, especially when Purdue won its fifteenth in a row, for their best start since 1931–32, defeating Michigan State, 78–67.[74]

Iowa was also bound to rise after beating Illinois 93–79 in Iowa City. Both coaches had insightful comments. Tom Davis noted that this "probably was the best game we played this year. By far the best for a full 40 minutes." Lou Henson, by contrast, saw his Illini as "tentative; we were timid and we were scared."[75]

Bob Knight, never a good loser, decided to take radical action against Ohio State on January 27 by starting two freshmen: Lyndon Jones, who scored 21 points, and Jay Edwards, who had 11 points and nine assists, in a 75–71 victory in Columbus. Keith Smart, the 1987 championship game hero, played only two minutes in the second half, and Ricky Calloway never left the bench. Knight had no comment about his decision. Three nights later, the Hoosiers knocked off Purdue 82–79 to end the Boilermakers' sixteen-game win streak. Calloway remained on the bench, and Smart played two minutes, once again.[76] Michigan gained a tie for first in the conference with Purdue by defeating Illinois 76–74 in Ann Arbor.

Down the Stretch

February began with Michigan traveling to Syracuse for a nationally televised intersectional game. After the Wolverines crushed the Orange, Linda Young of the *Chicago Tribune* addressed these big nonconference games played in the conference season at the behest of television. Her conclusion was that Big Ten coaches don't like such contests in- season but can't pass on the national exposure, the money generated, and the recruiting benefits.[77]

Michigan kept up its strong play, taking down Iowa in a real run-and-gun contest in Ann Arbor, 120–103. It was a Crisler Arena record for most points against a Big Ten opponent by Michigan and Iowa's seventy-seven-point second half was a school record, after they were down 61–26 at halftime.[78]

The next night Illinois stumbled at Ohio State 64–60, while Indiana crushed Minnesota in Bloomington 92–63. Lou Henson said of his Illini, "It came down to the same old thing. We're just not shooting the ball."[79] Two nights later Indiana added to the Illini woes by topping them in Champaign 75–74, and Iowa blasted Michigan State in Iowa City 101–72. Indiana's win was keyed by Jay Edwards who had 27 points, 24 in the second half.[80]

Seeing a chance to take first place and to beat their closest competitor on their own floor, Purdue topped Michigan 91–87 in another nationally televised contest. In a game with great shooting from the floor from both squads, Purdue shot 58 percent and Michigan 55.5 percent. Reserve guard Tony Jones hit three of four free throws in the last twenty-three seconds to seal the win for Purdue. Gene Keady, understating, thought "it was a very good game to watch."[81]

Illinois solidified its standing with a 118–86 win against Ohio State in Champaign. Five Illini scored in double figures. The next night, Indiana kept pace with a 95–58 romp over Michigan State in Bloomington.[82]

Purdue was still ranked #2 (behind Temple) nationally: they had a great team but no standout star. (Their leading scorer, Troy Lewis, averaged just over seventeen points per game.) Jud Heathcote credited their success to their coach. "It's Gene Keady. . . . Sometimes great teams don't have one individual to rely on, but the team approach. That's the way Purdue is. It's the image of the coach." Purdue demonstrated such tight team play in its defeat of Indiana 95–85.[83] Indiana came back to defeat Wisconsin 84–74, but Bob Knight was not impressed. He noted, "This is not a team of ours that going to be put in basketball's intellectual hall of fame. We make mistakes . . . we don't concentrate."[84]

Illinois went to Purdue, and the Illini were soundly beaten 93–79. Purdue had now won twenty or more games six years in a row. Michigan, also on the road, was beaten in Iowa City 95–87.[85] Illinois defeated Indiana in Bloomington 75–65. This was Coach Lou Henson's five hundredth college victory. What was most striking about this game was the difference in rebounds, with Illinois snaring 48 and IU just 26. Bob Knight observed, "Sometimes rebound statistics are deceptive, but I don't think they were tonight."[86]

The last week of conference play was filled with surprises. First, Ohio State defeated Purdue 71–60 in Columbus. That same evening, Illinois toppled Michigan in Champaign 85–74. Gary Grant scored just eight points; it was the first time he had been under double figures since his freshman year.[87]

In more predictable results, Indiana topped Minnesota 91–85 as Jay Edwards hit 8 of 9 three pointers, while scoring 36 points; Iowa humbled Wisconsin 103–70; and Northwestern lost its twelfth in a row, this time to Michigan State, 55–53. Indiana closed its conference season with a 116–89 win over Iowa, and got a measure of revenge for the previous year's game in which Indiana gave up a hundred points.[88]

In the final Big Ten standings for 1987–88 Purdue was 16–2, three games better than Michigan (13–5). In individual honors, Gene Keady was named UPI's Coach of the Year by the conference coaches for the second time, having also won in 1984. John Chaney of Temple was named national Coach of the Year by the USBA for the second year in a row: this had only happened twice before, in 1961 and 1962, when Fred Taylor of Ohio State was named, and in the period 1969–73 when UCLA's John Wooden won five times in a row. Glen Rice of Michigan led league scoring (22.9), Richard Coffey led in rebounds per game (8.9), and Gary Grant led in assists per (6.5).

As the season drew to a close, various honors were being awarded. Gene Keady was named Coach of the Year in District IV of the USBA. He would be a candidate for the national honor, as his team maintained its #2 national ranking and a record of 24–2. The Boilermakers kept winning and clinched the Big Ten title with a 80–67 win over Michigan in West Lafayette. This was the first time that Purdue had won consecutive Big Ten titles since 1935–36. Indiana won over Ohio State 85–77 to provide Bob Knight with his 210th Big Ten win, moving him to second in conference history behind "Piggy" Lambert's 213 while at Purdue.[89] The Big Ten's successes in national rankings (three teams in the top eleven) were tainted by the release of new NCAA sanctions against Minnesota's basketball program. Most of the violations had been committed in the period 1984–86 under Jim Dutcher—but not exclusively. The men's basketball program was put on probation for three years with no postseason tournament opportunities for two years. Only two coaches would be allowed to recruit off-campus during that period. One of the sanction years was suspended, and one year of postseason prohibition was also suspended because of the university's cooperation with the investigation.[90]

The Tournaments

Five teams were invited into the NCAA field. Purdue was a #1 seed in the Midwest, Illinois a #3 seed in the Southeast, Indiana a #4 seed in the East. Michigan, a #3 seed, and Iowa, a #5 seed, were placed in the West. Ohio State was invited to the NIT.

In the NIT, Ohio State acquitted itself very well, topping Old Dominion 86–73, Cleveland State 86–80, and New Mexico 68–65 in Albuquerque. The Buckeyes went to New York, where they topped Colorado State 64–62 in the NIT semis before losing to Connecticut 72–67 in the NIT final.[91]

Purdue and Michigan opened NCAA play on March 17 with wins: Purdue won 94–79 over Fairleigh Dickinson and Michigan prevailed 63–58 over Boise State. Indiana opened the next night and was the first Big Ten team to be eliminated: in this case it was twelve-seeded Richmond that pulled off the 72–69 upset in Hartford.[92]

Illinois and Iowa won their openers. The Illini topped the University of Texas–San Antonio 81–72, while Iowa outgunned Florida State 102–98. Michigan won 108–85 over Florida in a real shootout, and Purdue crushed Memphis State, 100–73 in what was almost a home game in South Bend. The Wolverines impressed Coach Bill Frieder, who commented, "I think we played a perfect game."[93]

Illinois broke the Big Ten win parade by losing to Villanova 66–63 in Cincinnati. The Illini gave the game away by shooting 10 of 23 from the free-throw line. By contrast, Iowa made 31 of 46 free throws in toppling UNLV in Los Angeles 104–86. The Big Ten was now 6–2 in the tournament.[94]

In off-the-court Big Ten news, Rickey Calloway, the Big Ten Freshman of the Year who had averaged 11 ppg and 4 rpg in 1987–88, was reportedly ready to transfer to Kansas. In a poll of Big Ten writers and broadcasters, Gene Keady was chosen Coach of the Year, with Bill Frieder second and Tom Davis, third. There were rumors that Keady would take the top job at Texas, but he labeled the gossip "ridiculous." He told his players, "You can quit worrying about that. I'm going to come back to get after your ass next year."[95]

But then the Big Ten was blown out on March 25. Arizona, the #1 seed in the West, sent Iowa home after a 99–79 rout in Seattle. Tom Davis observed, "We looked like we were a step slow the whole second half." Michigan also lost in Seattle 78–69 to North Carolina. The Tar Heels shot 71 percent in the second half. Purdue opened up a 10–0 lead on Kansas State in the Silverdome in Pontiac, Michigan, then faded at the end and lost 73–70. "The poise, the mistake-free basketball which had made Purdue the favorite to win the regional, suddenly wasn't there," wrote Skip Mylenski.[96]

In early April, Gary Grant was named winner of the *Chicago Tribune* Silver Basketball as the Big Ten Player of the Year, but it was bittersweet for Grant and the conference after the disappointing showing in the NCAA tourney. There was great anticipation for Big Ten successes for 1988–89 with so many top players returning. But off-season rule changes would make this an overly optimistic prediction.

CHAPTER 11

THE END OF THE 1980s AND INTO THE 1990s

There was great anticipation among Big Ten coaches and teams as the 1988–89 season approached. There were no coaching changes, most of the biggest stars were back, and the best teams were almost totally intact. Top finishes in the NCAA tournament were expected by many, but the league's excellence would also mean a very tough conference season.

Just before the season began, a series of events and rule alterations had already shrouded the upcoming season in apprehension and uncertainty. Two prominent basketball programs were found guilty of violations and placed on probation by the NCAA. Kansas, the defending NCAA champion, was found guilty of various recruiting violations under coach Larry Brown, who had absconded to the NBA's San Antonio Spurs, not long after his team had won the championship. The University of Cincinnati was declared a violator in both their football and basketball programs and placed on four- to six-year probation. Although neither was a Big Ten institution, there was increased scrutiny at top basketball programs, which included most of the Big Ten; however, no violations were seen.[1]

The Big Ten was tightening its standards for eligibility, specifically as they related to Proposition 48 recruits, meaning players had to meet more academic standards to become eligible to play. The conference would now require junior college recruits who did not meet Proposition 48 mandates to sit out their first season in the Big Ten, the only conference to adopt such a stringent rule. It was disliked by both junior college and Big Ten coaches, but it had been voted into place by the Big Ten faculty athletic representatives. Seeing the obvious disadvantages that this would have on recruiting, the Big Ten would now request that the NCAA adopt Proposition 48 for all institutions at its annual meeting in January, but the coaches and league administrators were not optimistic that this would happen.[2]

The first preseason AP national poll on November 14 had four Big Ten teams ranked in the top twenty, Michigan at #3, Iowa at #7, Illinois at #9 and Ohio State at #17. Bill Jauss was especially taken with the Illini, despite the fact that they "lack an extremely tall starter." He went on to note, "Nick Anderson, Ken Battle, Lowell Hamilton, Steven Bardo and Marcus Liberty all reach the 6–5 to 6–8 range and run the floor like track men."[3] The Illini would go on to be undefeated in preconference play, including wins over two ranked teams, Missouri (#10) 87–84 and #19 Florida 97–67.[4]

Another key college battle was the preseason Big Apple NIT tournament, which began with Indiana defeating Illinois State 83–48. Two nights later, Jay Edwards had 27 and Todd Jadlow 23, as IU defeated Stanford 84–73, both games in Bloomington. IU would move on to New York to play in the Big Apple NIT semifinals against Syracuse. Things were not pretty for the Hoosiers as the #7 Orangemen ran Indiana out of the Garden 102–78. This was the most points ever allowed by a Bob Knight–coached team in his twenty-four years of coaching. Some called it a rematch of the 1987 NCAA championship game, but with so many players having graduated from those squads, the comparison was not accurate, although Syracuse coach Jim Boeheim's pleasure at obtaining a degree of payback was certainly palpable. It got no better for IU in the third-place game: they gave up a hundred points for the third time in Knight's career, losing 106–92 to the University of North Carolina. It was noteworthy that Jay Edwards shot 6 of 10 from three-point range in racking up 31 points in the loss.[5]

As expected, most of the Big Ten teams were beating lesser opponents. Purdue, in particular, looked impressive, even as they lost to Kansas State 81–77.[6] Indiana lost to Louisville in Indianapolis at the Big Four Classic 101–79; it was the third time the Hoosiers had given up a hundred points in their last four games—they were just 3–3 for the season. Indiana would also lose to Notre Dame 84–71, as they were outrebounded 43–27. Things did not look good for Indiana. But then they won seven in a row heading into conference play, with a big win over Kentucky 75–52 at Rupp Arena, the Wildcats' first home loss to Indiana in sixty-two years.[7]

The Big Ten had three unbeatens (Michigan State, Michigan, and Illinois), for the second time ever as the teams headed toward conference play.[8] Ohio State was quietly building an enviable record as they captured the ECAC Holiday Classic in Madison Square Garden, topping hometown favorite St. John's 77–72. Jay Burson, the tourney MVP, scored 23 overall and 19 in the second half after picking up 37 in their recent victory over Florida.[9] Illinois remained unbeaten and in the top five, as they won the Rainbow Classic 96–87 over Hawaii, hitting 41 of 68 from the floor (60 percent) against the Rainbow Warriors. Nick Anderson had 26 and was named tourney MVP, despite teammate Kenny Battle getting 29 in the championship contest.[10]

Big Ten Play Begins

On opening night Indiana immediately inserted itself into the race by topping Ohio State 75–65 in Bloomington.[11] The first real battle was Indiana's win in West Lafayette 74–73 over Purdue. The win was Knight's 214th as Indiana coach: it was a new record for Big Ten coaches, passing Ward "Piggy" Lambert who had 213 wins at Purdue from 1916 to 1946.[12]

The NCAA helped the Big Ten in recruiting by adopting changes to Proposition 48, similar to the more stringent Big Ten rules. As of 1990, there would be no "partial qualifiers" and Proposition 48 admits would now have only three years of eligibility and would have to pay the tuition for their freshman year. They also would be prohibited from playing or practicing with the basketball team that year. The NCAA also rejected, by a 2–1 margin, a Big Ten proposal to make Proposition 48 casualties who attend a junior college sit out a year of competition after transferring to a four-year institution, a rule only the Big Ten had to abide by.[13]

Number two Illinois, now known as the "Flyin' Illini," went to 15–0 by defeating #6 Michigan 96–84 in Champaign (prompting Michigan coach Bill Frieder to comment, "That's a hell of a basketball team"). Indiana defeated Northwestern 92–76, Ohio State won by two in East Lansing 83–81, and Purdue won in Madison 68–62. The Hoosier victory was Bob Knight's five hundredth as a college coach.[14]

Five of the top twenty ranked teams were now from the Big Ten, making for an impressive showing but also indicating how tough it would be for Illinois to stay undefeated and for teams to win on the road in conference play.[15]

The turning point of the Big Ten season occurred on January 23 in Champaign in a game against nationally ranked Georgia Tech. Near the end of the game a Tech player came down on Kendall Gill's foot, fracturing it and sidelining him for an estimated seven weeks. Gill had 19 points at that time, and the Illini defeated the Bulldogs 103–92. In voting released the next day, Illinois had risen to #1, nationally. They had many coaches who were in awe of their play, including Ohio State coach Gary Williams, who said, "They might be the best in the country." Gene Keady said, "They've worked on their weaknesses," while Iowa coach Tom Davis remarked, "The question is how much better they can get." These comments were made before the extent of Gill's injury was known.[16]

The Illini traveled to Minnesota three days later and were beaten by the Golden Gophers 69–62; Illinois scored just twenty-four points in the first half, but the Illini did bounce back to defeat Indiana, ending the Hoosier thirteen-game win streak 75–65, after the Illini were down ten at the half.[17]

Glen Rice, Big Ten Player of the Year, 1989.
(Courtesy of Bentley Historical Library, University of Michigan)

The next night, two games had national implications as Michigan won at Purdue 99–88, and Ohio State stepped out of the conference to surprise #3 Louisville in Freedom Hall 85–79. In the former game, Glen Rice had thirty-four points for the Wolverines, eliciting this postgame comment from Purdue coach Gene Keady: "Rice is a great shooter. I think the best in America."[18]

Indiana was still the league leader at 7–1, despite their 17–5 record. Illinois was now 5–1 and 18–1 overall. The Big Ten continued to look like the most competitive conference in the nation.[19] Minnesota deflated Ohio State with a 76–73 win in Minneapolis, while Purdue did the same to Illinois 76–72 in West Lafayette. In the continued round-robin of wins, Minnesota, then lost 66–62 to Indiana despite a Gopher lead of 28–22 at the half.[20]

With the conference race more than halfway over, every game took on added importance, and no team could afford a home loss. Illinois edged Ohio State in Champaign 62–60 in a game notable for poor shooting. Michigan struggled in Iowa City but managed to win in double overtime 108–107, in a game where six players had at least eighteen points. Michigan then lost in Minnesota 88–80 as the Gophers were dominant on the boards, 41–21.[21]

Indiana kept winning. The Hoosiers edged Purdue in Bloomington 64–62, and they moved up in national rankings to ninth. In the conference race they still had a two-game lead as of February 15.

Ohio State suffered an injury equal to Illinois's loss of Kendall Gill when Jay Burson was diagnosed with a neck fracture, suffered in the Iowa game where he had scored twenty-five points in an 83–75 loss in Iowa City. It was initially uncertain how long he would be out. But then it was announced that he would be wearing a halo traction device, a neck stabilizer, for three months, which meant his Ohio State career was over.[22]

In mid-February was the game of the week, if not the season, for the Hoosiers and Wolverines, with Indiana winning in Bloomington 76–75, on Jay Edwards's three pointer at the end of the game. Despite this, both teams seemed destined for the NCAA tourney and, in fact, seven teams appeared to have a good chance to get in.[23] The NCAA tourney was shaping up to be an expensive ticket, as the Tier One tickets, with a face-value of $55, were selling for $900 to $1250 from ticket brokers, and Tier 3 tickets selling for $250 to $400 at the Kingdome in Seattle. Bid announcements were three weeks away.[24]

Indiana continued to roll on the road, winning their ninth straight contest when they defeated Ohio State in Columbus 73–66 to clinch a tie for the Big Ten title. Michigan matched IU with wins in Columbus over OSU, at home against Wisconsin, and on the road at Michigan State. Their scoring was led by Glen Rice, Rumeal Robinson, and Loy Vaught. Illinois bounced

Ohio State easily, but their best news was that Kendall Gill would be in uniform and might play on March 8.[25]

Michigan managed a fusillade of scoring in downing Iowa 119–96, with the Wolverines shooting 44 of 70 (63 percent) from the floor. The Wolverines seemed to be peaking but then lost in their final home game at Crisler Arena to Illinois, 89–73, their worst home loss since 1985. Coach Bill Frieder said that except for the Indiana NCAA champions of 1976, Illinois was "the best basketball team I've seen in my 16 years at Michigan." He also added that had Kendall Gill played all season, the Illini might have gone undefeated.[26]

Still, the title was Indiana's to lose, and they defeated Wisconsin 75–64 to clinch their tenth Big Ten championship, a conference record. In their last game at Iowa, title in hand, the Hoosiers lost to Iowa 87–70, as Knight played mostly reserves in the game.[27] IU was 15–3, a game ahead of Illinois at 14–4.

The NCAA announced teams and seedings for the upcoming NCAA tourney, which would end in Seattle on April 3. Five conference teams were invited. In the Midwest, Illinois was a #1 seed. In the West, Indiana was a #2 seed. In the Southeast, Michigan received a #3 seed, and in the East, Iowa was a #4 and Minnesota #11. Three other Big Ten teams were invited to the NIT, Ohio State, Michigan State, and Wisconsin, leaving just Northwestern and Purdue uninvited because of losing records.

At this point, an unusual incident took some of the attention off the Big Ten teams and onto Big Ten leadership. Arizona State had been seeking a new coach and had pursued Purdue mentor Gene Keady. But after some consideration, he decided to remain at Purdue. He turned it down because "I simply did not like Arizona State as well as I liked things at Purdue."[28]

Once Keady turned down the Arizona State offer, ASU moved to their next candidate: Michigan coach Bill Frieder. When Keady returned home from his visit to Tempe, Frieder called him and asked if he was taking the ASU job. When Keady said no, Frieder's response was, "Hot dog, I'm out of here." Publicly, Frieder said that he "picked the wrong time to leave Michigan for ASU."[29]

The NCAA field was announced on March 13; Frieder announced his departure on March 14, and the next day, Michigan athletic director and head football coach Bo Schembechler announced, "I don't want someone from Arizona State coaching Michigan." And with that, they named assistant coach Steve Fisher to lead the Wolverines in the NCAA tourney. Fisher was a thirty-six-year-old assistant with two years' experience as an assistant at Western Michigan before his seven years as an assistant at Michigan.[30] It was difficult to assess what effect all this might have on the Michigan squad.

It was hard to tell, but most observers saw Fisher as a "place holder," and there was much speculation regarding the naming of the new Wolverine coach.[31]

The NIT opened on March 15, and both Wisconsin and Ohio State won opening matches at home, Wisconsin topping New Orleans 63–61 and OSU defeating Akron 81–70.[32] The next day, Michigan State kept the Big Ten NIT win streak going with a 83–69 win over Kent State in Detroit.[33]

Opening games in the NCAA's sixty-four-team tournament were on March 16. Illinois squeezed by #16 McNeese State 77–71 in Indianapolis, while Minnesota topped Kansas State 86–75 in Greensboro. Indiana followed the next night with a 99–85 win over George Mason in Tucson, and Iowa had little trouble with Rutgers in Providence 87–73, behind 35 points from B. J. Armstrong and 24 from Roy Marble.[34]

Illinois, Minnesota, Indiana, and Michigan all won second-round games, but Iowa lost 102–96 in overtime to North Carolina State. Illinois downed Ball State 72–60; Minnesota topped Siena, 80–67; Indiana cruised by UTEP 92–69 with five Hoosiers scoring in double figures; and Michigan struggled against Southern Alabama but won 91–82. Michigan had slipped by Xavier 92–87 in their first game under acting coach Fisher.[35] Four Big Ten teams were in their respective regional semifinals, along with four ACC and three Big East teams, accounting for eleven of the sixteen squads left.

In the NIT, Wisconsin was eliminated by St. Louis 73–68 in Madison, while Michigan State topped Wichita State 79–67 in East Lansing, and Ohio State defeated Nebraska in Columbus 85–74. Michigan State, behind thirty-four points from Steve Smith then beat Villanova 70– 63 to advance to the NIT semis in Madison Square Garden. Ohio State lost at home to St. John's 83–80. In the semis, Michigan State lost to St. Louis 74–64 then 78–76 to Alabama-Birmingham in the game for third place.[36] It was during the tournaments that the Big Ten writers and broadcasters named their Coach of the Year in the conference, and the award went to Bob Knight.[37]

In the Southeast regional semifinals, Michigan surprised #2 seed North Carolina 92–87 as Glen Rice (with 34) topped the Wolverine scoring. In the regional finals, Michigan humiliated #5 Virginia 102–65, led by Rice (32) and Sean Higgins (31). The Wolverines would be heading to Seattle to meet the winner of the Midwest regional.[38]

In the Midwest, Illinois, playing in Minneapolis, topped Louisville 83–69. Two nights later, the Illini defeated Syracuse 89–86, with Nick Anderson scoring 24 along with 16 rebounds; Anderson would win the Midwest MVP award.[39] Illinois would face Michigan in one national semifinal. In the East, Minnesota lost to Duke 87–70. In the West, Indiana was beaten by Seton

The "Flyin'" Illini at the Final Four, 1989. (*Courtesy of University of Illinois Athletics*)

Hall 78–65, with neither team shooting well but IU shooting particularly bad, with just 18 of 46 from the floor (39 percent).[40]

Two Big Ten teams would be in the Final Four, the only conference to have two teams there three different times since the 1975 tournament expansion. Bob Knight recalled the 1976 title game when his Hoosiers defeated Michigan for the national title and said this game reminded him of that battle. He expanded on that remark, relating it to the upcoming contest: "We were up four with 10 minutes to go and won by 18 . . . (Illinois is) a team that you have to beat for 40 minutes. If Michigan plays well and makes a game of it, they can win. Unless Illinois plays as well as it can play. Then, no one can beat them." He noted that the Illini had two key players, Anderson and Battle, who were "the best pair of offensive forwards in the country."[41]

Just before the national title semifinal games, it was announced by the Associated Press that their Coach of the Year was Bob Knight, who easily outdistanced runner-up, P. J. Carlesimo of Seton Hall, with Lute Olson of Iowa third. Only one of those had a team in the Final Four.[42]

In a surprisingly easy contest, Seton Hall defeated Duke 95–78 to get to the NCAA championship game.[43] Seton Hall would meet Michigan, who finally defeated the Illini in their third meeting of the year, 83–81. It was a memorable contest with Rice leading Michigan with 28. Illinois was led by Battle with 29 and Anderson with 17. It was a bitter pill for Illinois who had beaten Michigan handily in their previous two meetings.[44]

The championship game, which had the highest television rating for an NCAA basketball championship since 1985, and was second all-time to the Michigan State victory of 1979, went to overtime before Michigan emerged with an 80–79 victory. Glen Rice had 31 and 11 rebounds, while Rumeal Robinson had 21 with 11 assists.[45]

The Michigan win capped a great season for the Big Ten, but it also meant a disappointing ending for Illinois, despite their semifinal appearance. Michigan would lose only Glen Rice, but this was significant since he had been the Big Ten scoring leader two seasons in a row. But Demetrius Calip would be looked to as a starter along with Robinson, Vaught, Higgins, and Mills; a week after the championship game, they would be joined by Steve Fisher, who was named coach for the next season.[46]

Another new name for the next season was Jim Delaney, who was announced as the next commissioner of the Big Ten, succeeding the retiring Wayne Duke. Delaney had played basketball at North Carolina under Dean Smith and was a tri-captain of the team in 1969–1970. He was the commissioner of the Ohio Valley Conference and chair of the NCAA Men's Basketball Committee.[47] As Delany stepped into the office, there were some who already lamented the loss (or at least recalled fondly) the work of Wayne Duke as commissioner. One of those was Bob Knight, who clarified what seemed at times to be a less than friendly relationship with Duke.

Knight said that he and Duke had had just three disagreements in eighteen years. He went on to compliment Duke for his efforts and successes in promoting Big Ten basketball. "It wasn't coincidental that, with Wayne's arrival as commissioner (1972), basketball became what it should be in the Big 10."[48]

The 1989–90 Season

During the summer, Gene Keady of Purdue coached the US team at the World University Games in Germany. He credited that experience with dramatically improving the play of his center, Steve Scheffler, who was a star

Steve Scheffler, All-American
at Purdue. *(Courtesy of Purdue
University Archives and
Special Collections)*

player on that gold medal team. "On that trip, Scheffler listened as some great players explained to him why basketball is so important. He learned a great deal from the practice drills that were incorporated into the World University Games team schedule. During his senior season, Scheffler responded by leading the nation in field-goal percentage."[49]

The Tip-Off Classic saw Arizona top Michigan, 82–75, despite Rumeal Robinson's 27 and Terry Mills' 16. The Wolverines came back to beat Boston University 73–65 two nights later.[50]

December had more nonconference games of varying intensity and then holiday tourneys. In a battle between longtime rivals Indiana and Kentucky, Indiana edged Kentucky in Indianapolis 71–69 as Laurence Funderbunke had 16 and Greg Graham 15. Indiana followed that with a home win over Notre Dame, 81–72, in a game where Bob Knight started four freshmen: Calbert Cheaney, Chris Reynolds, Greg Graham, and Funderfunke. In an unusual turn, there were no three pointers made in the contest, as each team shot just three. Ten days later, Funderbunke was kicked out of practice by Bob Knight, and the freshman then quit school. He would not appear in a Big Ten game again for two years after transferring to Ohio State, where he would play for three years (1991–94) and average nearly 15 points and 7 rebounds a game for the Buckeyes.[51]

In an important game, Michigan defeated visiting Duke in a fast-paced contest 113–108 in overtime. Sean Higgins had a career-high 32 for Michigan and shot 6 for 8 from three-point range.[52] Rivaling that contest was unbeaten Iowa's 84–74 defeat of North Carolina in Iowa City, which dropped the Tar Heels to 4–4, after they had been ranked in the top ten nationally at the outset of the season.[53]

Illinois, Indiana, and Michigan were all ranked and defended their status with some tough contests. Illinois beat Temple in Champaign 78–61; the Illini rebounding was most impressive as they out-rebounded the Owls 49 to 29. Temple coach John Chaney said of Illinois, "They're as good a ballclub as I've seen." They followed that win with victory in the "border clash," beating #4 Missouri 101–93 in St. Louis. The Hoosiers went to 8–0, roaring past Iowa State 115–66 and "looking a lot like champions."[54] The conference seemed to be in top form once again as they headed to the conference season, with every team in the Big Ten having a winning record.

The Big Ten Season Opens

The day before the conference season began, #20 Iowa was shocked by a loss to University of Northern Iowa in Cedar Falls 77–74 before more than twenty-two-thousand fans, the first win for UNI in the series since 1913.[55]

Surely aware of this outcome, Illinois took the floor at Champaign, both focused and relieved, the latter being because Gill and Bardo, who had been declared ineligible for a brief period, were both exonerated by the NCAA just hours before the game. Both were sidelined by Illinois while the university investigated bank loan applications for financing the purchase of used cars. Illinois's cautious action, was set aside initially by the NCAA, interpreting the NCAA rules differently. Illinois had its way with the Badgers 73–59, with Gill leading the way with twenty points.[56]

Three nights later Illinois traveled to Minneapolis and the Illini were beaten badly by the Gophers 91–74. That same night Ohio State surprised #9 Indiana by coasting to a 79–73 win in Columbus.[57] The beginning of the season already had unexpected consequences, and the first week had not even ended.

The highlight of the first week would have been the Michigan visit to Indiana, despite the fact that IU had lost eight letter winners from the prior season, as well as Lawrence Funderbunke. Michigan was missing only Glen Rice from their NCAA champions. The contest went from a rout, with Indiana down twenty in the first half, to a surprise, as Indiana edged Michigan 69–67. Coach Steve Fisher said, "We lost our poise, composure and the game, in that order."[58]

The NCAA annual convention was being held that same week and passed Proposition 26, modifying Proposition 42, which had altered the rules for the recruitment and eligibility of "partial qualifiers," that is, those that either hadn't met the test scores or the predicted/minimum GPAs to make them immediately eligible. Proposition 26 altered this in that partial qualifiers would be able to receive financial aid from the institution on a needs-based determination but would still not be eligible for initial athletic scholarships. Basketball schedules would be reduced to twenty-five regular season games, from twenty-eight, and preseason or exhibition tournaments would be limited to only once every four years, beginning in the fall of 1992.[59]

Minnesota went into Purdue with a ten-game winning streak but was smacked down by the Boilermakers 86–78, as Purdue dominated the boards, outrebounding the Gophers, 37–22.

That same night, Wisconsin surprised Iowa in Madison, topping them 73–69 in overtime. The Hawks may have been reeling from the loss of three starters-Ray Thomson and Brian Garner who were declared academically ineligible by the NCAA and Acie Earl, who had been suspended indefinitely for undisclosed reasons.[60] Purdue's victory sent them into Bloomington with some confidence, and they emerged with even more, after topping Indiana 81–79 in overtime, despite being down 42–29 to the Hoosiers at the half. That same night Michigan took down Minnesota in Ann Arbor 87–83. The biggest disparity in the contest was free throws, where Michigan was 26 of 37 (on 26 fouls) and Minnesota was just 3 of 9 (on 15 Michigan fouls). When asked about this after the game, Coach Clem Haskins of Minnesota said, "I want to coach the next game, so I'm not going to comment on the officiating."[61]

Michigan kept it up, defeating Illinois 74–70 and ending the Illini twenty-eight-game home winning streak. The Wolverines were relentless on the boards, taking 41 to Illinois's, 31, and outshot the Illini 52 percent (28–54) to 41 percent (29–71). Coach Lou Henson observed this disparity and commented, "For us to beat Michigan, we've got to shoot the ball. I don't know anyone on our schedule we'll beat shooting 40 percent."[62]

Illinois started a new home winning streak against Michigan State 73–64[63] then came into West Lafayette with a need for a road win, but Purdue handled them easily 81–68. Steve Scheffler had twenty points to take game scoring honors. (He was also leading the nation in field goal percentage at that time, shooting 78 of 107, 72.9 percent.)[64]

It was truly an unexpectedly mixed-up conference, and Gene Keady summarized his view of it from his Purdue coaching helm. "If somebody told me last August we'd have this record (5– 0), I'd have told them they're crazy," Jud Heathcote, observing Indiana's continued excellence and anticipating his upcoming clash in Bloomington commented, "Bob Knight motivates so well. He gets so much out of so many different players at different times."[65]

Whether Heathcote's comment was made to spur his players or soften the blow (were his Spartans to lose) was forgotten after Michigan State crushed Indiana 72–57 behind 30 of 54 team shooting.[66] The next night Illinois squeaked by Wisconsin in Madison 66–63, and Purdue hammered Ohio State in Columbus 78–66. The Illini game was played with the specter of NCAA penalties looming. The inquiry, which had begun with the recruiting of Deon Thomas as well as that of LaPhonso Ellis by assistant coach Jimmy Collins, had dire consequences for Illinois if found guilty: the university, as a repeat offender within five years, could receive the "death penalty" (i.e., no basketball for one year).[67]

Purdue stayed unbeaten in the conference, crushing Iowa 80–59, while Michigan stayed close, beating Michigan State in Ann Arbor 65–63 on a last second shot by Rumeal Robinson. Indiana did not keep pace, falling badly in Minnesota 108–89, in what was the most points ever yielded by a Bob Knight team in his nineteen years in Bloomington.[68]

Despite impressive wins by Purdue, Gene Keady was still skeptical of his squad's dominance. Coach Steve Fisher of Michigan agreed with Keady that the Big Ten had no dominant team, but Purdue certainly looked the part against Fisher's Wolverines, crushing them in Ann Arbor, 91–73. After the game, Fisher said, "I saw Purdue do this on the tapes. They did it to Illinois. They did it to Minnesota. But they did it to us here." Purdue was now 8–0 in the conference.[69]

Purdue's unbeaten streak ended at home three nights later against a Michigan State team that had lost two nights before in East Lansing to Minnesota 79–74.[70] So, halfway through the conference season, Purdue was still the only team with one loss (8–1), with three teams (Minnesota, Michigan, Michigan State) two games back at 6–3.

The next week, Michigan had an easy time defeating Illinois 93–79, behind twenty-nine from Robinson, and Minnesota recovered from their pounding at Illinois and ended Purdue's winning ways by edging the Boilers 73–72 in Minneapolis.[71] The next night, Michigan State won at Iowa 80–70, in a game where Kirk Manns of MSU set a Big Ten record for three pointers in a game as he hit 8 of 13 attempts, while scoring 30 points. At this points, Manns was leading the Big Ten in scoring with 20.8 ppg, followed by Rex Walters of Northwestern at 20.5 ppg. Manns also led in three-point percentage with 44 of 88 for 50 percent, and Walters was 24 of 49 for 49 percent.[72]

Purdue struggled against Wisconsin but finally prevailed at home, 62–55 then defeated Indiana 72–49 to hold on to a tie for first place with Michigan State, who topped Illinois 70–63. Purdue's Steve Scheffler had 18 points, 8 assists and 4 rebounds, prompting Bob Knight to declare him "the most valuable player in the Big 10." Skip Mylenski, a *Chicago Tribune* writer called the conference "the best basketball show in college," the day before Illinois surprised Purdue with a 90–78 win in Champaign.[73]

The next week saw no big upsets and led to serious speculation that the Big Ten could have seven teams in the NCAA tournament. There were two losses of note. Michigan State, in its 72–66 victory over Indiana, lost Kirk Manns to a stress fracture in his right foot, sidelining him for at least two weeks, and Illinois was beaten 86–80, by Ohio State.[74] Purdue shot itself in the foot, losing in Iowa 64–63 to fall into a tie for first with Michigan State, who topped Michigan in East Lansing 78–70.[75]

Both first place teams won again, setting up a clash for the title on the last day of the season when Purdue traveled to East Lansing, the same day that the NCAA sixty-four-team field was announced. The Spartans got twenty-two points from Steve Smith to edge Purdue 72–70, and the result was a #1 seeding for MSU in the Southeast and a #2 seeding for Purdue in the Midwest. Gene Keady's recollection of that loss to MSU was as follows: "We had a lead late in the game, but Michigan State fouled the hell out of us, stole the ball and made a layup just ahead of the buzzer to beat us, 72–70."[76] Michigan State was 15–3, winning the title by two games over Purdue at 13–5.

The NCAA Tournament

Seven Big Ten teams were selected for the NCAA field, all but Wisconsin, Iowa, and Northwestern. The first day of tournament play was disappointing for the Big Ten as both Illinois and Indiana lost, the former to Dayton 88–86 in Austin and the latter to Cal 65–63 in Hartford. Illinois played with "little emotion," according to coach Lou Henson. Bob Knight's take on his team's loss was even harsher: "This team has a lot of holes. . . . We've got too many who can't shoot and too many who have to work harder."[77]

Michigan State, Michigan, Purdue, Ohio State, and Minnesota all won their first round contests, but none in dominant fashion, with two games going into overtime. In Knoxville, MSU managed to slip by Murray State in overtime 75–71 thanks to the return of Kirk Manns and his 21 points and Steve Smith's 22. In Salt Lake City, Ohio State defeated Providence in overtime 84–83. Michigan won over Illinois State 76–70 in Long Beach. Purdue was sluggish in a 75–63 win over Northeast Louisiana in Indianapolis and Minnesota also went into overtime before beating UTEP 64–61. The Big Ten teams would have to play better in order to advance farther.[78]

The second round began with Michigan State struggling to beat UC–Santa Barbara 62–58 in Knoxville and Ohio State falling 76–65 to UNLV in Salt Lake City. Then the bigger upsets started, as both Michigan and Purdue lost, the latter 73–72 to Texas in Indianapolis in a game where Gene Keady lashed out afterward at the referees. "Throughout the game, our players took six or seven charges, but the officiating crew would not actually call a charging foul on Texas."[79] Michigan's loss was breathtaking, as Loyola Marymount shot 40 three-pointers, made 21, and won 149–115. Minnesota managed to stay alive with an 81–78 win over Northern Iowa in Richmond, becoming the first Gopher team to make it to the Sweet Sixteen in consecutive years.[80]

Minnesota was the only Big Ten team to get to the Elite Eight as Michigan State lost in overtime to Georgia Tech 81–80, and the Gophers topped Syracuse 82–75 by shooting 79 percent in the second half. In the MSU contest, a disputed last-second shot was the difference, and it led Coach Jud Heathcote to assert after the game, "In crucial games, I'm not sure we shouldn't be using instant replay" (usage would begin the next year).[81]

Minnesota then lost to Georgia Tech 93–91 in the Southeast regional final; the Gophers outshot the Techsters from the floor, with 39 field goals to GT's 29, but it was at the free-throw line where an enormous disparity made the difference. Minnesota was 5 of 11, while Georgia Tech was 27 of 35.[82]

So, the Final Four was set with Georgia Tech, Arkansas, Duke, and UNLV. In the final game, UNLV humbled Duke with a 103–73 victory. This was a surprise and disappointment for the Blue Devils, but no more surprising or disappointing than the Big Ten's poor showing in the NCAA tournament. The seven conference teams compiled a record of 8–7, which was the worst showing since 1986 and especially disappointing after their 16–5 record in the 1989 tournament with just five Big Ten teams. Since 1980, the Big Ten had gone 80–53 (.600) in the NCAA tournament.[83]

In addition to the conference disappointment, Illinois was still under a cloud of uncertainty because of the NCAA probe, which required a response from Illinois to the various recruiting charges by April 16. This led directly to the loss of a top Illinois All-Stater who had initially announced for Connecticut or Illinois, Cuonzo Martin, who instead decided on Purdue. Sean Higgins of Michigan decided to skip his senior season and turn pro. Northwestern's leading scorer, Rex Walters, announced that he was transferring to Kansas.[84]

The NCAA meetings during the tournament resulted in a number of important decisions for the next season. First, despite the National Association of Basketball Coaches wanting to move the three-point line back to 20 feet, 6 inches, the NCAA basketball committee voted to retain the 19 feet, 9 inches distance for the shot, but three free throws would be awarded for a foul on a three-point attempt. The use of replay would now be part of the tournament, although the specifics were still to be clarified.[85]

All of these rule changes, transfers, and NCAA investigations could not alter the fact that Big Ten basketball had underperformed severely when it most counted: in the NCAA tournament. Coaches and players were eager and anxious about the 1990–91 season and cautiously optimistic that the conference would reclaim its position as the premier college league in the nation. It would be a long summer to ponder what had gone wrong.

CHAPTER 12

THE LAST YEARS OF JUST TEN

1990–92

It was a new season, 1990–91, and no team had a lead in the polls yet. Prognostications from the media had Michigan State and Indiana as favorites for the conference title, with Ohio State, Minnesota, and Purdue not far behind.[1] At Illinois, there were significant losses, with just Larry Smith and Andy Kaufmann returning as both Big Ten first-teamers; Kendall Gill and Steven Bardo left after four years; and Marcus Liberty decided to go pro early and sign with the Denver Nuggets after two years of varsity play.[2]

Initial punishment for Illinois not following recruiting rules was three-year probation, no off-campus recruiting for one year and no paid campus visits for recruits for one year. There was also a one-year postseason ban and a two-year limitation on scholarships. The good news was that Illinois was cleared of the major allegations regarding Deon Thomas and LaPhonso Ellis (who had enrolled at Notre Dame). Assistant coach Jimmy Collins was "vindicated," but the university was still cited for "failure of institutional control of the basketball program."[3]

In Bloomington, Indiana showed that it would be formidable by defeating the touring Soviet team, which had won the 1988 Olympic title in Seoul, 93–88.[4] Indiana's cofavorite for the Big Ten title, Michigan State, began the exhibition season with a 94–91 loss to the touring Athletes in Action team (AIA), despite twenty-nine points from Steve Smith. Smith, coincidentally, was praised after that game by Bob Knight, who noted, "I can't tell you how much I enjoy seeing a kid like Smith make the transformation from a talented player to being a talented *and* competitive player."[5]

Michigan State (ranked #5 nationally), had a tighter game against Furman than anticipated, winning 78–73 behind Steve Smith's twenty-four points, then they lost to Nebraska in Lincoln 71–69. They continued to stumble at Bowling Green, losing 98–85, despite Smith's twenty-nine points.[6]

Illinois continued to be up and down, losing a shocker to Illinois-Chicago 71–60 in Champaign but then crushing Eastern Illinois 106–87. The

Andy Kaufmann, All-American at Illinois. *(Courtesy of University of Illinois Athletics)*

Illini followed with a trip to Penn State, the new Big Ten team, whose games would not count in the conference standings until the next season. Illinois was a fine guest, losing 78–68, as Penn State had five players in double figures and went 24 of 25 from the free-throw line.[7]

At this point, the Big Ten race looked to be much more of a toss-up than had been anticipated, not because of great play but because of inconsistency. The Big Ten was assuaged by the signing of a new NCAA formula regarding television revenue, and the conference was the big winner, getting $7.1 million of the $70 million in the package.[8]

Illinois, in the Illini Classic, destroyed Oregon State 112–78 then soundly defeated Georgia Southern 85–67. Andy Kaufmann had 24 against Oregon State and 28 against Georgia Southern; he was awarded the MVP trophy in the tourney.[9]

Indiana also won their classic in Indianapolis, beating Niagara 101–64 and San Diego 91–64, as Calbert Cheaney captured MVP honors with 19 in the first game and 25 in the championship clash. Indiana followed that championship with two very impressive wins, first against Kentucky in Bloomington 87–84 then against Iowa State in Ames 87–76.[10] Title co-favorite Michigan State handled Detroit 83–61, squeaked by Cincinnati 65–63, then were trounced by UNLV at the Palace in Auburn Hills 95–75.[11]

Purdue was up and down. Against Georgia, they were up, beating the Bulldogs in Athens 64–63 to stop their fifteen-game home win streak. The Purdue players were always trying to please Coach Keady. Chuckie White said, "It's like a father-son relationship. No one wants to let his dad down, especially Coach Keady who has so much fire to him. . . . His fire rubs off on us."[12]

Minnesota was back in the news for the wrong reasons. They were being investigated for a series of major NCAA violations in both the football program helmed by Lou Holtz and the basketball program of Clem Haskins. Regarding the latter, there were three accusations, and Minnesota responded by claiming that an athletic department employee, Oliver Darville, was responsible for all the violations and was convicted of swindling $186,000.[13]

The Conference Season

Into the conference fray plunged the Big Ten squads, and favorites took opening games. Indiana, led by Cheaney's thirty points, wasn't pressed by Illinois and coasted to a 109–74 win, the second worst Illini defeat in history. Ohio State was pushed hard before edging Iowa in Columbus 63–59, ending a ten-game Iowa win streak. Michigan State rolled over Michigan in East Lansing 85–70.[14]

In mid-January Ohio State traveled to Bloomington for the first and most vital game of the conference season. Before tip-off, the latest AP rankings were released and had Indiana at #3 and Ohio State #4 nationally. The upcoming game would force those rankings to change. In a rugged battle, OSU won on their shooting and rebounding. OSU shot 33 of 53 from the floor (60 percent) to Indiana's 43 percent (28 of 65) and outrebounded the Hoosiers 37–28. The score was 93–85.[15]

Michigan State was not as fortunate, losing 62–51 at Purdue. Meanwhile, Ohio State went to 17–0 after winning at Minnesota, 80–70.[16] In Bloomington, the Hoosiers hung the Spartans out to dry, 97–63. Jud Heathcote summed it up: "Indiana did everything right."[17]

Halfway through the conference season, MSU had faded, and Illinois now seemed to be the top rival to Indiana and Ohio State. Jimmy Jackson kept Ohio State on top by scoring twenty-two at Purdue as the Buckeyes won 66–59. Coach Gene Keady declared Jackson "one of the top five players in the nation . . . certainly a great player, especially for a sophomore." Indiana took advantage of the OSU loss by winning in Minneapolis 77–66, after being down seven at the half.[18] The Big Ten was still impressive outside the conference. Seven Big Ten teams had played teams leading their respective leagues, and the Big Ten squads were 11–3 against this group. Maybe the league's parity was hiding how strong the individual teams really were.

On February 7, Bob Knight was elected to the Naismith Memorial Basketball Hall of Fame, based on his coaching record of 553–200 with his twenty-year Indiana record at 451–150.[19]

Michigan State continued to underperform, losing at Wisconsin in double overtime 84–78.[20] The Spartan stumbling paled in comparison to that of Northwestern, which dropped its twelfth in a row, this one to Ohio State 94–64 in Columbus. Iowa lost in Ann Arbor, as they fell to 5–6 in conference just ahead of Michigan's 4–6.[21]

Indiana continued its hot play, dumping Purdue 81–63 to move a half-game in front in the Big Ten race. But then they met an even hotter team, Ohio State, in Columbus, where the game went to two overtimes before OSU won 97–95 in what the *Chicago Tribune* called a win "for the ages."[22]

As Indiana and Ohio State asserted themselves, only Illinois seemed strong enough to assure itself an NCAA berth. At this point (mid-February), nine of ten conference teams had winning records overall, but only five were more than one game above .500.

Both IU and OSU teams had poor games following their epic battle, with Ohio State beating Illinois in Champaign 73–64 and Indiana collapsing at home against Iowa in overtime, 80–79.[23] Ohio State managed to eke out its next win 63– 62 in Minnesota but not without some controversy, as coach Clem Haskins said that the officials "put the big-time screws to us at the end," Indiana would rebound from its loss by demolishing Michigan in Bloomington 112–79.[24]

The magical month of March was near and, as a prelude, Indiana defeated Michigan State 62–56 in East Lansing in a less than stellar contest. Both coaches agreed, "It didn't look good" and found the officiating "wanting."[25]

On March 3, Ohio State edged Michigan State in Columbus 65–64 to secure a share of the Big Ten title, an honor the Buckeyes had not achieved since 1971. Jimmy Jackson (20 points, 10 rebounds) paced the Bucks. It was a rugged game with relatively few fouls called.[26]

The Big Ten did not seem as strong a league as in previous years, and the speculation about how many teams might make the NCAA tournament was rife among the league media. Illinois was ineligible because of the NCAA sanctions; it appeared that only three teams might be in the mix: Indiana, Michigan State, and Ohio State. Lou Henson thought four or five would be proper, with Iowa and Purdue being his other choices. He also felt that the league was weakened by the fact that it did not hold a conference end-of-the-year tournament.[27]

Iowa and Michigan State helped their own causes with big wins in the last week of the conference season. Iowa upset Ohio State in Iowa City 80–69 the day after the Buckeyes captured a #1 tournament seed for the Midwest regional. Iowa's win may have tipped the balance getting them into the tournament, although the timing was such that this was probably a fait accompli. The Hawks were given a #7 seed in the Midwest and would play their opener in Minneapolis.[28]

Lou Henson's view prevailed as five Big Ten teams were selected for the tourney. Besides Ohio State and Iowa, Michigan State was a #5 seed in the West and would open in Tucson; Indiana would be a #2 seed in the Southeast and open in Louisville. Purdue was selected as a #7 seed in the East and would open in College Park, Maryland.

Before the tournament opened, the Big Ten still had games to play. Indiana finished its conference season with a 70–59 victory in Champaign. After the hard-fought game, coaches Henson and Knight engaged in a shouting match. In their postgame interviews, Henson said Knight's "entire life is based on intimidation, but the big bully won't intimidate me." Knight mocked Henson's recruiting but would not answer any questions, saying that he was tired. Three days later both coaches were censured by the Big Ten for their conduct.[29]

Randy Ayres, Ohio State head coach, 1989–1997. *(Courtesy of Ohio State Athletics)*

The Big Ten had two other teams invited to the NIT: Michigan, who would travel to Boulder to play Colorado, and Wisconsin, who would host Bowling Green. Both of these Big Ten teams finished with losing conference records but at .500 for the season.[30]

The All-Big Ten team selected by writers and broadcasters consisted of Jackson, Calbert Cheaney (IU), Steve Smith (MSU), Jimmy Oliver (Purdue), and Patrick Tompkins (WI), with Jackson as Player of the Year, Damon Bailey (IU) as First Year Player of the Year, and Randy Ayres of OSU as Coach of the Year. The US Basketball Writers Association also named Ayres as National Coach of the Year, and the Big Ten coaches agreed with the writers and broadcasters, naming Jim Jackson winner of the *Chicago Tribune* Silver Basketball for the Most Valuable Player in the Big Ten.

The Tournaments: The NIT

For the Big Ten, Wisconsin opened first with a win at home in overtime 81–79. That same night Colorado ended Michigan's season with a 71–64 win in Boulder, despite twenty-nine points from Demetrius Calip of the Wolverines. The Wisconsin joy didn't last as they dropped the next game at home to Stanford, the eventual NIT champion, 80–72.[31]

The NCAA

Indiana opened in Louisville with a close win against #15 seed Coastal Carolina 79–69. That same night, Iowa eked out a 76–73 win against East Tennessee State in Minneapolis. Purdue was unable to keep the Big Ten's win streak going as they were surprised by the great shooting of Temple (30 of 46 field goals for 65 percent). Gene Keady said, "Their kids were at a magic level and just gave us an old-fashioned fanny-kicking." The score was 80–63.[32]

The next night saw two more Big Ten teams advancing. In Tucson at the West regional, #5 Michigan State edged #12 Wisconsin-Green Bay 60–58 on a twenty-footer by Steve Smith at the buzzer. Jud Heathcote noted, "We have a go-to guy and the go-to guy hit the shot at the end."[33]

In Syracuse, the newly invited Big Ten member, Penn State, derided because of its weak schedule and seemingly mediocre basketball history, followed up its Atlantic Ten Conference championship with a victory over the fourth-seeded UCLA Bruins 74–69. The victory silenced (or at least muffled temporarily) some of those critical of Penn State's basketball program.

In Dayton, at the midwest regional, #1-seed Ohio State had a surprisingly close 97–86 win over Towson State. The Buckeyes seemed to be fading as their last four wins had been by two points or less, and they had lost their last two Big Ten contests. These were not good omens, but the Buckeyes stayed lucky in their next game, winning 65–61 over Georgia Tech in what was termed an "ugly win," by the *Chicago Tribune*'s Skip Mylenski, in Dayton.[34]

Indiana looked powerful in defeating Florida State 82–60 in Louisville, but Duke looked just as strong in topping Iowa 85–70 in Minneapolis.[35] Michigan State could not overcome Utah's enormous free-throw advantage in Tucson and fell to the Utes in double overtime, 85–84. Utah was 28 of 46 from the line while MSU was just 13 of 17.[36]

The Big Ten was now down to two teams in the tournament, Ohio State and Indiana, playing in regional semifinal contests. In the first, Kansas crushed the Hoosiers 83–65 in Charlotte, and Bob Knight's summation was, "They're a better basketball team right now." Knight later noted, "They hit six three-point shots in the first seven minutes and just buried us before we could even get started, 13–2, 23–4, as badly as I've ever had a good team outscored at the start of the game."[37]

Ohio State, meanwhile, was pounded in the Silverdome in Pontiac, Michigan, 91–74 by #4-seed St. John's before a crowd of 30,461. The Redmen (Red Storm, as of 2009) outshot the Bucks from the floor (34 of 54 to OSU's 30 of 62) and the line (20 of 26 to 11 of 19) to thoroughly rout OSU. No Big Ten teams would make it to the Elite Eight, where Duke emerged as NCAA champion with a 72–65 win over Kansas.[38]

It was an abrupt and embarrassing ending for the Big Ten after a wildly inconsistent season. The hope, of course, was that the last year of the Big Ten as a ten-team league would be better for the conference since most of the young stars returned for 1991–92.

1991–92 Season

At a Big Ten luncheon stop, Coach Bruce Parkhill of Penn State (whose team would join conference play in 1992–93) talked about his team's campus location, which had been lamented by Bob Knight. Parkhill assured Big Ten fans that "Penn State is not as difficult to get to as everyone thinks. And next year we'll have all the roads paved."[39]

No team would be subjected to more hype and high expectations from its incoming class than Michigan, with five high school All-Americas: Chris Webber, Jalen Rose, Ray Jackson, Juwan Howard, and Jimmy King. Only Eric Riley, the seven-foot center, who had led the team in rebounding and blocked shots in 1990–91, seemed assured of starting ahead of them as the season began.

Bob Knight was looking forward to the new season after the successes of 1990–91. "We won a Big Ten co-championship in 1991, the sophomore year

Damon Bailey, Big Ten Freshman of the Year, 1991. (*Courtesy of Indiana University Archives*) for the Cheaney class and Bailey's freshman year. The next year we added the final two pieces-Alan Henderson from Indianapolis Brebeuf and Brian Evans from Terre Haute South."[40]

The Tip-Off Classic in Springfield, Massachusetts, began with a surprise, as UCLA blasted Indiana 87–72. Indiana got 20 from Alan Henderson and 18 from Damon Bailey, but Calbert Cheaney failed to show up, shooting just 2 of 9 from the floor, totaling only eight points.[41]

Lou Henson felt good about his team, which he called "a pretty good ball club," as they headed into the new season, led by Deon Thomas and Rennie Clemons. But he was not happy with their 65–60 loss at home against future Big Ten foe Penn State, after leading 16–0. Henson said, "I don't like the way we caved in during the second half" (after leading 30–22 at halftime).[42]

In Hawaii, Michigan State upset #2 Arkansas 86–71 for the championship of the Maui Classic. At that same tourney, Minnesota lost to Arkansas 92–83 but beat Providence 89–82 and Arizona State 69–37.[43] Michigan State continued their undefeated pace, stretching it to ten games as they headed into Big Ten play. The 10–0 start was the best in school history.[44]

The last day of November brought something new: a Northwestern victory, after nineteen losses in a row over two seasons. The Wildcats defeated Columbia 78–60 with freshman Cedric Neloms scoring 26 points and taking 10 rebounds. Ohio State, by contrast, was winning everything and ranked #5, nationally after a seventy-two-point win over Chicago State, 116–44. Northwestern went to 3–0 after beating Vanderbilt 83–81.[45]

Indiana shook off the beating by UCLA by topping Butler 97–73 and Notre Dame 78–46, before losing in Indianapolis to Kentucky 76–74 on a last second shot. After the Notre Dame rout, coach John McLeod said, "Gentlemen, I pick Indiana to win the NBA championship." But Kentucky put a pause in that direction, hitting a last-minute shot and going 11 of 23 on three pointers as Indiana made zero in five attempts from that distance. Indiana would not lose again for nearly two months. Bob Knight claimed that his real focus was not on victory, which he always hoped for; he was "only interested in teams playing as well as they can and that's my objective this year."[46]

After the hiding Henson administered to his Illini following the Penn State loss, his team seemed to awaken, winning four in a row. The fun ended in Philadelphia for Illinois when they were smashed in their first road contest by Temple 92–56. This was the worst loss for Illinois under Henson, as well as their worst loss in seventeen years. Illinois would continue a year of inconsistent play.[47]

After four easy wins over weak opponents, Michigan took defending national champion Duke to overtime before succumbing 88–85 in Ann Arbor.

The game foreshadowed the end-of- season contest in which the two would meet again. After the game, Jalen Rose said, "I figured we could win. But we didn't. But I don't believe in moral victories. The difference was they made their free throws (31–36). They only made one field goal out of their last 17 points."[48]

After the deflating loss, the Wolverines won four in a row. Chris Webber made Michigan's intentions clear when he stated, "We dream of a national championship this year. . . . We're a team to be reckoned with."[49]

Heading into conference play, Michigan State was 10–0; Michigan and Ohio State were both 8–1; Indiana was 9–2 and Iowa 8–2. Every Big Ten team had a winning record, and the conference was 81–26, compared to the prior season's 90–32 in overall nonconference play.

Ohio State began with a rout of Michigan State 62–46 in Columbus. Coach Jud Heathcote said that "their pressure bothered us the way it has bothered us all year." Illinois barely defeated Purdue 74–72 in overtime in Champaign, eliciting the following statement from Coach Henson: "In over-time, I thought we played as well as we could play." It was hard to tell if this was a compliment or just an observation.[50]

The first test for the Michigan "Fab Five" was in Iowa, and the Wolverines won in overtime 80–77, powered by Jalen Rose's 34 points on 12 of 19 shooting from the field.[51]

Indiana had no problem in Bloomington with Minnesota, handing the Gophers their worst loss in their school's history, 96–50. Minnesota came back two nights later to beat Michigan in Minneapolis 73–64 in a sloppy, turnover-laden contest.[52]

Indiana beat their arch rival, Ohio State, in Bloomington 91–83, led by Graham and Bailey with twenty-five each. Lawrence Funderbunke had twelve points in his first game in Bloomington since transferring to Ohio State. In earlier comments, Funderbunke said that Knight wasn't being fair when he suspended him but that he felt Knight was concerned for him, having his best interests at heart. Funderbunke apologized for leaving IU as precipitously as he did. But he felt his departure was inevitable because the "timing was off."[53]

Michigan continued to display the kind of inconsistency expected from a freshmen-heavy starting five, as they lost at home to Purdue 65–60 then won 68–61 at Illinois.[54] The Wolverines lost their next game 89–74 in Bloom-ington.

Indiana won its thirteenth straight game 106–65, handing Purdue the worst loss of the ninety-one-year intrastate rivalry. Michigan went to East Lansing and defeated Michigan State in overtime 89–79, with the top scorers on both teams living up to expectations. Rose had 24 and Webber 21 for Michigan while Respert had 26 and Peplowski 16 for MSU. Jud Heathcote was certainly enamored of Michigan's young players: "Michigan's freshmen dominated the stats. They are not just a good team. They are on the threshold of becoming a great team."[55]

Michigan State came back in their next game to end Indiana's thirteen-game win streak 76–60, as the #4-ranked Hoosiers shot a season-low 39 percent from the floor (23 of 59), while the Spartans shot 57 percent (29 of 51) and out-rebounded Indiana 40–24. The Hoosiers went on to Illinois and started a new streak with a 76–65 victory.[56]

Ohio State came into Ann Arbor and topped the Wolverines 68–58 to reassert their position at the top of the conference standings.[57] It had become a volatile and confusing race in the conference; at almost the halfway point on February 5; Indiana was 7–1 and OSU 6–1 to lead the conference.

The two leaders won easily in their next contests, but on February 12, the Hoosiers were surprised in Minneapolis 71–67. Indiana then defeated Northwestern 91–60 before facing Michigan State in Bloomington. The #11 Spartans were coming off a 70–59 pounding of Michigan, outscoring the Wolverines 18–3 in the last six minutes of the contest. In that game, Steve Fisher noted that "we didn't have enough poise under pressure when Michigan State made its run."[58] But in the MSU-Indiana game, it was no contest, as the #7 Hoosiers cruised to a 103–73 win, out-rebounding MSU 38–21.[59]

In the most vital conference game so far that season, Indiana defeated Ohio State in Columbus 86–80. Cheaney had 28, while Jackson (24) topped the losers. Bob Knight was gracious in praising Jackson, exclaiming, "I'm not sure I've ever used the word marvelous, but Jimmy Jackson is a marvelous basketball player." Of course, victory allows you to be generous in praise of others.[60]

That week also saw the first Big Ten coaching casualty of the season as Steve Yoder, Wisconsin's coach, resigned at the end of the season after being pushed to do so by the university. Yoder had been reprimanded and was on the verge of being let go in 1986 when it was determined that he had knowledge of a 1982 loan by a booster to Cory Blackwell, former Badger star. Yoder was 127–160 overall and 49–125 in conference play. Big Ten coaches spoke out strongly in support of Yoder and, ironically, the Badgers had their biggest win of the season the next day as they crushed #17 Michigan 96–78 in Madison.[61]

Ohio State kept the pressure on Indiana by defeating Purdue in West Lafayette, 71–64 and winning a struggle in East Lansing over #12 Michigan State 78–65. After the MSU game, coach Randy Ayres said, "Our challenge has been to play a solid 40 minutes. Today we played well for 35, and our All American Jimmy Jackson, made some crucial baskets." Mike Peplowski had thirteen to top MSU and said after the contest, "If anybody comes along and says, 'It's just a game,' they're lying. . . . It's an emotional struggle—for yourself, your team, your school, and your coach. It's a fit of passion."[62]

Both Indiana and Ohio State now faced tough contests, OSU hosting Michigan and IU at Iowa, but both emerged victorious. In the latter contest, Cheaney scored a season-high 29 points on 13 of 17 from the floor to overcome the cold shooting by the rest of his team (8 of 42).[63]

Michigan finally seemed to be growing stronger and took down Indiana 68–60 in a rugged game in Ann Arbor. Cheaney had his worst game of the year, shooting just 3 for 13 for 10 points. The Wolverines had won a big game and, as Webber noted, "We needed this for our pride."[64]

Indiana and Ohio State both coasted in their next conference games, the Hoosiers over Wisconsin 66–41 and the Buckeyes over Minnesota 94–63, which clinched the Big Ten title for Ohio State. That was reinforced by Purdue upsetting Indiana in the season finale 61–59. Michigan continued to play better as the conference season closed, sending Illinois to a 76–65 defeat, which put Illinois out of tournament consideration with a record of 13–15 for the year.

Five Big Ten teams were invited to the sixty-four-team NCAA tourney and two (Minnesota and Purdue) to the thirty-two-team NIT. Penn State, a competitor in next season's Big Ten race, was also selected.

The All-Big Ten first team, as selected by the media, consisted of Jimmy Jackson of OSU, named Player of the Year; Calbert Cheaney (Indiana); Mike Peplowski (MSU); Woody Austin (Purdue), and Acie Earl (IA). Randy Ayres of OSU was named Coach of the Year, and Chris Webber was named Frosh of the Year.[65]

The 1992 NIT

Purdue, playing at home, pounded Butler, 82–56, led by WoodyAustin's twenty-four points. Coach Gene Keady's summation of the contest was, "When you shoot the ball well, you look good," and the Boilermakers did just that. Minnesota and Penn State were not as fortunate. The Gophers went to Pullman and lost to Washington State 72–70, and the Nittany Lions were upset by Pittsburgh in State College 67–65 to close at 21–8 and set to enter Big Ten competition the next season.[66]

Purdue won again at home, topping Texas Christian 67–51. Two nights later, however, Florida ended the Boilermaker season in Indianapolis with a 74–67 defeat. Coach Keady observed, "We were outhustled and outplayed."[67]

That same day there was a surprise announcement from the University of Wisconsin, naming Stu Jackson the new head coach of the Badgers. Jackson had coached under Rick Pitino at Providence, had been director of basketball operations for the NBA and head coach of the New York Knicks, among a number of other positions in the fifteen years since he had graduated from Oregon. He would lead the Badgers to the 1994 NCAA tournament before returning to pro basketball.[68]

The NCAA Tournament

In what one writer called a "crazy season," six teams were selected from the Big Eight, five from the ACC and the Big East, as well as the Big Ten. Four of the five were in the top twenty-five. Iowa was seeded #9 in the East. Michigan was a #6 seed in the Southeast, where Ohio State was the #1 seed. In the West, Indiana was a #2 seed and, in the West, Michigan State was a #5 seed.[69]

Both Indiana and Ohio State rolled to easy wins in the first round, the Buckeyes beating Mississippi Valley State in Cincinnati 83–56. Indiana won 94–55 over Eastern Illinois in Boise. Iowa also won that night, defeating Texas in Greensboro, 98–92. The victory put Iowa in line to play #1 Duke.[70]

The next night both Michigan squads won, moving five conference teams forward in the tourney. Michigan State slipped by Southwest Missouri State 61–54 in Dayton, while Michigan defeated Temple 73–66 at Rupp Arena in Lexington, Kentucky. Jud Heathcote was happy to win but recognized his team's luck in doing so: "We didn't play very well, but their aggressive pressure defense really took us out of our offense."[71]

Indiana won its second-round game over LSU in Boise. Shaquille O'Neal had 36 points and 12 rebounds, but it was not enough. Ohio State crushed Connecticut in Cincinnati 78–55. Iowa was the first Big Ten team to fall, but they gave top-ranked Duke a scare in the second half, after being down 48–24 at the half. The final was 75–62, and an unusual NCAA record was set as the teams combined for eighteen blocked shots.[72]

Michigan won easily the next night in a real shootout against East Tennessee State in Atlanta 102–90, but Michigan State fell to Cincinnati 77–65 in Dayton.[73]

All three remaining Big Ten teams advanced into their respective regional finals. In the West, Indiana outshot Florida State to win 85–74 in Albuquerque. The Hoosiers were 27 of 54 from the floor and 25 of 34 from the line—in addition to 6 of 18 from three-point range to win easily. FSU coach Pat Kennedy said admiringly, "Since the Purdue game, they're playing like a team possessed." They would face UCLA in the West final.[74]

At Rupp Arena in Lexington, Michigan advanced by edging Oklahoma State 75–72, as Jalen Rose was spectacular with 25 points and 11 rebounds. Ohio State eliminated North Carolina in that same regional 80–73 after being down by five at the half. This would set up an all–Big Ten regional final in the Southeast.[75]

Indiana crushed UCLA 106–79, avenging an early season loss to the Bruins. It was no contest from the start, and Indiana held a 44–29 lead at the half. Michigan joined Indiana by beating Ohio State in overtime 75–71. Rose had twenty points and directed the floor, winning Most Outstanding Player for the regional. Jimmy Jackson (who had twenty points for OSU) summed up Michigan's play for the game and the year: "They grew up. They executed down the stretch the way they needed to."[76]

So the Big Ten went from three teams in the Elite Eight to two teams in the Final Four. Indiana would meet Duke, and Michigan would take on Cincinnati in Minneapolis on April 4. In the first game, Michigan topped Cincinnati 76–72, with four players in double figures for the Wolverines. In the second game, Duke held off Indiana 81–78.[77]

Two nights later, Duke embarrassed Michigan with a 71–51 win in the championship contest. It was 48–45 with seven minutes to go in the game before Duke took it up a notch on defense, and Michigan ended up shooting just 9 of 31 in the second half, while Duke scored on its last twelve possessions. The fifty-one points were the second lowest total in a championship game since 1949, when Kentucky defeated Oklahoma A&M (now Oklahoma State) 46–36. Despite the loss, the Big Ten still had the most all-time NCAA tournament victories with 189 to the ACC's 188.[78]

After the crushing defeat, Juwan Howard predicted an NCAA title for Michigan in 1993, assuming all his teammates returned. The Wolverines did get to the championship game, once again, before losing to UNC 77–71, but that's another story.[79]

AFTERWORD

The Big Ten conference closed the 1991–92 basketball season with ten teams and the eleventh member of the conference, Penn State University, waiting in the wings. (The Big Ten kept the name of the conference but modified its logo to show an eleven within the words "Big Ten.") The Nittany Lions had fashioned a 21–8 record in 1991–92, with big wins over Illinois and Marquette and an invitation to the NIT, where they met and lost to Pitt, 67–65 to close their last season as an independent. Their entrance into the Big Ten in the 1992–93 season came after losing three of their top four scorers, and expectations were not high for their initial year competing in the Big Ten. Not surprisingly, Penn State finished at the bottom of the conference standings, going 2–16 in the league and 7–20 overall, with a starting line-up relying on freshmen and sophomores. In the 1993–94 season they moved to eighth in the conference. In the 1994–95 season they earned a 9–9 record in Big Ten play, which allowed them to return to postseason play in the NIT tournament.

The Big Ten would be stable for almost twenty years until Nebraska joined the conference in 2010, followed by Maryland and Rutgers in 2014, creating two seven-team divisions and making for a tougher basketball league. The 1990s would be a much more difficult decade for Big Ten basketball, at least in terms of Final Four appearances (four appearances, two of which were later vacated), but the first decade of the twenty-first century would see at least one Big Ten team in the Final Four in seven of the eleven years from 2000–2010. Conferences were incorporating more teams and a number of conferences dissolved. It was an unsettled period for college basketball, but the Big Ten continued to show strength and stability.

APPENDIX 1
BIG TEN COACHES 1972–93

Illinois	Harve Schmidt (1967–74), Gene Bartow (1974–75), Lou Henson (1975–96)
Indiana	Bob Knight (1971–2000)
Iowa	Dick Schultz (1970–74), Lute Olson (1974–83), George Raveling (1983–86), Tom Davis (1986–1999)
Michigan	Johnny Orr (1968–80), Bill Frieder (1980–89), Steve Fisher (1989–97)
Michigan State	Gus Ganakas (1969–76), Jud Heathcote (1976–95)
Minnesota	Bill Musselman (1971–75), Jim Dutcher (1975–86)*, Clem Haskins (1986–99)
Northwestern	Brad Snyder (1969–73), Tex Winter (1973–78), Rich Falk (1978–86), Bill Foster (1986–93)
Ohio State	Fred Taylor (1958–76), Eldon Miller (1976–86), Gary Williams (1987–89), Randy Ayres (1990–97)
Purdue	George King (1965–72), Fred Schaus (1972–78), Lee Rose (1978–80), Gene Keady (1980–2005)
Wisconsin	John Powless (1969–76), Bill Cofield (1976–82), Steve Yoder (1982–92), Stu Jackson (1993–94)

*Jimmy Williams was interim coach in 1986 for eleven games after Dutcher resigned on January 25, 1986.

APPENDIX 2

FINAL FOURS AND THE BIG TEN, 1973–92

1973   Indiana loses to UCLA in semis 70–59,
defeats Providence for third, 97–79.

1976   Indiana defeats Michigan 65–51 in semis.
Michigan defeats Rutgers 86–70.
Indiana wins championship, 86–68.

1979   Michigan State 101 Penn 69 in semis.
Michigan State wins championship over Indiana State, 75–64.

1980   Louisville 80 Iowa 72 in semis.
UCLA 67 Purdue 62 in semis.
Purdue 75 Iowa 58 for third nationally.

1981   Semis, Indiana 67 LSU 49.
Indiana wins championship, 63–50 over UNC.

1987   Semis, Indiana 97-UNLV 93.
Indiana wins championship, 74–73 over Syracuse.

1989   Semis, Michigan 83 Illinois 81.
Michigan wins championship 80–79 over Seton Hall.

1992   Semis, Duke 81 Indiana 78, Michigan 76 Cincinnati 72.
Duke wins championship, 71–51 over Michigan.

Six Big Ten teams were represented in the twelve appearances. During this same period, the Atlantic Coast Conference (ACC) had more Final Four appearances (fourteen), but six of those were by Duke and five by UNC.

APPENDIX 3

A SHORT LOOK AT THE CAREERS OF BIG TEN MVP AWARD WINNERS

1972 MVP: Jim Brewer, Minnesota

1973–79 Cleveland Cavaliers; 1979 Detroit Pistons; 1979–80 Portland Trail Blazers; 1980–82 Los Angeles Lakers; 1982–85 Ford/Jollycolombani Cantu (Italy)

1973 MVP: Steve Downing, Indiana

1973–74 Boston Celtics; 1979–2001 Indiana University Associate Athletic Director; 2001–2011 Texas Tech Senior Associate Athletic Director; 2011–present Athletic Director Marian University, Indianapolis

1974 MVP: Campy Russell, Michigan

1974–80 and 1984 Cleveland Cavaliers; 1980–82 New York Knicks; 1984–85 Detroit Spirits (Continental League); currently Director of Alumni Relations for Cleveland Cavs

1975 and 1976 MVP: Scott May, Indiana

1976–81 Chicago Bulls; 1981–82 Milwaukee Bucks; 1982 Detroit Pistons; 1983 Cidneo Brescia; 1983–86 Berloni Torino; 1986 Virtus Banco di Roma; 1986–88 Enichem Lavorno (All Italian League). Late 1970s started buying apartment units around Bloomington, Indiana, and now owns more than two thousand units in the area.

1977 MVP: Kent Benson, Indiana

1977–80 Milwaukee Bucks; 1980–86 Detroit Pistons; 1986–87 Utah Jazz; 1987–88 Cleveland Cavs; 1988–89 Vismara Cantu (Italian League). Lives in New Castle, Indiana. Preacher, Bibles for Ballers. Color commentator for vintage auto auctions (Kruse International). Owns a telecommunications company that develops wireless internet services for rural America.

1978 MVP: Mychal Thompson, Minnesota

1978–86 Portland Trailblazers; 1986–87 San Antonio Spurs; 1987–91 Los Angeles Lakers; 1991–92 Juvecaserta Basket. Lakers and ESPN LA commentator. Father of Klay (Golden State Warriors) and Trayce (Major League Baseball player for Chicago White Sox, LA Dodgers, and Oakland A's).

1979 MVP: Earvin "Magic" Johnson, Michigan State

1979–96 and (player-coach) 1994 Los Angeles Lakers; president of Lakers, 2017–19; president of Magic Johnson Enterprises (2007–present, includes various businesses and companies)

1980 MVP: Mike Woodson, Indiana

1980–81 New York Knicks; 1982 Nets; 1982–86 Kings (K.C. and Sacramento); 1986–88 Los Angeles Clippers; 1988–90 Houston Rockets; 1991 Cleveland Cavs; Lakers head coach, 1996–99; Bucks assistant coach; 1999–2001 Cavs assistant coach; 2001–03 76ers assistant coach; 2004 Pistons assistant coach; 2004–2010 Atlanta head coach; 2011–12 Knicks assistant coach; 2012–14 Knicks head coach; 2014–18 Clippers assistant coach

1981 MVP: Ray Tolbert, Indiana

1981 New Jersey Nets; 1981–83 Seattle Supersonics; 1983–84 Detroit Pistons; 1984–85 Reyer Venezia Mestre; 1985 Tampa Bay Thrillers; 1985–86 Bay State Bombadiers; 1986–87 La Crosse Catbirds; 1987 Pensacola Tornados; 1987 New York Knicks; 1987–88 Los Angeles Lakers; 1988–89 Atlanta Hawks; 1989–90 Aurora Desio; 1991 Malaga; 1993–94 Fort Wayne Fury; 2006–07 Anderson Champions (ABA) coach; current high school assistant coach Fishers, Indiana.

1982 MVP: Clark Kellogg, Ohio State

1982–86 Indiana Pacers; 1993–present, color and play-by-play basketball announcer for ESPN, CBS Sports

1983 MVP: Randy Wittman, Indiana

1983–88 Atlanta Hawks; 1988–89 Sacramento Kings; 1989–92; Indiana Pacers; 1992–93 Pacers assistant coach; 1993–94 Dallas Mavericks assistant coach; 1994–99 Minnesota Timberwolves assistant coach; 1999–2001 Cleveland Cavaliers head coach; 2001–2005 Minnesota Timberwolves assistant coach; 2005–06 Orlando Magic assistant coach; 2006–08 Minnesota Timberwolves head coach; 2009–2012 Washington Wizards assistant coach, 2012–2016 head coach, and 2017 consultant

1984 MVP: Jim Rowinski, Purdue

1988 Long Island Knights; 1988–89 and 1989–90 Topeka Sizzlers; 1989 Detroit Pistons; 1989 76ers; 1990 Miami Heat; 1990–91, 1991–92, and 1995–96 Yakima Sun Kings; 1991 CB Breogan; 1991–92 BC Castors Braine; 1992, 1995, and 1997 Long Island Surf; 1992–94 Karsiyaka; 1995 Miami Tropics; 1995 Memphis Fire

1985 MVP: Roy Tarpley, Michigan

1986–91 Dallas Mavericks; 1991–92 Wichita Falls Texans; 1992–93 Aris (Greece); 1993–94 Olympiacos (Greece); 1994–95 Dallas Mavericks; 1996 Iraklis (Greece); 1998–99 Apollon Limassol; 1999 Esperos Kallitheas (Greece); 1999–2000 Ural Great (Russia); 2000–01 Bejing Olympians (China); 2003–04 Sioux Falls Skyforce (NBA G League); 2005 Dodge City Legend (United States Basketball League); 2005–06 Michigan Mayhem (Continental Basketball League). Died in 2015 of liver failure after years of addiction problems.

1986 MVP: Scott Skiles, Michigan State

1986–87 Milwaukee Bucks; 1987–89 Indiana Pacers; 1989–94 Orlando Magic (set NBA record with thirty assists in one game in 1990); 1994–95 Washington Bullets; 1995–96 Philadelphia 76ers; 1996–97 PACK, Thessaloniki (Greece) player and coach; 1997–99 Phoenix Suns assistant coach and 1999–2002 head coach; 2003–07 Chicago Bulls head coach; 2008–13 Milwaukee Bucks head coach; 2015–16, Orlando Magic head coach

1987 MVP: Steve Alford, Indiana, and Dennis Hopson, Ohio State

Steve Alford

1987–88 Dallas Mavericks; 1988–89 Golden State Warriors; 1989–91 Dallas Mavericks; 1991–95 Manchester College head coach; 1995–99, Southwest Missouri State head coach; 1999–2007, University of Iowa head coach; 2007–2013, University of New Mexico head coach; 2013–2018, UCLA head coach; 2019–present, University of Nevada head coach

Dennis Hopson, Ohio State

1987–90 New Jersey Nets; 1990–91 Chicago Bulls; 1991–92 Sacramento Kings; 1992–94 Natwest Zaragoza (Spain); 1994–95 Cholet Cedex Basket (France); 1995–96 Le Mans (France); 1996 Purefoods Carne Norte (Philippines); 1996–97 Galatasaray (Turkey); 1997 Hapoel Eliat (Israel); 1997–98 Maccabi Rishon LeZion (Israel); 1998–99 Maccabi Giv'at Shmuel; 1999 Gaiteros del Zulia (Venezuela); 1999–2000 Maccabi Kiryat Motzkin; 2000 Maccabi Giv'at Shmuel; 2000–? ran trucking company in Columbus, OH; 2001(?)–2006 Toledo Royal Knights (ABA) head coach; 2008–09(?) Northwood University (FL), assistant coach; 2009–14 Bowling Green assistant coach; 2014–15 Temperance High School (MI), head coach; 2019 Lourdes University (OH) head coach

1988 MVP: Gary Grant, Michigan

1988–95 Los Angeles Clippers; 1995–96 New York Knicks; 1996–97 Miami Heat; 1997 Yakima Sun Kings (CBA); 1998 Portland Trail Blazers; 1998–99 Aris (Greece); 1999–2000 Portland Trail Blazers; 2001–2002 Peristeri (Greece)

1989 MVPs: Glen Rice, Michigan and Jay Edwards, Indiana

Glen Rice

1989–95 Miami Heat; 1995–99 Charlotte Hornets; 1999–2000 Los Angeles Lakers; 2001–2003 Houston Rockets; 2003–04 Los Angeles Clippers

Jay Edwards

1989–91 Los Angeles Clippers; 1991 Rapid City Thrillers (CBA); 1991–92 Fort Wayne Fury (CBA); 1993 Argal Huesca (Spain); 1993 Fort Wayne Fury (CBA); 1993–94 Rochester (MN) Renegades (CBA); 1994–95 Rockford Lightning; 1995–96 Fort Wayne Fury; 1996 Connecticut Pride (CBA); 1996–97 Yakima Sun Kings (CBA); 1997–2000 Eitzur Ashkelon (Israel); 2001 Gimnasia de Comodoro (Argentina)

1990 MVPs: Steve Smith, Michigan State, and Steve Scheffler, Purdue

Steve Smith

1991–94 Miami Heat; 1994–99 Atlanta Hawks; 1999–2001 Portland Trail Blazers; 2001–2003 San Antonio Spurs; 2003–2004 New Orleans Hornets; 2004–2005 Charlotte Bobcats; 2005 Miami Heat; 2006–2009 Basketball analyst for Atlanta Hawks television and Big Ten Network. Currently basketball analyst for Turner Sports.

Steve Scheffler

1990–91 Charlotte Hornets; 1991–92 Quad City Thunder (CBA); 1992 Denver Nuggets; 1992–97 Seattle Supersonics; 1998–99 Quad City Thunder; 1999 Yakima Sun Kings (CBA)

1991 and 1992 MVP: Jim Jackson, Ohio State

1992–97 Dallas Mavericks; 1997 New Jersey Nets; 1997–98 Philadelphia 76ers; 1998 Golden State Warriors; 1999 Portland Trail Blazers; 1999–2001 Atlanta Hawks; 2001 Cleveland Cavaliers; 2001–2002 Miami Heat; 2002–2003 Sacramento Kings; 2003–2004 Houston Rockets; 2005–2006 Phoenix Suns; 2006 Los Angeles Lakers. Basketball analyst for Big Ten Network and Fox Sports. Son, Traevon, played point guard for University of Wisconsin, 2001–2015.

MVP Team Totals

Indiana 8
Michigan 4
Michigan State 3
Minnesota 2
Ohio State 3
Purdue 1

APPENDIX 4

CHICAGO TRIBUNE SILVER BASKETBALL WINNERS, 1973–92

1973	Steve Downing, Indiana
1974	Campy Russell, Michigan
1975	Scott May, Indiana
1976	Scott May, Indiana
1977	Kent Benson, Indiana
1978	Mychal Thompson, Minnesota
1979	Earvin Johnson, Michigan State
1980	Mike Woodson, Indiana
1981	Ray Tolbert, Indiana
1982	Clark Kellogg, Ohio State
1983	Randy Wittman, Indiana
1984	Jim Rowinski, Purdue
1985	Roy Tarpley, Michigan
1986	Scott Skiles, Michigan State
1987	Steve Alford, Indiana
1988	Gary Grant, Michigan
1989	Glen Rice, Michigan
1990	Steve Smith, Michigan State
1991	Jim Jackson, Ohio State
1992	Jim Jackson, Ohio State

The selection process consisted of teams nominating their MVP. Then the coaches and media selected the league winner from the ten team nominees.

APPENDIX 5
KNIGHT V. KEADY, 1972–92

Bob Knight began his Big Ten coaching career in the 1972–73 season and Gene Keady began in 1980. During their overlapping time, Keady won three Big Ten championships (he would win a total of six before retiring) and Knight won ten (he would win eleven overall). Keady was Big Ten Coach of the Year seven times and National Coach of the Year five times. Knight was Big Ten Coach of the Year eight times and AP National Coach of the Year three times. Both have been inducted into the College Basketball Hall of Fame.

1972–73	Purdue 72 IU 69	IU 77 Purdue 72	
1973–74	IU 80 Purdue 79		
1974–75	IU 104 Purdue 71	IU 83 Purdue 82	
1975–76	IU 71 Purdue 67	IU 74 Purdue 71	
1976–77	Purdue 80 IU 63	Purdue 86 IU 78	
1977–78	Purdue 77 IU 67	IU 65 Purdue 64	
1978–79	IU 63 Purdue 54	Purdue 55 IU 48	
1979–80	IU 69 IU 58	Purdue 56 IU 51	Purdue 76 IU 69 NIT
1980–81	IU 69 Purdue 61	Purdue 68 IU 66	
1981–82	IU 77 Purdue 55	Purdue 76 IU 65	
1982–83	IU 81 Purdue 78	IU 64 Purdue 41	
1983–84	Purdue 74 IU 61	IU 78 Purdue 69	
1984–85	Purdue 62 IU 52	Purdue 72 IU 63	
1985–86	IU 71 Purdue 70 (OT)	Purdue 85 IU 68	
1986–87	IU 88 Purdue 77	Purdue 75 IU 64	
1987–88	IU 82 Purdue 79	Purdue 95 IU 85	
1988–89	IU 74 Purdue 73	IU 64 Purdue 62	
1989–90	Purdue 81 IU 79 (OT)	Purdue 72 IU 49	
1990–91	IU 65 Purdue 62	IU 81 Purdue 63	
1991–92	IU 106 Purdue 65	Purdue 61 IU 59	

Totals:
Regular season Big Ten wins IU (21), Purdue (17)
One NIT win for Purdue
Knight 21, Keady 18

NOTES

1. The Early 1970s: The Big Ten Asserts Its Strength as a League

1. Roy Damer, "Big 10 Cagers Have Muscle, Maturity," *Chicago Tribune*, December 3, 1972, 2:3.

2. Damer, "Big 10 Cagers," 2:3.

3. Damer, "Big 10 Cagers," 2:3.

4. Damer, "Big 10 Cagers," 2:3.

5. Damer, "Big 10 Cagers," 2:3.

6. "Hoosiers Win Behind Sophs," *Chicago Tribune*, December 10, 1972, 3:2.

7. "Gophers Beat Loyola in Final Two Minutes," *Chicago Tribune*, December 17, 1972, 2:3; "Minnesota (Unbeaten) Tops Oregon State 83–80 to Win Far West Classic in Portland, OR," *Chicago Tribune*, January 1, 1973, 3:2.

8. "IU loses 74–65 to UTEP in Sun Bowl Final," *Chicago Tribune*, January 1, 1973, 3:2; "Indiana Trounces Ball State," *Chicago Tribune*, January 4, 1973, 2:3.

9. "Hawkeyes Upset Minnesota 65–62," "Michigan Defeats Ohio State," and "Indiana Holds off Wisconsin," *Chicago Tribune*, January 7, 1973, 3:1.

10. "Michigan Stalls Iowa; Illinois Wins," *Chicago Tribune*, January 9, 1973, 3:1.

11. "Illini Top Iowa 80–78 on Two Free Throws by Sub Foster," *Chicago Tribune*, January 14, 1973, 3:2.

12. "Michigan Rally Wins 78–71," *Chicago Tribune*, January 14, 3:2.

13. "Gophers Dump Marquette," *Chicago Tribune*, January 17, 1973, 3:1.

14. "Indiana Dulls Gophers' 'Golden Hopes,'" *Chicago Tribune*, January 21, 1973, 3:1; Roy Damer, "Indiana's Laskowski 'Super Sub,'" *Chicago Tribune*, January 19, 1973, 3:3.

15. "Indiana Beats Mich. 79–73, Leads Big Ten" and "Ohio State Trips Purdue Out of Lead," *Chicago Tribune*, January 28, 1973, 3:1.

16. "Indiana Wins 6th Straight in Big Ten" and "Gophers Nip Purdue on Boards, Win 70–53," *Chicago Tribune*, February 4, 1973, 3:1.

17. "Ohio State Nips Indiana," *Chicago Tribune*, February 6, 1973, 3:2.

18. Richard Dozer, "Ohio State, Minnesota 'Rematch' Today," *Chicago Tribune*, February 10, 1973, 2:1; Dozer, "Gophers Strong Off Pressure to Win," *Chicago Tribune*, February 11, 1973, 3:1.

19. Cooper Rollow, "Purdue Wins over Hoosiers 72–69," *Chicago Tribune*, February 11, 1973, 3:1.

20. Roy Damer, "Downing, Hoosiers Rout Illini 87–66," *Chicago Tribune*, February 13, 1973, 3:1.

21. Roy Damer, "Knight Calls Morning Drill," *Chicago Tribune*, February 16, 1973, 3:5.

22. Damer, "Knight Calls Morning Drill," 3:5.

23. Roy Damer, "25,000 Await Key Indiana-Gopher Clash Tonight," *Chicago Tribune*, February 17, 1973, 3:2.

24. Roy Damer, "Hoosiers Fall 82–75 to Gophers," *Chicago Tribune*, February 18, 1973, 3:1.

25. Roy Damer, "Taylor Wants End to System of 3 Referees," *Chicago Tribune*, February 22, 1973, 3:4. Apparently, the Big Eight experiment with a shot clock was not well received by the coaches and was dropped.

26. "Kendrick Bags 22, Purdue Wins" and "Indiana Gets by Wisconsin, 57–55," *Chicago Tribune*, February 25, 1973, 3:2.

27. Roy Damer, "Gophers Jolt Purdue, 79–66," *Chicago Tribune*, March 4, 1973, 3:1.

28. "Gophers Upset by Iowa," *Chicago Tribune*, March 6, 1973, 3:1.

29. "Musselman Stays; 3 Big Ten Jobs under Fire," *Chicago Tribune*, March 6, 1973, 3:4. "Big Ten Faculty Reps OK Redshirt Rule," *Chicago Tribune*, March 8, 1973, 3:1.

30. Roy Damer, "Surging NU Jolts Minnesota Out 79–74," *Chicago Tribune*, March 11, 1973, 3:1.

31. John Husar, "Hoosiers Turn Back Purdue," *Chicago Tribune*, March 11, 1973, 3:1.

32. Roy Damer, "Snyder Resigns as N.U. Cage Coach," *Chicago Tribune*, March 13, 1973, 3:1. "Knight Tops in Big 10," *Chicago Tribune*, March 16, 1973, 6:1.

33. Roy Damer, "Hoosiers' Charge Runs over Marquette 75–69," *Chicago Tribune*, March 16, 1973, 3:1.

34. Roy Damer, "Hoosiers Win Mideast Crown 72–65," *Chicago Tribune*, March 18, 1973, 3:1.

35. Bob Knight with Bob Hammel, *Knight: My Story* (New York, St. Martin's Press, 2002), 136.

36. Steve Delsohn and Mark Heisler, *Bob Knight, the Unauthorized Biography* (New York: Simon & Schuster, 2006), 91–92.

37. Bill Walton with Gene Wojciechowski, *Nothing but Net* (New York: Hyperion, 1994), 160.

38. Roy Damer, "UCLA Wins 7th Straight Title 87–66," *Chicago Tribune*, March 27, 1973, 3:1; Knight with Hammel, *Knight: My Story*, 118; Roy Damer, "Downing Named Big 10's M.V.P.," *Chicago Tribune*, April 17, 1973, 3:1.

39. Roy Damer, "N.U. Names Tex Winter Basketball Coach," *Chicago Tribune*, March 5, 1973, 3:1.

40. Delsohn and Heisler, *Bob Knight, the Unauthorized Biography*, 92.

41. "Hoosiers Beat Kansas; Green Stars" and "Purdue Loses to Clemson 81–80," *Chicago Tribune*, December 6, 1973, 3:2. "South Carolina Beats Michigan State, 74–63," "Wolverines Whacked by Detroit 70–59," and "Miami Shades Purdue in Overtime," *Chicago Tribune*, December 9, 1973, 3:1.

42. "Indiana Humbles Kentucky 77–68," *Chicago Tribune*, December 9, 1973, 3:1; "Indiana Upset by Irish 73–67," *Chicago Tribune*, December 12, 1973, 3:2.

43. "Purdue Tops MSU," *Detroit News*, January 6, 1974, D3.

44. Gene McGivern, *Here's Johnny Orr* (Ames: Iowa State Press, 1992), 112.

45. "Illinois Beats OSU 75–73," Badgers Whip Wildcats 87–53 in Big 10 Opener," "Michigan's 2d Half Salvo Upsets Hoosiers 73–71," and "Iowa Is 66–55 Winner," *Chicago Tribune*, January 6, 1974, 3:1 and 3:2.

46. Govonor Vaughan and Mannie Jackson both joined the Illini in 1957–58.

47. Roy Damer, "No Black Cagers at Illinois," *Chicago Tribune*, January 10, 1974, 3:1.

48. "Purdue Beats N.U. 89–76," "Michigan Wins at Buzzer over MSU," "Badgers Hit Early to Rout Illini," and "Indiana Outlasts Stubborn Iowa 55–51," *Chicago Tribune*, January 20, 1974, 3:1.

49. "Purdue Wins in OT," *Chicago Tribune*, January 22, 1974, 3:1.

50. Roy Damer, "Big 10 Basketball Action Runs Close," *Chicago Tribune*, February 1, 1974, 3:3.

51. "Spartans Shock Purdue, 76–74," *Chicago Tribune*, February 3, 1974, 3:1.

52. Roy Damer, "Hoosiers Just Love That Second Time Around," *Chicago Tribune*, February 14, 1974, 3:4.

53. Roy Damer, "Michigan vs. Indiana Today for Big Ten Lead," *Chicago Tribune*, February 16, 1974, 2:2.

54. Roy Damer, "Hoosiers Triumph; Take Big 10 Lead," *Chicago Tribune*, February 17, 1974, 3:1. Regarding his fouling out, Steve Grote said that he had played the entire second half of the earlier Indiana game, which Michigan had won, with four fouls; so being in the game with four fouls halfway through the second half in this contest was not a radical deviation for Coach Orr's defense, which relied on quickness and helping out (defenders switching to cover players who had beaten their man), according to Grote in his June 27, 2018, interview with the author.

55. "Nixon Okays Quizzing By House," *Chicago Tribune*, March 7, 1974, 1:1.

56. "Schultz Quits at Iowa," *Chicago Tribune*, March 8, 1974, 3:1; David Condon, "Illini Coach Announcement Today?" *Chicago Tribune*, March 9, 1974, 2:1.

57. Roy Damer, "A Hot Knight in the O. Town Tonight," *Chicago Tribune*, March 3, 1974, 3:1.

58. Bill Halls, "U-M Bombs MSU to Tie for Title," *Detroit News*, March 10, 1974, D1; "Indiana, Michigan Win; Tie for Title," *Chicago Tribune*, March 10, 1974, 3:1.

59. Roy Damer, "Michigan Wins 75–67 for NCAA Spot," *Chicago Tribune*, March 12, 1974, 3:1.

60. McGivern, *Here's Johnny Orr*, 117.

61. Delsohn and Heisler, *Bob Knight, the Unauthorized Biography*, 94. It was not held again after 1974.

62. "Michigan Shocks Notre Dame," *Chicago Tribune*, March 15, 1974, 3:1.

63. Roy Damer, "Warriors Edge Michigan 72–70," *Chicago Tribune*, March 17, 1974, 3:1.

64. "Norm Sloan Top Coach; Orr 4th," *Chicago Tribune*, April 4, 1974, 3:3.

65. Tom Pastorius, "Midwest Fearless Forecast," *Basketball News 1974–1975 College Yearbook*. (New York: National Sports Publishing, 1974).

66. Tom Pastorius, "Midwest Fearless Forecast for 1974–75," *Basketball News 1974–1975 College Yearbook*, 66.

67. "Indiana Gets By Kansas in Overtime," *Chicago Tribune*, December 5, 1974, 4:5; "Hoosiers Blast Kentucky," *Chicago Tribune*, December 8, 1974, 3:3.

68. "Purdue Upset by California 76–73," *Chicago Tribune*, December 7, 1974, 2:2.

69. Roy Damer, "Hoosiers Get Lucky Un-break," *Chicago Tribune*, December 13, 1974, 6:3.

70. Roy Damer, "Purdue's Super-Subs: Soul-Patrol," *Chicago Tribune*, December 16, 1974, 6:7.

71. "Hoosiers Rout Michigan for 13th in Row" and "Gophers Bury Hapless Illini," *Chicago Tribune*, January 7, 1975, 4:1.

72. Roy Damer, "Bartow Says Big Ten's Physical," *Chicago Tribune*, January 11, 1975, 2:3.

73. "Indiana Rips Iowa by 53" and "Michigan State Upsets Michigan," *Chicago Tribune*, January 12, 1975, 2:3; "Hoosiers Roll to 15th Win," *Chicago Tribune*, January 14, 1975, 4:1.

74. Roy Damer, "Best Basketball Coach in the Country," *Chicago Tribune*, February 6, 1975, 2:1.

75. Roy Damer, "Indiana's Knight Wants New Setup for NCAA Tourney," *Chicago Tribune*, February 20, 1975, 4:4.

76. Chad Carlson, *Making March Madness: The Early Years of the NCAA, NIT and College Basketball Championships, 1922–1951* (Fayetteville, AR: University of Arkansas Press, 2017), 314.

77. Roy Damer, "Indiana Defense Destroys UTEP," *Chicago Tribune*, March 16, 1975, 3:1.

78. Roy Damer, "Orr's Lament, 'We Outplayed UCLA,'" *Chicago Tribune*, March 17, 1975, 3:3.

79. Delsohn and Heisler, *Bob Knight: The Unauthorized Biography*, 98.

80. Roy Damer, "Kentucky's Shots, Refs Beat Hoosiers," *Chicago Tribune*, March 24, 1975, 4:8.

81. Roy Damer, "Kentucky's Shots, Refs Beat Hoosiers," 4:8.

82. Knight with Hammel, *Knight*, 99.

2. Indiana All the Way

1. Roy Damer, "Illini Upset over Bartow Leaving," *Chicago Tribune*, March 4, 1975, 4:1.

2. Roy Damer, "Illini Pick DeVoe Basketball Coach," *Chicago Tribune*, March 5, 1975, 2:1; "Trustees OK Henson as Illini Cage Coach," *Chicago Tribune*, March 17, 1975, 4:3.

3. "Report Smith Ousted as Michigan State AD," *Chicago Tribune*, October 1, 1975, 4:2; "MSU Ousts Smith as AD," *Chicago Tribune*, October 2, 1975, 5:5.

4. Bill Jauss, "Hoosiers Teach Russ 94–78 Cage Lesson," *Chicago Tribune*, November 4, 1975, 4:2.

5. Roy Damer, "Big 10 Cage Race: Who'll Be Second?" *Chicago Tribune*, November 28, 1975, 4:3; Steve Grote, interview with author, June 27, 2018. Grote thought that Green was the fastest player in college basketball.

6. "ACC Coaches Support Knight," *Chicago Tribune*, December 4, 1975, 4:3.

7. "Hoosiers Easily Top UCLA 84–6," and "Minnesota 96 SD State 74," *Chicago Tribune*, November 30, 1975, 3:2.

8. "Victory over UCLA a Charm to Knight," *Chicago Tribune*, December 1, 1975, 6:4. "Wildcats Shock Kentucky 89–77," *Chicago Tribune*, December 2, 1975, 4:1.

9. "Michigan Loses by 1," *Chicago Tribune*, December 7, 1975, 3:8.

10. Roy Damer, "Local Cage Scene Holds Great Promise," *Chicago Tribune*, December 8, 1975, 4:6.

11. "Minnesota Reports 128 Cage Violations," *Chicago Tribune*, December 13, 1975, 2:3.

12. Steve Delsohn and Mark Heisler, *Bob Knight, the Unauthorized Biography* (New York: Simon & Schuster, 2006), 99.

13. "Hoosiers Subdue Aroused Kentucky," *Chicago Tribune*, December 16, 1975, 4:1.

14. Roy Damer, "Tex 'Floors' Wildcats," *Chicago Tribune*, December 16, 1975, 4:6.

15. Mark Bender, *Trial by Basketball: The Life and Times of Tex Winter* (Lenexa, KS: Addax, 2000), 110–111. The court in this version cost $20,000, rather than $7,000.

16. Roy Damer, "Early Play Backs Cage Forecasts," *Chicago Tribune*, December 22, 1975, 4:5.

17. Roy Damer, "Who Misses Bartow? Illini 7–2 with Henson," *Chicago Tribune*, December 24, 1975, 2:5.

18. Neil Milbert, "Hawkeyes Rout Illini," "Hoosiers Edge Stubborn Bucks," and "Purdue 111, Minnesota 110," *Chicago Tribune*, January 4, 1976, 3:2.

19. "Hoosiers Rip Cats" and "Michigan Wins 95–72," *Chicago Tribune*, January 6, 1976, 4:1.

20. "Spartan Shatters Records," *Chicago Tribune*, January 6, 1976, 4:1.

21. "Hoosiers Roll 80–74," *Chicago Tribune*, January 11, 1976, 3:2; Robert Cross, "Knight's Guys Finish First," *Chicago Tribune*, January 11, 1976, 20.

22. Cross, "Knight's Guys Finish First," 21.

23. Cross, "Knight's Guys Finish First," 30.

24. "Hoosiers Romp 69–57," and "Wolverines Edge Ohio St.," *Chicago Tribune*, January 13, 4:1.

25. Roy Damer, "Henson Pulls Illinois Out of the Gloom," *Chicago Tribune*, January 16, 1976, 4:5. Roy Damer, "Wildcats, Gophers Hope for Better Days," *Chicago Tribune*, January 17, 1976, 2:5; Roy Damer, "Northwestern Defeats Thompson-less Gophers 85–77," *Chicago*

Tribune, January 18, 1976, 3:2; "Purdue Defense 'Up' for Hoosiers," *Chicago Tribune*, January 19, 1976, 6:7.

26. Bill Jauss, "Thompson Wins Delay, Can Play," *Chicago Tribune*, January 19, 1976, 6:8.

27. "Hoosiers Edge Purdue," *Chicago Tribune*, January 20, 1976, 4:1; Bill Jauss, "Cats Upset Iowa in OT," and "Thompson Leads Gophers," *Chicago Tribune*, January 20, 1976, 4:1.

28. Roy Damer, "Poor Shooting May Bench Buckner," *Chicago Tribune*, January 21, 1976, 4:5.

29. "Hoosiers Gun Down Gophers" and "Michigan Sneaks In," *Chicago Tribune*, January 25, 1976, 3:1 and 3:2.

30. Roy Damer, "Indiana Prevails at Iowa," *Chicago Tribune*, January 27, 1976, 4:1.

31. "U-M Is Upset; Indiana Ties Record," *Detroit News*, January 27, 1976, D2.

32. "Indiana Beats U-M in Overtime," *Detroit News*, February 8, 1976, D1.

33. Roy Damer, "Wolverines Face 'Must' Saturday," *Chicago Tribune*, February 6, 1976, 4:4; Roy Damer, "Hoosiers Win in OT," *Chicago Tribune*, February 8, 1976, 3:1.

34. Roy Damer, "Knight Apologizes for 'Temper Tantrum,'" *Chicago Tribune*, February 11, 1976, 4:4.

35. "Powless Quits as Wisconsin Cage Coach," *Chicago Tribune*, February 12, 1976, 4:4.

36. "Indiana Trips Up Illinois," *Chicago Tribune*, February 15, 1976, 3:1. Roy Damer, "Tale of Two Tips Keeps Michigan's Orr in Tizzy," *Chicago Tribune*, February 13, 1976, 4:2. "Michigan Stops Spartans," *Chicago Tribune*, February 15, 1976, 3:2. Bill Hall, "U-M Cagers Rout Outmanned MSU," *Detroit News*, February 15, 1976, D1.

37. Rick Talley, "Reasons Taylor Quit Ohio State Cage Pos," *Chicago Tribune*, February 15, 1976, 3:3. See Murry R. Nelson, *Big Ten Basketball, 1943–1972* (Jefferson, NC: McFarland, 2017), 208–212 for details of the Minnesota–Ohio State altercation of 1972.

38. Roy Damer, "Boilermakers Last Hurdle for Unbeaten Hoosiers," *Chicago Tribune*, February 16, 1976, 6:6. Roy Damer, "Hoosiers Thwart Plucky Purdue," *Chicago Tribune*, February 18, 1976, 4:2.

39. "Wolverines Romp," "Iowa Rips OSU," *Chicago Tribune*, February 22, 1976, 3:2.

40. "Indiana Clinches Share of Big 10 Title," "Spartans Win," "Illini Bow 90–75," and "Gophers Triumph," *Chicago Tribune*, February 24, 1976, 4:2.

41. "Indiana Wraps Up Title 96–67," *Chicago Tribune*, February 27, 1976, 4:1; "Michigan Clinches," and "Purdue to Third," *Chicago Tribune*, February 29, 1976, 6:3.

42. Roy Damer, "Hoosiers Outclass Wildcats 76–63," *Chicago Tribune*, March 2, 1976, 4:2; Roy Damer, "Hoosiers Give Taylor a Farewell Blast," *Chicago Tribune*, March 7, 1976, 3:1.

43. Bob Knight with Bob Hammel, *Knight: My Story* (New York: Thomas Dunne, 2002), 163–64.

44. Knight with Hammel, *Knight*, 163.

45. Roy Damer, "Faith in God Rewarding Benson," *Chicago Tribune*, March 9, 1976, 4:2.

46. "Minnesota Put on Probation for 3 Years," *Chicago Tribune*, March 10, 1976, 6:3.

47. Roy Damer, "Indiana and Marquette Launch NCAA Title Bids," *Chicago Tribune*, March 13, 1976, 2:2.

48. "Knight Tabbed AP Coach of the Year," *Chicago Tribune*, March 13, 1976, 2:3; Bill Jauss, "Coaches Tab Hoosiers," *Chicago Tribune*, March 15, 1976, 6:2.

49. "Hoosiers in Rout," *Chicago Tribune*, March 14, 1976, 3:1; "Green's Jumper Wins for Michigan 74–73," *Chicago Tribune*, March 14, 1976, 3:4.

50. Dave Condon, "Cofield Ends a Long Haul," *Chicago Tribune*, March 18, 1976, 4:3.

51. Roy Damer, "Indiana, Marquette Not Looking Ahead," *Chicago Tribune*, March 18, 1976, 4:1.

52. "Hoosier Fans Get Ban Lifted," *Chicago Tribune*, March 18, 1976, 4:5; Bill Jauss, "Michigan Tops Irish 80–76," *Chicago Tribune*, March 19, 1976, 4:1.

53. Roy Damer, "Indiana, Marquette Win in Mideast," *Chicago Tribune*, March 19, 1976, 4:1.

54. Roy Damer and Bill Jauss, "May Rescues Indiana; Michigan Wins," *Chicago Tribune*, March 21, 1976, 3:1.

55. Roy Damer, "Indiana's Wins Typical of Season," *Chicago Tribune*, March 22, 1976, 6:5; Roy Damer, "UCLA Alive, Well, Looking for Revenge," *Chicago Tribune*, March 23, 1976, 4:2. "Two 'Firsts' Mark Finals in NCAA Tourney," *Chicago Tribune*, March 25, 1976, 4:2.

56. Roy Damer, "NCAA Finals Pay Off Big and Will Be Bigger!" *Chicago Tribune*, March 24, 1976, 6:2.

57. "Buckeyes Pick Cage Coach Today," *Chicago Tribune*, March 26, 1976, 4:2; "Ohio State Names Miller as Head Basketball Coach," *Chicago Tribune*, March 27, 1976, 2:5.

58. Bill Halls, "'M' to Face Indiana in NCAA Final," *Detroit News*, March 28, 1976, E1.

59. Bill Halls, "'M' Blends Talent," *Detroit News*, March 26, 1976, E1.

60. Roy Damer, "NCAA Final: All in the Big 10 Family," *Chicago Tribune*, March 28, 1976, 3:1; Halls, "'M' to Face Indiana in NCAA final," E1.

61. For more details on these teams see Nelson, *Big Ten Basketball, 1943–72*; or Peter Bjarkman, *Big Ten Basketball* (Indianapolis: Masters Press, 1995).

62. Besides Benson, the rest of the all-tournament team consisted of Scott May and Tom Abernathy of Indiana, Rickey Green of Michigan, and Marques Johnson of UCLA.

63. Roy Damer, "Unbeaten Hoosiers Prove Unbeatable," *Chicago Tribune*, March 30, 1976; Bill Jauss, "Wilkerson Only Casualty of Cage World War III," *Chicago Tribune*, March 30, 1976, 4:1.

64. Bill Halls, "Hoosiers Stagger 'M,'" *Detroit News*, March 30, 1976, D1.

65. "Spartans Fill Cage, Grid Spots," *Chicago Tribune*, April 6, 1976, 4:1; "Heathcote Takes Over MSU Post," *Chicago Tribune*, April 13, 1976, 4:4.

66. Mike O'Hara, "MSU Cage Plans Bared," *Detroit News*, April 13, 1976, D1.

67. Richard Sandomir, "Jud Heathcote, 90, Coach Who Led Michigan State to '79 N.C.A.A. Title," *New York Times*, August 31, 2017, B15.

68. The overall nonconference record of Big Ten teams, not counting the NCAA tourney, was an impressive 65–24.

69. Roy Damer, "Michigan's Orr Believes Green Will Be Back Next Season," *Chicago Tribune*, April 23, 1976, 4:7.

3. Coaching in the 1970s in the Big Ten, the Knight Effect

1. Dan Fife interview in Murry R. Nelson, *Big Ten Basketball, 1943–72* (Jefferson, NC: McFarland, 2016), 2.

2. Dave Bliss, telephone interview with author, September 30, 2016.

3. Bliss interview.

4. Nelson, *Big Ten Basketball, 1943–72*, 208–13.

5. Jerry Sichting, telephone interview with author, July 25, 2018.

6. Steve Delsohn and Mark Heisler, *Bob Knight, the Unauthorized Biography* (New York: Simon & Schuster, 2006), 53. Also see Bob Knight with Bob Hammel, *Knight: My Story* (New York: St. Martin's Press, 2002), 88.

7. Dale Koehler, telephone interview with author, June 29, 2018.

8. Brian Colbert, telephone interview with author, June 28, 2018. Powless seemed to still possess all of those qualities when I talked with him on the phone in 2018.

9. Gene McGivern, *Here's Johnny Orr* (Ames: Iowa State Press, 1992), 93.

10. McGivern, *Here's Johnny Orr*, 93–96.

11. C. J. Kupec, telephone interview with author, June 30, 2018.

12. Steve Grote, telephone interview with author, June 27, 2018.

13. Kupec interview. It should be noted that Kupec played in the NBA for three years and then in Europe for a number of years after graduating from Michigan. So his assertion should be seen in that context, where only the top players get to perform.

14. "Stoltz Quits; Ganakas Fired," *Chicago Tribune*, March 17, 1976, 6:1.

15. "Spartans Fill Age, Grid Spots," *Chicago Tribune*, April 6, 1976, 4:1; "Heathcote Takes Over MSU Post," *Chicago Tribune*, April 13, 1976, 4:4.

16. Bliss interview.

17. Bliss interview.

18. David Israel, "'Real' Work Begins for Knights, Orrs," *Chicago Tribune*, November 26, 1979, 5:1.

4. The Big Ten in the Late 1970s

1. Jim Bukata, "15 Freshmen of Influence," in *Street and Smith's Official College, Pro and Prep Yearbook, 1976–77* (New York: Conde Nast, 1976), 14.

2. Bob Pille, "Midwest" in *Street and Smith's*, 60.

3. "Hurtin' Hoosiers," *Chicago Tribune*, October 16, 1976, 2:1; Roy Damer, "Benson Is Knight's Choice for Hoosiers' Captain," *Chicago Tribune*, October 28, 1976, 4:4.

4. Roy Damer, "Gophers' Programs in Jeopardy," *Chicago Tribune*, October 26, 1976, 4:4; "Minnesota Can Blame Itself for Team Eligibility Woes," *Chicago Tribune*, November 2, 1976, 4:1.

5. Steve Delsohn and Mark Heisler, *Bob Knight: The Unauthorized Biography* (New York: Simon & Schuster, 2006), 113. Bender transferred to Duke, where he started on the 1978 team that made the NCAA Finals. Valavicius transferred to Auburn, where he was a starter.

6. Bob Knight with Bob Hammel, *Knight: My Story* (New York: St. Martin's Press, 2002), 181.

7. Roy Damer, "Michigan, Indiana Rated Top Teams," *Chicago Tribune*, November 25, 1976, 6:4.

8. Pille, "Midwest," 61.

9. Bill Jauss, "Toledo Snaps Indiana's 33-Game Winning Streak 59–57," *Chicago Tribune*, December 2, 1976, 4:1.

10. "Gophers Score Court Victory," *Chicago Tribune*, December 3, 1976, 4:1.

11. Roy Damer, "Kentucky Beats Indiana," *Chicago Tribune*, December 7, 1976, 4:1.

12. Roy Damer, "Big 10 Best: Badgers' Cofield," *Chicago Tribune*, December 13, 1976, 5:5.

13. Bill Jauss, "Marquette Loses 2d in Row," *Chicago Tribune*, December 22, 1976, 6:1.

14. "Michigan, Green Edge S. Carolina," *Chicago Tribune*, January 3, 1977, 3:2.

15. "Purdue 80 Indiana 63," *Chicago Tribune*, January 7, 1977, 4:2; Roy Damer, "Purdue Hastens King's Fall," *Chicago Tribune*, January 7, 1977, 4:3.

16. Jerry Sichting, telephone interview with author, July 25, 2018.

17. Roy Damer, "Parkinson Injury 'Break' for Purdue," *Chicago Tribune*, January 8, 1977, 2:4.

18. "Michigan Wins; Orr Irate," *Chicago Tribune*, January 9, 1977, 3:8; Bill Halls, "Cold Michigan Cagers Edge Frigid Badgers," *Detroit News*, January 9, 1977, D1.

19. Bill Jauss, "Boiler Heat Stifles Gopher Streak," *Chicago Tribune*, January 16, 1977, 3:3.

20. Roy Damer, "Michigan's 'Best' Leaves Iowa Mumbling," *Chicago Tribune*, January 18, 1977, 4:1.

21. "Late Foul Shots Enable MSU to Trip Indiana," *Chicago Tribune*, January 18, 1977, 4:4; "Michigan Dumps Iowa; Spartans Stun Indiana," *Detroit News*, January 18, 1977, C1.

22. Roy Damer, "Michigan Sits Alone in Top Spot," *Chicago Tribune*, January 21, 1977, 4:1; Roy Damer, "Rickey's Good News Is Bad for Foes," *Chicago Tribune*, January 22, 1977, 2:5; Roy Damer, "Illini Heat Can't Wilt Hubbard," *Chicago Tribune*, January, 23, 1977, 3:2.

23. Roy Damer, "What If Minnesota Ends Up 1st or 2nd?" *Chicago Tribune*, January 26, 1977, 4:4.

24. Mark Bender, *Trial by Basketball: The Life and Times of Tex Winter* (Lenexa, KS: Addax, 2000), 113.

25. "McKinney Perfect; NU Wins," *Chicago Tribune*, January 28, 1977, 4:3; Roy Damer, "McKinney, Northwestern Marvelous," *Chicago Tribune*, January 30, 1977, 3:1.

26. Bender, *Trial by Basketball*, 114.

27. Bender, *Trial by Basketball*, 114.

28. "Purdue Outlasts Stubborn Illini," *Chicago Tribune*, January 30, 1977, 3:2; Roy Damer, "Wolverines Tip Indiana," *Chicago Tribune*, February 4, 1977, 4:1; "Purdue 92 NU 85," *Chicago Tribune*, February 4, 1977, 4:2; "'Pride' Provides Minnesota's Fuel," *Chicago Tribune*, January 6, 1977, 3:2.

29. Roy Damer, "Tex Likes Gophers in Showdown," *Chicago Tribune*, February 7, 1977, 2:5; "Grote Shot Sinks Gophers," *Chicago Tribune*, February 8, 1977, 4:1.

30. "Badgers Upset Boilermakers," "Minnesota 91 Ohio State 65," *Chicago Tribune*, February 11, 1977, 4:3; Roy Damer, "Parker Gives Lesson in Statistics to NU," and "Minnesota 61 Iowa 58," *Chicago Tribune*, February 13, 1977, 3:2.

31. David Condon, "Hoosiers Tighten Big 10 Title Race," *Chicago Tribune*, February 14, 1977, 6:1.

32. "Gophers Dump Indiana," *Chicago Tribune*, February 16, 1977, 4:3; "Illinois Ends Hoosiers' Hex," *Chicago Tribune*, February 18, 1977, 4:3.

33. Bill Halls, "Shoddy 'M' Victory Irks Orr," *Detroit News*, February 18, 1977, D1.

34. Roy Damer, "Green Comes Alive and Michigan Rolls," *Chicago Tribune*, February 18, 1977, 4:3; Roy Damer, "Michigan Captures Control of Big 10," *Chicago Tribune*, February 20, 1977, 3:2.

35. Mike O'Hara, "'M' Buries Gophers," *Detroit News*, March 20, 1977, D1.

36. Bill Jauss, "Boilermakers Surge and Hoosiers Fold," *Chicago Tribune*, February 21, 1977, 6:2; "Benson College Career Over," *Chicago Tribune*, February 24, 1977, 4:1. Benson did return to basketball the next year and eventually played eleven seasons in the NBA.

37. Roy Damer, "Gopher Pair Finds Gold in OT," *Chicago Tribune*, February 25, 1977, 4:1; Roy Damer, "Illini Boot Upset Bid," *Chicago Tribune*, February 27, 1977, 3:2.

38. Roy Damer, "Purdue Could Win Way into Tourney," *Chicago Tribune*, February 28, 1977, 6:5; Roy Damer, "Purdue Topples Michigan State," "Minnesota 64 Wisconsin 61," and Michigan Clinches Tie," *Chicago Tribune*, March 4, 1977, 4:2; Bill Halls, "'M' Wraps Up NCAA Tourney Berth," *Detroit News*, March 4, 1977, D4.

39. "U-M Tops Purdue for Outright Title," *Detroit News*, March 6, 1977, D1.

40. Roy Damer, "Blue Top Purdue Sans Green," *Chicago Tribune*, March 6, 1977, 3:2; Neil Milbert, "Minnesota Crashes McKinney's Party," *Chicago Tribune*, March 6, 1977, 3:2.

41. Bill Jauss, "Michigan's Orr: We Deserve Top," *Chicago Tribune*, March 7, 1977, 5:3.

42. Bruce Ramsey, "Oh, So Close," in *Lafayette Journal and Courier Presents Most Memorable Moments in Purdue Basketball History* (Champaign, IL: Sports Publishing, 1998), 76.

43. "Purdue Falls Victim to Tar Heels," *Chicago Tribune*, March 13, 1977, 3:2; Roy Damer, "Rickey Runs Michigan Show," *Chicago Tribune*, March 14, 1977, 5:1.

44. Bill Halls, "U. of D., Wolverines Make a Date," *Detroit News*, March 14, 1977, D1.

45. Roy Damer, "Wolverines Soar Past Tough Titans," *Chicago Tribune*, March 18, 1977, 4:1; Roy Damer, "Cornbread Upsets No.1," *Chicago Tribune*, March 20, 1977, 3:1.

46. Roy Damer, "Big 10 Mulls Basketball Meet," *Chicago Tribune*, April 7, 1977, 4:3.

47. "Minnesota Obeys NCAA," *Chicago Tribune*, October 25, 1977, 4:1; Roy Damer, "Minnesota Had No Out, Ended Feud," *Chicago Tribune*, October 26, 4:2.

48. "Listening In," *Chicago Tribune*, November 10, 1977, 4:1; "Thompson Out for 7 Games," *Chicago Tribune*, November 15, 1977, 4:3.

49. Bill Jauss, "Purdue Places Title Hopes on 'More Aggressive' Carroll," *Chicago Tribune*, November 24, 1977, 6:3; "Hubbard to Have Knee Surgery," *Chicago Tribune*, October 26, 1977, 4:3.

50. Jim Cohen, "Midwest" in *Street and Smith's*, 92.

51. Bill Jauss, "Big Bird Crushes Purdue," *Chicago Tribune*, November 29, 1977, 4:1.

52. Bill Jauss, "Carroll Comes of Age as Boilermakers Roll," *Chicago Tribune*, December 4, 1977, 3:3.

53. Bill Jauss, "Kentucky Tips Indiana," *Chicago Tribune*, December 6, 1977, 4:3; "Marquette in Romp," *Chicago Tribune*, December 7, 1977, 6:3; "Michigan Loses First," *Chicago Tribune*, December 8, 1977, 4:3; Jim Spadafore, "Louisville Steals Victory from U of M," *Detroit News*, December 8, 1977, F1.

54. Roy Damer, "Holcomb Pays to Be an Illini," *Chicago Tribune*, December 9, 1977, 5:2; Delsohn and Heisler, *Bob Knight*, 114–15.

55. "Purdue Puts End to Arizona Streak," *Chicago Tribune*, December 11, 1977, 3:1.

56. Roy Damer, "Earvin Johnson Excites Spartans," *Chicago Tribune*, December 12, 1977, 6:8.

57. Bill Jauss, "Purdue Flattens Illini," *Chicago Tribune*, January 6, 1978, 5:1; "MSU Rally Catches Minnesota," "Michigan 80 Northwestern 65," *Chicago Tribune*, January 6, 1978, 5:3.

58. "Indiana 69 Iowa 51," *Chicago Tribune*, January 6, 1978, 5:3; "Illini Stop Indiana Streak," *Chicago Tribune*, January 8, 1978, 3:1.

59. "Michigan Frosh too Much," *Chicago Tribune*, January 9, 1978, 3:1.

60. Bill Jauss, "Earvin's Magic Mystifies Illinois," *Chicago Tribune*, January 13, 1978, 5:2; Bill Jauss, "Johnson 'Magic' Indeed," *Chicago Tribune*, January 14, 1978, 4:1.

61. "Little 'Magic' in NU Loss" and "Iowa 66 Purdue 60," *Chicago Tribune*, January 15, 1978, 4:3; Richard Dozer, "Home Folks Watch Judson Save Illinois," *Chicago Tribune*, January 15, 1978, 4:3.

62. "Michigan State 60 Purdue 51" and "Michigan 83 Wisconsin 64," *Chicago Tribune*, January 20, 1978, 6:6; Bill Halls, "MSU's Johnson Stifles Purdue," *Detroit News*, January 20, 1978, D1.

63. "Purdue 72 Minnesota 64," *Chicago Tribune*, January 29, 1978, 3:3; "Indiana Stuns Spartans" and "Purdue 80 Michigan 65," *Chicago Tribune*, January 31, 1978, 4:3; Bill Halls, "Boilermaker Cagers Whip U-M, 80–65," *Detroit News*, January 31, 1978, D1.

64. Roy Damer, "Michigan's Own Magic Sinks Michigan State" and "Purdue Gets Share of Big 10 Lead," *Chicago Tribune*, February 3, 1978, 5:1.

65. Roy Damer, "Michigan State Rallies to Win," *Chicago Tribune*, February 5, 1978, 3:2.

66. "Purdue's Early Eruption Enough," *Chicago Tribune*, February 5, 1978, 3:3.

67. Roy Damer, "MSU Takes Title Hopes on the Road," *Chicago Tribune*, February 6, 1978, 5:3. Roy Damer, "'Magic' Johnson no Hot Dog—He's Just Emotional," *Chicago Tribune*, February 9, 1978, 4:1.

68. Bill Halls, "Spartans End U-M Whammy in 73–62 Stroll," *Detroit News*, February 12, 1978, D1.

69. Roy Damer, "Purdue Turns It On Early," *Chicago Tribune*, February 17, 1978, 6:3.

70. Bill Jauss, "Michigan State Drubs Illinois for Share of Title," "Frosh Eclipses Minnesota Star," and "Purdue Still Lives in Big 10," *Chicago Tribune*, February 26, 1978, 3:3.

71. "Spartans Rip Illini, Clinch Share of Title," *Detroit News*, February 26, 1978, D1.

72. "Big Ten Teams Named," *Chicago Tribune*, March 2, 1978, 4:1 and 4:4.

73. Bill Jauss, "Heathcote, Magic Bring MSU Title," *Chicago Tribune*, March 3, 1978, 6:1.

74. Bill Halls, "Graceful Spartans Glide to First Crown since '59," *Detroit News*, March 3, 1978, C1.

75. "Lee Rose Fills Purdue Post," *Chicago Tribune*, April 8, 1978, 2:3.

76. Bill Jauss, "MSU Stomps Providence," *Chicago Tribune*, March 12, 1978, 2:3; Roy Damer, "'Fortunate' Indiana Survives Furman," *Chicago Tribune*, March 13, 1978, 6:1; Bill Halls, "It's Spartans in a Breeze," *Detroit News*, March 12, 1978, D1.

77. Neil Milbert, "Villanova Stuns Indiana," *Chicago Tribune*, March 18, 1978, 2:3.

78. Roy Damer, "MSU, Kentucky Romp," *Chicago Tribune*, March 17, 1978, 6:3.

79. Roy Damer, "Purdue Refugee Is Kentucky Hero," *Chicago Tribune*, March 19, 1978, 3:3.

80. Roy Damer, "NCAA Basketball Tournament," *Chicago Tribune*, March 24, 1978, 5:2.

81. "Tex Winter Leaves NU," *Chicago Tribune*, April 7, 1978, 6:1.

82. Seth Davis, *When March Went Mad* (New York: Times Books, 2010), 11–12.

5. The 1978–79 Season: The Big Ten Proves Its Mettle and Tenacity

1. Robert Markus, "Illinois Center Impresses Soviets," *Chicago Tribune*, November 17, 1978, 5:1.

2. Roy Damer, "Talent 'Explosion' Forecasts Hot Race," *Chicago Tribune*, November 21, 1978, 5:1.

3. Damer, "Talent 'Explosion.'"

4. Robert Markus, "Bird, Indiana St. Pick Purdue Clean," *Chicago Tribune*, November 28, 1978, 4:3.

5. "Pepperdine Tips Indiana," *Chicago Tribune*, November 25, 1978, 2:4; "Texas A&M 54 IU 49," *Chicago Tribune*, November 26, 1978, 4:12.

6. Roy Damer, "New Players Bolster Illinois' Lineup," *Chicago Tribune*, November 30, 1978, 4:4.

7. "Michigan Gets 2-Star Win," *Chicago Tribune*, December 1, 1978, 6:3; "Michigan 99 Alabama 84," *Chicago Tribune*, December 3, 1978, 4:12; Bill Jauss, "Loyola Falls in 2 OTs," *Chicago Tribune*, December 3, 1978, 4:1.

8. "Louisville 86 Michigan 84," *Chicago Tribune*, December 7, 1978, 4:3; "Michigan 66 Dayton 61," and "Michigan St. 92 Cal-Fullerton 89," *Chicago Tribune*, December 10, 1978, 4:4.

9. "Knight Dumps Three Players," *Chicago Tribune*, December 12, 1978, 4:1.

10. "Coach Knight Ousts 3 Players, Places 5 on Probation at Indiana," *New York Times*, December 13, 1978, https://www.nytimes.com/1978/12/13/archives/coach-knight-ousts-3-players-places-5-on-probation-at-indiana.html.

11. David Israel, "Knight's Principles Outrank Victories," *Chicago Tribune*, December 12, 1978, 4:1.

12. Robert Markus, "Kentucky Bows so Knight Talks," *Chicago Tribune*, December 7, 1978, 4:1.

13. "N. Carolina Ends MSU Streak at 3," *Chicago Tribune*, December 7, 1978, 4:3.

14. Roy Damer, "MSU Benevolence Lets UNC Off Hook," *Chicago Tribune*, December 18, 1978, 5:7.

15. "'Outhustled Us,' Heathcote Says," *Detroit News*, December 18, 1978, E8.

16. "31,683 Fans See Spartans Ramble," *Chicago Tribune*, December 20, 1978, 5:5.

17. *Lansing State Journal*, December 21, 1979, cited in Seth Davis, *When March Went Mad* (New York: Times Books, 2010), 68.

18. "Ohio State, Williams Upset Top-Ranked Duke," *Chicago Tribune*, December 30, 1978, 2:1; "MSU, 'Magic' Rout Hoosiers for Title," *Chicago Tribune*, December 31, 1978, 4:5.

19. Fred Rothenberg, "College Recruiting Is a Vicious Business," *Chicago Tribune*, December 24, 1978, 4:1.

20. Fred Rothenberg, "Why Cheating Pays Off," *Chicago Tribune*, December 25, 1978, 5:3. Forty years later, one still smells the taint of Pitino and his recruiting practices.

21. Fred Rothenberg, "NCAA Enforcement Ineffective When Schools Flout Rules," *Chicago Tribune*, December 27, 1978, 6:1.

22. Mike Kiley, "Illinois Duo Vents Anger on Hoosiers," *Chicago Tribune*, January 5, 1979, 4:3; Don Pierson, "Ohio Resists Purdue," *Chicago Tribune*, January 5, 1979, 4:3.

23. Dave Nightingale, "Ailing Michigan's Worries Prove Needless," *Chicago Tribune*, January 5, 1979, 4:3; Roy Damer, "Michigan's Hubbard Not the Same," *Chicago Tribune*, January 6, 1979, 2:1.

24. Bill Halls, "Gophers Scare MSU," *Detroit News*, January 7, 1979, D1.

25. Roy Damer, "Illinois Fans in a Dither for Mich.St," *Chicago Tribune*, January 8, 1979, 6:6; David Condon, "Illinois Basketball Fans Making Own Kind of Music," *Chicago Tribune*, January 11, 1979, 4:1.

26. Davis, *When March Went Mad*, 94.

27. Bill Jauss, "Last Second Shot Lifts Unbeaten Illini," *Chicago Tribune*, January 12, 1979, 6:1.

28. Robert Markus, "Michigan, Hubbard Run Afoul of Purdue," "McHale Paces Minnesota Win," *Chicago Tribune*, January 12, 1979, 6:3.

29. Bill Jauss, "Big Victory Ignites Illini and Fans," *Chicago Tribune*, January 13, 1979, 2:1; Rick Talley, "Ohio State Free Throws Foul Up Illinois" and "Loss Doesn't Ruin Illini's Real Dream," *Chicago Tribune*, January 14, 1979, 4:1.

30. Robert Markus, "Purdue Shoots Down Michigan St," *Chicago Tribune*, January 14, 1979, 4:1; Davis, *When March Went Mad*, 95, 96; Dave Nightingale, "Badgers Win Stunner," *Chicago Tribune*, January 14, 1979, 4:3; Roy Damer, "MSU Still Team to Beat, but Now Illini a Threat," *Chicago Tribune*, January 14, 1979, 4:13.

31. "Long Day's Journey to Another NU Loss," January 16, 1979, 4:3.

32. "Ohio State 83 Minnesota 80" and "Boyle Paces Iowa Victory," *Chicago Tribune*, January 19, 1979, 5:3; Bill Jauss, "'Magic' Whisks MSU Out of Jam," *Chicago Tribune*, January 19, 1979, 5:3.

33. Bill Halls, "OSU Drops Wolverines, 78–69," *Detroit News*, January 21, 1979, E1.

34. Davis, *When March Went Mad*, 99.

35. Roy Damer, "Ransey Pushes Ohio State Past Michigan" and "Purdue 69 Illinois 57," *Chicago Tribune*, January 21, 1979, 4:3; Richard Dozer, "Michigan State Beats Iowa in OT," *Chicago Tribune*, January 21, 1979, 4:1.

36. "Michigan Free Throw Beats Michigan State" and "Ohio State Beats NU, Protects Big 10 Lead," *Chicago Tribune*, January 26, 1979, 6:1.

37. Robert Markus, "Dead End for Spartan Magic, Irish Luck" and David Israel, "'Magic' Act Losing Its Edge," *Chicago Tribune*, January 28, 1979, 4:1; Bill Halls, "MSU Jolted; 'M' Wins at Horn," *Detroit News*, January 28, 1979, D1.

38. "Ohio State Defeats Indiana in 'Routine' Overtime," *Chicago Tribune*, January 28, 1979, 4:3.

39. "Iowa 81 Minnesota 64," *Chicago Tribune*, January 28, 1979, 4:3; Roy Damer, "Fickle No.1 Points at Indiana St," *Chicago Tribune*, January 29, 1979, 5:5.

40. Roy Damer, "Limping Johnson Sparks Michigan St. Past Ohio," *Chicago Tribune*, February 2, 1979, 5:3.

41. Neil Milbert, "Indiana's Erratic, but Ohio's a Loser" and "Iowa Jumps to Top by Blitzing Minnesota," *Chicago Tribune*, February 4, 1979, 4:1; Roy Damer, "Michigan State Avenges Loss to Northwestern," *Chicago Tribune*, February 4, 1979, 4:1.

42. Roy Damer, "'Perfect' Michigan State Romps," *Chicago Tribune*, February 5, 1979, 5:1; Roy Damer, "Michigan State Knocks Iowa Out of Tie for First," *Chicago Tribune*, February 9, 1979, 6:1.

43. "Iowa Vaults into Top 20," *Chicago Tribune*, February 6, 1979, 4:3; David Israel, "Knight Answers Critics Who Paint Him as Villain," *Chicago Tribune*, February 9, 1979, 6:1.

44. Robert Markus, "Purdue Kicks Illini," *Chicago Tribune*, February 9, 1979, 6:3; Richard Dozer, "Michigan State Scrambles Ohio," "Iowa Staves off Wisconsin," and "Purdue 76 Northwestern 64," *Chicago Tribune*, February 11, 1979, 4:1 and 4:3.

45. Roy Damer, "Carroll Hits 36, but Iowa Nips Purdue," *Chicago Tribune*, February 16, 1979, 6:1; "Ohio State 74 Minnesota 68" and "MSU, at Home on Road, Raps Indiana," *Chicago Tribune*, February 16, 1979, 6:3.

46. Tom Duffy, "Most Teams Need Both Talent, Luck for NCAA Berth," *Chicago Tribune*, February 25, 1979, 4:2.

47. "Iowa Slips; Ohio State Alone at Top," *Chicago Tribune*, February 23, 1979, 5:1; Bill Jauss, "Michigan State Denies Purdue," *Chicago Tribune*, February 23, 1979, 5:1; Bill Halls, "MSU Chains Purdue Ace," *Detroit News*, February 23, 1979, F1.

48. "Michigan State Is in Control," *Chicago Tribune*, March 2, 1979, 5:1; Robert Markus, "Ohio State Stumbles Again," "Michigan 61 Iowa 53," and "Purdue 55 IU 48," *Chicago Tribune*, March 2, 1979, 5:1.

49. Bill Halls, "Spartans Clinch Tournament Bid," *Detroit News*, March 2, 1979, F1.

50. Robert Markus, "55-Footer Beats Michigan State," *Chicago Tribune*, March 4, 1979, 4:1; "Iowa, Purdue Like Crowds-at Top of Big 10, That Is," *Chicago Tribune*, March 4, 1979, 4:3.

51. "Ohio State Runs Away with Its NIT Opener," *Chicago Tribune*, March 8, 1979, 4:3; Robert Markus, "Purdue Is in a Riot in NIT Opener" and "Indiana 78 Texas Tech 59," *Chicago Tribune*, March 9, 1979, 6:1.

52. Robert Markus, "Indiana Stops Alcorn Advance," *Chicago Tribune*, March 13, 1979, 4:1; Bill Jauss, "Purdue Wins—So?" *Chicago Tribune*, March 13, 1979, 4:1; "Ohio State Magnifies Misery of ACC," *Chicago Tribune*, March 13, 1979, 4:3.

53. Robert Markus, "Purdue Struggles On," *Chicago Tribune*, March 16, 1979, 6:1.

54. Robert Markus, "NIT Final Will Be All-Indiana Affair," *Chicago Tribune*, March 20, 1979, 4:1.

55. "Iowa's Season Ends with the Buzzer," *Chicago Tribune*, March 11, 1979, 4:1.

56. Bill Jauss, "Relaxed Magic Leads Spartans' Rout of Lamar," *Chicago Tribune*, March 12, 1979, 5:3; Davis, *When March Went Mad*, 160.

57. Bill Jauss, "Steal, Dunk, Slap! Spartans Romp into Final," *Chicago Tribune*, March 17, 1979, 2:3.

58. Davis, *When March Went Mad*, 172; Bill Jauss, "Michigan State, Notre Dame Ready for Their 'Physical,'" *Chicago Tribune*, March 18, 1979, 4:5.

59. Bill Halls, "MSU Rides Pink Cloud to Final 4," *Detroit News*, March 19, 1979, D1.

60. Bill Jauss, "Michigan State Lobs Throw Irish for Loop," *Chicago Tribune*, March 19, 1979, 5:1; Davis, *When March Went Mad*, 174–77.

61. Bill Halls, "Mismatch: MSU 101–67," *Detroit News*, March 25, 1979, H1.

62. "ISU 76 DePaul 74," *Chicago Tribune*, March 25, 1979, 4:1; Bill Jauss, "Michigan State Overwhelms Penn," *Chicago Tribune*, March 25, 1979, 4:3; "Ray Meyer's Tourney Diary," *Chicago Tribune*, March 26, 1979, 5:3.

63. "Magic Puts Crown on Michigan St.," *Chicago Tribune*, March 27, 1979, 4:1. The game is worth watching in its entirety at https://www.youtube.com/watch?v=KUWrYFobpxo.

64. Bill Halls, "MSU Wins It All in 5 Easy Pieces," *Detroit News*, March 27, 1979, C1; Bill Halls, "Vincent Limps with Joy," *Detroit News*, March 27, 1979, C3.

65. Murry Nelson, "Larry Bird vs. Magic Johnson, 1979" in *Replays, Rivalries and Rumbles; the Most Iconic Moments in American Sports*, ed. Steven Gietscher (Urbana: University of Illinois Press, 2017), 153–60.

66. Roy Damer, "Watch out for Big 10 Next Season, Too," *Chicago Tribune*, April 1, 1979, 4:15.

67. Fred Mitchell, "Indiana Leads Thomas Chase," *Chicago Tribune*, April 8, 1979, 4:5; Fred Mitchell, "Isiah Decides—Indiana Happy, Mother Wary," *Chicago Tribune*, April 10, 1979, 4:1; "Knight Rejects Celtics' Offer," *Chicago Tribune*, April 18, 1979, 6:3.

6. Into the 1980s: The Big Ten Remains Assertive

1. Bill Halls, "'Pollsters' Respect for MSU Disappears Just Like Magic," *Detroit News*, November 20, 1979, D:1.

2. Larry Donald, "Midwest," in *Street & Smith's Official Yearbook 1979–80 College, Pro, Prep Basketball* (New York: Conde Nast), 69.

3. Robert Markus, "Indiana, Ohio State Just a Shade Above Rest of the Best," *Chicago Tribune*, November 30, 1979, 6:2.

4. "Street & Smith's All America," in *Street & Smith's Official Yearbook 1979–80*, 66.

5. "Indiana 78 Soviet Nationals 50," *Chicago Tribune*, November 18, 1979, 4:5.

6. "Indiana, Isiah Rate a 'So-So,'" *Chicago Tribune*, December 2, 1979, 4:1; Bob Knight with Bob Hammel, *Knight: My Story* (New York: St. Martin's Press, 2002), 195.

7. "Michigan State Falls to Talented St. John's," *Chicago Tribune*, December 2, 1979, 4:3; Bill Jauss, "Big 10 (11–1) Living Up to Its Notice," *Chicago Tribune*, December 3, 1979, 4:6.

8. Dave Nightingale, "Michigan's 'Man' Beats Marquette," *Chicago Tribune*, December 9, 1979, 4:3.

9. Roy Damer, "Big 10 Basketball Best Says a Coach Who Should Know," *Chicago Tribune*, December 10, 1979, 5:6.

10. Robert Markus, "Isiah Helps Indiana Fight Off Stubborn Georgetown," *Chicago Tribune*, December 12, 1979, 5:3; Bill Jauss, "Thomas Fouls Out, Indiana Falls," *Chicago Tribune*, December 16, 1979, 4:1.

11. "Woodson Out 'Indefinitely,' Lost for at Least Two Weeks," *Chicago Tribune*, December 21, 1979, 6:3.

12. "Outmanned—N. Carolina Leans on Injured Indiana," *Chicago Tribune*, December 23, 1979, 4:3.

13. Don Pierson, "Kellogg Makes a Difference for Ohio State," *Chicago Tribune*, January 5, 1980, 2:5.

14. Gordon Edes, "Joe Barry Finds Indiana Defenders Wherever He Turns," Robert Markus, "Wisconsin Reserve's Only 3 Points Upset Ohio St," and Dave Nightingale, "Iowa 80 Minnesota 73," *Chicago Tribune*, January 27, 1980, 4:3.

15. Roy Damer, "The Eyes Have It for Isiah–His Best Game Destroys Iowa," "Purdue 68 NU 63," and "Ohio Slips Past Minnesota," *Chicago Tribune*, January 18, 1980, 4:3.

16. Dave Nightingale, "Ohio Bottoms Out of Fight for 1st," and. Gordon Edes, "Minnesota Gets Left Out," *Chicago Tribune*, February 3, 1980, 4:3; Robert Markus, "Purdue Winds Up the Sole Leader," *Chicago Tribune*, February 3, 1980, 4:3.

17. Robert Markus, "Ohio State Must Struggle to End Conference Skid," *Chicago Tribune*, February 8, 1980, 4:1; Dave Nightingale, "Purdue Tries, but Can't Miss Forever," *Chicago Tribune*, February 8, 1980, 4:1; Gordon Edes, "Michigan State Slowdown Can't Stop Iowa," *Chicago Tribune*, February 8, 1980, 4:3.

18. Roy Damer, "Woodson's Return Keys Indiana's Victory," *Chicago Tribune*, February 15, 1980, 5:3.

19. Don Pierson, "Ohio St. Flexes Its Muscle in Converting Win over Illinois," *Chicago Tribune*, February 17, 1980, 4:3.

20. "Ohio State 68 Northwestern 59," "Indiana 75 Michigan St. 72," and "Purdue Loses Share of Lead in Michigan," *Chicago Tribune*, February 22, 1980, 4:3.

21. Bill Jauss, "It's Ohio State-Indiana for Big 10 Title"; Roy Damer, "Free Throws Lift Hoosiers," *Chicago Tribune*, February 29, 1980, 4:1.

22. Roy Damer, "Carroll Makes Purdue's Chances for Bid Look Rosy," *Chicago Tribune*, March 2, 1980, 4:4.

23. Knight with Hammel, *My Story*, 196.

24. Robert Markus, "Illinois' Height, Strength Doom Loyola," *Chicago Tribune*, March 6, 1980. 4:1; "Minnesota Struggles Past Bowling Green," *Chicago Tribune*, March 6, 1980, 4:3; "Michigan Dumps Nebraska," *Chicago Tribune*, March 7, 1980, 4:3.

25. Robert Markus, "Iowa Looks Like Sleeper of Big Cast"; Roy Damer, "Carroll's 33 Points Power Purdue over LaSalle," *Chicago Tribune*, March 7, 1980, 4:1.

26. Robert Markus, "Iowa Looks Better and Better," *Chicago Tribune*, March 9, 1980, 4:1; Roy Damer, "Joe Barry and Purdue Tower over St. John's," *Chicago Tribune*, March 9, 1980, 4:5; Roy Damer, "Indiana Swarms to Win" and "Ohio State Flexes Its Muscles," *Chicago Tribune*, March 10, 1980, 5:1.

27. Robert Markus, "Illinois Zone Ends ISU Season," *Chicago Tribune*, March 11, 1980, 5:1; "McGee Michigan, Board Up UTEP" and "Minnesota 58 Mississippi 56," *Chicago Tribune*, March 11, 1980, 5:3.

28. Bruce Ramey, "Knight Credits Purdue's Tempo and Intensity," *Lafayette Journal and Courier Presents Most Memorable Moments in Purdue Basketball History* (Champaign, IL: Sports Publishing, 1998), 93.

29. Bill Jauss, "UCLA, Wilkes Sink Ohio State," *Chicago Tribune*, March 14, 1980, 3:1; Roy Damer, "Purdue Overpowers Indiana on Way to Duke Showdown," *Chicago Tribune*, March 14, 1980, 3:3.

30. Robert Markus, "Illini Stagger into NIT Semis," *Chicago Tribune*, March 14, 1980, 3:1; "Minnesota's Inside Power Crushes Southwestern La" and "Virginia 79 Michigan 68," *Chicago Tribune*, March 14, 1980, 3:3.

31. Robert Markus, "Illini Come Up Short against Minnesota," *Chicago Tribune*, March 18, 1980, 5:1; Robert Markus, "Sampson Leads Virginia Charge to NIT Crown," *Chicago Tribune*, March 20, 1980, 4:1.

32. Steve Perlstein, ed., *Gopher Glory: 100 Years of University of Minnesota Basketball* (Minneapolis: Layers, 1995), 100.

33. "Iowa Shoots Past Syracuse," *Chicago Tribune*, March 15, 1980, 2:1; Robert Markus, "Waite Pays Off in Iowa Win," *Chicago Tribune*, March 17, 1980, 5:1.

34. Roy Damer, "Third-Place Purdue in Final 4," *Chicago Tribune*, March 16, 1980, 4:1.

35. Bill Jauss, "Three Factors Make Big 10 Top League," *Chicago Tribune*, March 18, 1980, 5:1.

36. Mike Kiley, "UCLA Foils Purdue," *Chicago Tribune*, March 23, 1980, 4:1.

37. Bill Jauss, "Griffith Ousts Iowa," *Chicago Tribune*, March 23, 1980, 4:1; Skip Mylenski, "A Career Ends at the Foot of a Stepladder," *Chicago Tribune*, March 23, 1980, 4:4.

38. Mike Kiley, "Purdue, Carroll Win Curious Consolation," *Chicago Tribune*, March 25, 1980, 5:5; Bill Jauss, "Louisville Subdues UCLA," *Chicago Tribune*, March 25, 1980, 5:1.

39. Roy Damer, "Iowa St. Gives Orr 'Anything,'" *Chicago Tribune*, March 26, 1980, 5:1. As of fall 2018, the highest-paid college coach in the country was John Calipari at $8 million. The top Big Ten coach salary-wise was Tom Izzo of Michigan State, with an annual salary of just under $4 million.

40. Roy Damer, "Whither Rose?" *Chicago Tribune*, April 1, 1980, 5:3; Roy Damer, "Lee Rose Quits Purdue to Coach South Florida," *Chicago Tribune*, April 4, 1980, 5:1.

41. Jeff Washburn, "Keady Ready to Start Recruiting Purdue," in *The Lafayette Journal and Courier Presents Most Memorable Moments in Purdue Basketball History (Champaign, IL: Sports Publishing, 1998)*, 104.

42. "Purdue Picks a New Coach," *Chicago Tribune*, April 11, 1980, 4:3.

43. "Illini Play Exhibition," *Chicago Tribune*, November 17, 1980, 4:3; Roy Damer, "Illini Top South Koreans in Basketball Exhibition," *Chicago Tribune*, November 18, 1980, 6:2; Roy Damer, "Illinois Big 10 Title Chances Given Boost by 2 New Guards," *Chicago Tribune*, November 19, 1980, 5:3.

44. Jim Bukata, "Freshmen of Influence," in *Street & Smith's Official Basketball Yearbook, 1980–81* (New York: Conde Nast), 28.

45. Bill Jauss, "Indiana the Toughest of Tough Big 10 Lot," *Chicago Tribune*, November 30, 1980, 4:8.

46. "Cross' 25 Points Carry Purdue" and "Central Michigan 89 MSU 66," *Chicago Tribune*, November 30, 1980, 4:4; Bill Jauss, "Kentucky Outmuscles OSU," *Chicago Tribune*, December 3, 1980, 5:3; Bill Jauss, "Kentucky Steals Another Win," *Chicago Tribune*, December 7, 1980, 4:3; Roy Damer, "Paxson Passes Thomas Test," *Chicago Tribune*, December 10, 1980, 5:1.

47. "Best Illini Team Ever," *Chicago Tribune*, December 15, 1980, 5:2.

48. "South Alabama Shocks Ohio State" and "BYU 82 Michigan State 50," *Chicago Tribune*, December 17, 1980, 5:3; "Marquette 92 Minnesota 84," *Chicago Tribune*, December 18, 1980, 4:2; Roy Damer, "Brigham Young Hands Illinois Its First Loss," *Chicago Tribune*, December 20, 1980, 2:1.

49. Roy Damer, "Illinois, Johnson Rebound Nicely to Find Consolation against Iona" and "Carolina's 2d Half Downs Indiana," *Chicago Tribune*, December 21, 1980, 4:4 and 4:5.

50. Perlstein, *Gopher Glory*, 102.

51. "Gophers Control Louisville" and "Tulsa 90 Purdue 76," *Chicago Tribune*, December 23, 1980, 4:3; "Indiana 51 Kansas State 44," *Chicago Tribune*, December 24, 1980, 4:3.

52. "Clemson Sneaks Past Indiana," *Chicago Tribune*, December 30, 1980, 6:3; "Rainbow Classic" and "Michigan 85 Drake 68," *Chicago Tribune*, December 31, 1980, 3:2; Roy Damer, "Michigan Wins Opener," *Chicago Tribune*, January 4, 1981, 4:2.

53. Bill Jauss, "Purdue Stops Michigan; Cross's Big 10 Debut a Hit," *Chicago Tribune*, January 6, 1981, 5:1; Dick Ham, "Boilers' 75.5 Firing Sets Big Ten Mark," in *Lafayette Journal and Courier*, 109.

54. Bob Logan, "Kitchel's 40 Leads Indiana by Dazed Illini," *Chicago Tribune*, January 11, 1981, 4:1; Roy Damer, "Cross Stopped, but Not Purdue," *Chicago Tribune*, January 11, 1981, 4:8.

55. Bill Jauss, "Quick Illini Put Purdue on the Run," *Chicago Tribune*, January 16, 1981, 4:1.

56. "Minnesota Coasts by MSU" and "Iowa 76 Wisconsin 66," *Chicago Tribune*, January 16, 1981, 4:2; Bob Logan, "Ohio State Rips NU with Kellogg's 42," *Chicago Tribune*, January 16, 1981, 4:2; Roy Damer, "Twins Carry Michigan Past Indiana," *Chicago Tribune*, January 16, 1981, 4:2.

57. Roy Damer, "Iowa on the Road to Success After Easy Win over Mich" and "Win Cheers Purdue, not Performance," *Chicago Tribune*, January 18, 1981, 4:3.

58. David Israel, "Indiana's Victory Most Reassuring to Knight," *Chicago Tribune*, January 19, 1981, 4:1.

59. Linda Kay, "Illinois Scoring Hits New Low in Home-Court Loss to Wisconsin," *Chicago Tribune*, January 25, 1981, 4:3; Dave Nightingale, "Michigan St. Stifles Purdue" and "Ice-Cold Iowa Tumbles to Minnesota," *Chicago Tribune*, January 25, 1981, 4:3; Bob Logan, "Isiah's

Return no Party for Wildcats," *Chicago Tribune*, January 25, 1981, 4:3; Roy Damer, "Williams' Big 2d Half Powers Ohio St. into a Share of 1st," *Chicago Tribune*, January 25, 1981, 4:5.

60. "Sampson Scores 40, Virginia Rips Ohio St," *Chicago Tribune*, January 26, 1981, 4:2; Roy Damer, "Big 10 Has Reached Parity," *Chicago Tribune*, January 26, 1981, 4:2.

61. "Krafcisin Sparks Iowa" and "Ohio State 71 Wisconsin 67," *Chicago Tribune*, January 30, 4:3; John Husar, "Indiana Wins in OT, but Knight Not Happy," *Chicago Tribune*, January 30, 4:3.

62. Mike Kiley, "Illinois Gets Its Guard Up and Leaves Iowa Breathless," *Chicago Tribune*, February 1, 1981, 4:1; Roy Damer, "Indiana Gets Some Help in Victory over Purdue" and "MSU Stops Ohio State," *Chicago Tribune*, February 1, 1981, 4:3.

63. "Indiana Leads Big 10, but Chaos in Close 2d," *Chicago Tribune*, February 2, 1981, 5:2; Roy Damer, "Big 10 Tells Knight: Keep Hands off the Refs," *Chicago Tribune*, February 3, 1981, 4:3.

64. Roy Damer, "Iowa Takes 1st; Isiah's Ejected," *Chicago Tribune*, February 20, 1981, 4:1; Bob Logan, "Illini Come Back to Stop Michigan" and "Minnesota Rips OSU," *Chicago Tribune*, February 20, 1981, 4:1.

65. Bob Logan, "Illini Run Past Michigan State," *Chicago Tribune*, February 22, 1981, 4:1; Bill Jauss, "Indiana Wins 'Fight for Survival,'" *Chicago Tribune*, February 22, 1981, 4:4; John Husar, "Iowa Shuts Down Cross to Stay Atop the Big 10," *Chicago Tribune*, February 22, 1981, 4:4.

66. Bill Jauss, "Illinois' Big 10 Hopes Jolted by Minnesota," *Chicago Tribune*, February 27, 1981, 4:1; Neil Milbert, "Iowa Survives Michigan One-Man Show," *Chicago Tribune*, February 27, 1981, 4:3; Roy Damer, "The Other Thomas Lifts Indiana," *Chicago Tribune*, February 27, 1981, 4:3.

67. Roy Damer, "Indiana Wins Big 10 Title," *Chicago Tribune*, March 8, 1981, 4:1.

68. Lynn Henning, "Coaches Fume over NCAA Slight to Big Ten," *Detroit News*, March 9, 1981, D1.

69. Al McGuire, "McGuire Puts Rap on NCAA," *Detroit News*, March 12, 1981, D1.

70. "NCAA Irks Big 10 Coaches," *Chicago Tribune*, March 9, 1981, 5:1; "Purdue, Minnesota, Michigan Get Bids to NIT," *Chicago Tribune*, March 9, 1981, 5:2.

71. Jay Mariotti, "Schedule Favors U-M in NIT Play," *Detroit News*, March 11, 1981, 7E.

72. "McGee, Johnson Pace Michigan," *Chicago Tribune*, March 16, 1981, 5:7; Cooper Rollow, "Purdue Finally Comes to against a Hobbled Dayton" and "Tucker Can't Miss in Minnesota Win," *Chicago Tribune*, March 17, 1981, 6:1.

73. Skip Mylenski, "West Virginia, Jones Too Quick for Minnesota" and "Syracuse 91 Michigan 76," *Chicago Tribune*, March 20, 1981, 4:2.

74. Cooper Rollow, "Morris Leads Purdue into the Semifinal," *Chicago Tribune*, March 21, 1981, 2:2.

75. Cooper Rollow, "Purdue Falls to Syracuse, Gimpy Schayes," *Chicago Tribune*, March 24, 1981, 6:1; "Richardson Takes Tulsa to the Top," *Chicago Tribune*, March 26, 1981, 4:3.

76. Dave Condon, "Henson May Give the Illini Tourney Edge," *Chicago Tribune*, March 14, 1981, 2:1; Dave Nightingale, "Illini Topple Wyoming on Smith's Foul Shots," *Chicago Tribune*, March 15, 1981, 4:1.

77. Bill Jauss, "Indiana Thinks There's Room for Improvement," *Chicago Tribune*, March 16, 1981, 5:7.

78. Bill Jauss, "Isiah Nearly Perfect in Indiana Romp," *Chicago Tribune*, March 15, 1981, 4:3; Bob Logan, "Wichita State Ends Iowa's Dream," *Chicago Tribune*, March 16, 1981, 5:1.

79. Dave Nightingale, "Illinois Another Victim in Year of the Underdog," *Chicago Tribune*, March 20, 1981, 4:1.

80. Al McGuire, "Al McGuire," *Chicago Tribune*, March 19, 1981, 4:1; David Israel, "I'm for Indiana and Knight," *Chicago Tribune*, March 20, 1981, 4:2.

81. Bill Jauss, "Other Thomas Sparks Indiana by Ala.-Birmingham," *Chicago Tribune*, March 21, 1981, 2:1; Bill Jauss "Turner Turns into a Tiger, Indiana Roars to Finals," *Chicago Tribune*, March 23, 1981, 4:1.

82. Bill Jauss, "Absence of Isiah Can't Slow Indiana," *Chicago Tribune*, March 29, 1981, 4:1.

83. David Israel, "Just Call This NCAA Final 'the Best and the Brightest,'" *Chicago Tribune*, March 30, 1981, 4:2.

84. Knight with Hammel, *My Story*, 204.

85. Roy Damer, "7th Hoosier named Big 10 MVP," *Chicago Tribune*, April 20, 1981, 4:1.

7. The Big Ten, 1981–83

1. "Street & Smith's Pre-season Forecast," in *Street & Smith's Official Basketball Yearbook, 1981– 82*; ed. Jim O'Brien (New York: Conde Nast, 1981), 56.

2. "Cross Hurt," *Chicago Tribune*, November 12, 1981, 5:5.

3. Bill Jauss, "NU Hope to Give Foes a Pain," *Chicago Tribune*, November 13, 1981, 6:7; Bob Logan, "Iowa Will Inflict Payne on the Big 10," *Chicago Tribune*, November 20, 1981, 6:1; "Basketball: Landon Returns," *Chicago Tribune*, November 22, 1981, 4:12; Roy Damer, "Good News for Purdue," *Chicago Tribune*, November 24, 1981, 4:2.

4. Bill Jauss, "Illini Work Overtime to Hold Off Loyola," *Chicago Tribune*, November 29, 1981, 4:1; Roy Damer, "Indiana Barely Wins—to Knight's Disgust," and "2 Iowa Freshmen Show Their Value in Win over Northern Illinois," *Chicago Tribune*, November 29, 1981, 4:3; "Purdue 82 Tennessee 66," *Chicago Tribune*, November 29, 1981, 4:3.

5. Roy Damer, "Minnesota Slim Favorite in Big 10," *Chicago Tribune*, November 29, 1981, 4:7.

6. Mike Kiley, "Cross Beefs Up for Purdue Foes," *Chicago Tribune*, December 4, 1981, 6:7; Mike Kiley, "DePaul Unloads Its Depth Charge to Torpedo Purdue," *Chicago Tribune*, December 6, 1981, 4:1.

7. Roy Damer, "Louisville Sub Jumps on Purdue," *Chicago Tribune*, December 10, 1981, 5:3; "Oklahoma 80 Purdue 77," *Chicago Tribune*, December 13, 1981, 4:3.

8. "Big 10 Books Schedule That Will Add Class," *Chicago Tribune*, December 26, 1981, 2:5.

9. "Villanova Surprises Indiana in Holiday Meet," and "Sugar Bowl Tourney—Houston 59 Purdue 58," *Chicago Tribune*, December 29, 1981, 3:2; "Sugar Bowl Tourney Wake Forest 76 Purdue 68," "OSU 63 WSU 54," and "ECAC Kansas 71 Indiana 61," *Chicago Tribune*, December 30, 1981, 4:3.

10. "Pillsbury Classic—Minnesota 91 Arizona 62," *Chicago Tribune*, December 30, 1981, 4:3; Minnesota 75 Long Beach 67," and "Minnesota Guard Ruled Eligible," *Chicago Tribune*, January 3, 1982, 4:2.

11. Bill Jauss, "Big 10 Looking at 'Court' Victory by Gopher Star," *Chicago Tribune*, January 4, 1982, 6:2.

12. Bill Jauss, "Big 10 Coaches Fear Fallout on Hall Case," *Chicago Tribune*, January 7, 1982, 6:3.

13. Mike Kiley, "'New' Ohio State's Ok—Just Ask Minnesota," *Chicago Tribune*, January 8, 1982, 6:1; "Michigan St. Calls Out the Guards to Top Indiana," *Chicago Tribune*, January 8, 1982, 6:3; Roy Damer, "Boyle Makes His Point—It's Plenty for Iowa," *Chicago Tribune*, January 8, 1982, 6:3.

14. Bob Logan, "Good Knight! NU Stuffs Indiana," *Chicago Tribune*, January 10, 1982, 4:1.

15. Logan, "Good Knight!"

16. Roy Damer, "Indiana's Upset Has NU's Coach All Charged Up," *Chicago Tribune*, January 11, 1982, 4:5.

17. Mike Kiley, "Illinois Lets a Big One—Ohio State—Get Away," "Indiana Ends Mistakes, Losing Streak," and "Purdue 53 Michigan St. 47," *Chicago Tribune*, January 15, 1982, 4:3.

18. Bill Jauss, "Illini Use 'Bank Shot' for Last Minute Win," and "Indiana Ends Ohio St.'s Win Streak," *Chicago Tribune*, January 17, 1982, 4:1.

19. "Roy Damer, "Over a Lost Weekend, Illinois Finds Itself," *Chicago Tribune*, January 25, 1982, 4:14.

20. Bill Jauss, "Pass, Pick, Plunk! Kitchel and Co. Rip Illini," *Chicago Tribune*, February 12, 1982, 4:1; Roy Damer, "Indiana Shoots Past Iowa and into Big 10 Race," *Chicago Tribune*, February 14, 1982, 4:1.

21. Bob Logan, "Presto! Minnesota Turns into a Winner," *Chicago Tribune*, February 14, 1982, 4:2.

22. Bill Jauss, "College Coaches Disagree about Need for Shot Clock," *Chicago Tribune*, February 14, 1982, 4:1.

23. Roy Damer, "Illini, Tucker Lead the Way in Upsetting Big 10 Day," "Michigan Gives Iowa a Foul Feeling," and "Scearce a One-Man Gang in Purdue Victory," *Chicago Tribune*, February 21, 1982, 4:1 and 4:3.

24. "Mark Hall Hangs Up on Minnesota; Awaits Charges," *Chicago Tribune*, February 24, 1982, 4:3; Bill Jauss, "Minnesota's Hot Hands Cool Michigan," *Chicago Tribune*, February 26, 1982, 4:1; Roy Damer, "Minnesota Runs Out of Time—and Then Knocks Off Iowa," *Chicago Tribune*, February 28, 1982, 4:1.

25. Bill Jauss, "Minnesota Charges to Big 10 Lead," *Chicago Tribune*, March 5, 1982, 4:3; Bill Jauss, "Minnesota, Breuer Prove Who Is Best," *Chicago Tribune*, March 7, 1982, 4:1; Bob Logan, "'Jail the Officials!' Cries Iowa's Olson After Upset," *Chicago Tribune*, March 7, 1982, 4:3.

26. Bill Jauss, "Bradley Coach: We Deserve Bid, Indiana Doesn't," *Chicago Tribune*, March 8, 1982, 3:1.

27. Bob Logan, "That Was No Earthquake; That Was the Illini," *Chicago Tribune*, March 11, 1982, 5:1; Cooper Rollow, "Edmonson Paces Purdue NIT Win," *Chicago Tribune*, March 11, 1982, 5:2.

28. Bob Logan, "Revenge for a Reject; Illini Ousted from NIT," *Chicago Tribune*, March 16, 1982, 4:1; Cooper Rollow, "Purdue Turns on Speed, Runs Rutgers Out of NIT," *Chicago Tribune*, March 16, 1982, 4:2.

29. Bob Logan, "It's No Joke, Purdue Wins Again," *Chicago Tribune*, March 20, 1982, 4:2.

30. Bob Logan, "Purdue in NIT Final By a Hare," *Chicago Tribune*, March 23, 1982, 4:1; Bob Logan, "NIT Title Won't Just Be Consolation," *Chicago Tribune*, March 24, 1982. 4:2.

31. Bob Logan, "NIT Champion Bradley, Thirdkill, Prove the Experts Wrong," *Chicago Tribune*, March 25, 1982, 4:1; Bob Scott, "'Bradley Played Better,' Purdue's Keady Says," in *The Lafayette Journal and Courier Presents Most Memorable Moments in Purdue Basketball History* (Champaign, IL: Sports Publishing, 1998), 117–18.

32. Steve Daley, "Ohio State Learns a Painful Lesson," *Chicago Tribune*, March 12, 1982, 4:1; Bill Jauss, "Indiana Breezes in Opener," *Chicago Tribune*, March 12, 1982, 4:3; "Hansen Has a Big Hand in Iowa Win," *Chicago Tribune*, March 13, 1982, 2:3.

33. Bill Jauss, "Indiana Early KO Victim," *Chicago Tribune*, March 14, 1982, 4:1; "Idaho's Shot at Buzzer Bounces Iowa in OT," *Chicago Tribune*, March 15, 1982, 4:3.

34. Bill Jauss, "Size and Big Scorers Can't Save Minnesota," *Chicago Tribune*, March 19, 1982, 4:1.

35. "Big 10 Switches for More Money," *Chicago Tribune*, March 16, 1982, 4:2.

36. Roy Damer, "Kellogg Is MVP in Big 10," *Chicago Tribune*, April 4, 1982, 4:2.

37. "No Thanks, Wisconsin," *Chicago Tribune*, April 9, 1982, 4:2; "Eau Claire Coach Receives Wisconsin OK," *Chicago Tribune*, April 10, 1982, 2:2.

38. Ray Compton, "Young Pups Are Maturing; Indiana Rates as Top Dog," in *The Sporting News College and Pro 1982–83 Basketball Yearbook* (St. Louis: Sporting News, 1982), 76.

39. Compton, "Young Pups Are Maturing," 78.

40. Compton, "Young Pups Are Maturing," 81.

41. "9 Straight Points Late in the Game Help Soviets Beat Illini," *Chicago Tribune*, November 19, 1982, 4:4; "Basketball (Notes) PU 66 Soviets 63," *Chicago Tribune*, November 21, 1982, 4:10.

42. Bill Jauss, "Big 10 Long Shots? Not Indiana, Iowa," *Chicago Tribune*, November 28, 1982, 4:6.

43. Jauss, "Big 10 Long Shots?" 4:6.

44. "Cross, Purdue Win 5th in Row," *Chicago Tribune*, December 7, 1982, 3:3; Bill Jauss, "Indiana Stymies Paxson, Notre Dame," *Chicago Tribune*, December 8, 1982, 3:3; Bill Jauss, "Iowa Slices Marquette," *Chicago Tribune*, December 9, 1982, 4:3.

45. Bill Jauss, "Illinois and ISU: A Classic Final," *Chicago Tribune*, December 18, 1982, 2:1. "Illinois Socks It to ISU," *Chicago Tribune*, December 19, 1982, 4:1.

46. "Indiana Edges Kansas St.," *Chicago Tribune*, December 19, 1982, 4:3; Steve Daley, "UCLA Adds Iowa to List of Victims," *Chicago Tribune*, December 19, 1982, 4:3.

47. Bill Jauss, "A Fun Night for Indiana," *Chicago Tribune*, December 23, 1982, 3:1.

48. Bill Jauss, "Big Ten Preview," *Chicago Tribune*, January 6, 1983, 4:1.

49. "Michigan State Spoils Iowa Opening Night," *Chicago Tribune*, January 7, 1983, 4; Roy Damer, "NU's Defense Turns Off Michigan," *Chicago Tribune*, January 7, 1983, 4.

50. "Ohio State Trips No.1 Indiana," *Chicago Tribune*, January 9, 1983, 4:1.

51. Bob Logan, "1st in Big 10? It's NU," *Chicago Tribune*, January 9, 1983, 4:3; Bill Jauss, "The Long and Short of Things," *Chicago Tribune*, January 9, 1983, 4:3.

52. Roy Damer, "Iowa Shoots Past NU," *Chicago Tribune*, January 14, 1983, 4:1; Bill Jauss, "Indiana Gets Aid from Afar," *Chicago Tribune*, January 14, 1983, 4:3; "Ohio State Runs Afoul of Purdue Free Throws," *Chicago Tribune*, January 14, 1983, 4:3.

53. Roy Damer, "Hot Hoosiers Mean Business," *Chicago Tribune*, January 16, 1983, 4:3.

54. Bill Jauss, "Indiana Just a 'Little' Too Much," *Chicago Tribune*, January 23, 1983, 4:3.

55. Roy Damer, "Indiana Drops the Ax on Minnesota," *Chicago Tribune*, February 6, 1983, 4:3; Jerome Holtzman, "Mighty Mite Strikes," *Chicago Tribune*, February 6, 1983, 4:3.

56. Neil Milbert, "Indiana Gets Some Breathing Room," "Iowa Evens the Score," *Chicago Tribune*, February 11, 1983, 4:3.

57. "Absolute Perfection," *Chicago Tribune*, February 20, 1983, 4:1.

58. Bill Jauss, "Script for Illinois Loss Reads Like Fiction," *Chicago Tribune*, February 24, 1983, 3:1; Tom Kubat, "Boilermaker Scrub Patrol Shines in Win," in *The Lafayette Courier and Journal Presents Memorable Moments in Purdue Basketball History* (Champaign, IL: Sports Publishing, 1998), 119–20.

59. "Indiana Shot Down," *Chicago Tribune*, February 25, 1983, 4:1; "Ohio State Falls in 3 Overtimes," *Chicago Tribune*, February 25, 1983, 4:3; "Indiana's Backed into a Corner," *Chicago Tribune*, February 26, 1983, 2:1; "Ohio State Ties Indiana for Conference Lead," *Chicago Tribune*, February 27, 1983, 4:2.

60. Bill Jauss, "Illini's Douglas Comes of Age," *Chicago Tribune*, March 4, 1983, 4:1; Bob Logan, "Indiana Devours Purdue," *Chicago Tribune*, March 4, 1983, 4:1.

61. Bob Logan, "Ringing Up a Title," *Chicago Tribune*, March 6, 1983, 4:1; Bill Jauss, "Indiana Listens to Blab's Call," *Chicago Tribune*, March 13, 1983, 4:1.

62. Bill Jauss, "NCAA Meet Has a Definite Big 10 Look," *Chicago Tribune*, March 14, 1983, 4:1.

63. Mike Kiley, "DePaul's Cookin' at Home," *Chicago Tribune*, March 17, 1983, 3:1; Bill Jauss, "NU Paints Irish Purple," *Chicago Tribune*, March 18, 1983, 4:1; "Willis Stands Tall in Michigan St. Win," *Chicago Tribune*, March 19, 1983, 2:2; Mike Kiley, "It's DePaul by Long Shot," *Chicago Tribune*, March 22, 1983, 4:1; "Michigan St. Freezes so Fresno St. Breezes," *Chicago Tribune*, March 22, 1983, 4:3.

64. "Utah Sends Illinois Packing," *Chicago Tribune*, March 18, 1983, 4:1; Mike Kiley, "Purdue Can't Be Caught," *Chicago Tribune*, March 18, 1983, 4:3; Mike Kiley, "Crime Pays for Arkansas," *Chicago Tribune*, March 20, 1983, 4:3; Gene Keady with Jeff Washburn, *The Truth and Nothing but the Truth* (Champaign, IL: Sports Publishing, 2005), 46.

65. Roy Damer, "Iowa Shoots Past Utah St," *Chicago Tribune*, March 19, 1983, 2:3; Roy Damer, "Iowa's Big Is Clearly Better," *Chicago Tribune*, March 21, 1983, 3:1.

66. "Ohio St. Victory an Inside Job," *Chicago Tribune*, March 21, 1983, 3:3; Bob Logan, "North Carolina, Georgia Stay Alive," *Chicago Tribune*, March 26, 1983, 2:1.

67. Bill Jauss, "Indiana Getting Defensive," *Chicago Tribune*, March 21, 1983, 3:3; "Kentucky Rules Out Indiana," *Chicago Tribune*, March 25, 1983, 4:1.

68. Skip Mylenski, "Big 10 to Fill the Basket with Even More Bread," *Chicago Tribune*, March 29, 1983, 4:3.

69. Mylenski, "Big 10 to Fill the Basket," 4:3.

70. Roy Damer, "Stunned Hawkeyes Understand," and "George Raveling Is New Iowa Coach," *Chicago Tribune*, April 5, 1983, 4:2.

71. "News—No Shot Clock or 3 Point Shot Nationally," *Chicago Tribune*, April 7, 1983, 4:7.

72. "Big Ten Coaches Take the Air Out of 3-Pointer," *Chicago Tribune*. April 29, 1983, 4:4; "A.D.s Vote to Drop 3 Pointers and No Shot Clock," *Detroit News*, May 12, 1983, 3-E.

73. "Brad Sellers (WI) Will Transfer," *Chicago Tribune*, April 16, 1983, 2:4.

74. Roy Damer, "Valuable Piece of Property," *Chicago Tribune*, April 22, 1983, 4:3.

8. Rules and Referees

1. This matter is more fully discussed in Murry R. Nelson, "Three-Point Shot," in *American Sports; A History of Icons, Idols and Ideas*, ed. Murry R. Nelson (Santa Barbara: Greenwood, 2013), 1340–42. Much more on the ABL's short life can be found in Murry R. Nelson, *Abe Saperstein and the American Basketball League, 1960–63* (Jefferson, NC: McFarland, 2013).

2. Bob Knight with Bob Hammel, *Knight: My Story* (New York, St. Martin's Press, 2002), 208.

3. Steve Alford with John Garrity, *Playing for Knight* (New York: Simon & Schuster, 1989), 253.

4. "Survey Draws the Line: 3-Point Shot Will Stay," *Chicago Tribune*, March 27, 1987, 4:7.

5. Robert Markus, "3-Point Shot Stays, but Length May Vary," *Chicago Tribune*, April 2, 1987, 4:8.

6. "A.D.s Vote to Drop 3-Pointers and No Shot Clock," *Detroit News*, May 12, 1983, 3-E.

7. "Big 10 Approves Shot Clock," *Chicago Tribune*, April 26, 1984, 4:9.

8. Sam Smith, "NCAA Goes for the 3-Pointer," *Chicago Tribune*, April 3, 1986, 4:1.

9. Bill Halls, "Cold Michigan Cagers Edge Frigid Badgers," *Detroit News*, January 9, 1977, D1.

10. Some colleges began using three referees in the mid-1960s, but this was done on a conference-by-conference basis until the entire NBA adopted the procedure, and the NCAA adopted it shortly after that.

11. Roy Damer, "NU Coach Blasts 3 Big 10 Officials for Pounding Lumps on Wildcats," *Chicago Tribune*, December 7, 1978, 4:3; "Taylor Wants End to System of 3 Referees," *Chicago Tribune*, February 22, 1973, 3:4.

12. Bob Logan, "Jail the Officials! Cries Iowa's Olson after Upset," *Chicago Tribune*, December 7, 1981, 4:3.

13 "Big 10 Plans Review of Iowa's Complaint," *Chicago Tribune*, March 8, 1982, 3:10.

14. "Ref Admits Called Wrong Foul in Iowa-Purdue Game," *Chicago Tribune*, April 13, 1983, 3:7.

15. Bill Jauss, "NU Topples U. of C," *Chicago Tribune*, December 9, 1984, 3:3.

16. "Knight Ejected during Indiana Loss," *Chicago Tribune*, February 24, 1985, 4:3. Two technicals led to his ejection, but Knight acted so swiftly that he managed to achieve the third before he left the game.

17. Mike Conklin, "Apologetic Knight May Be Penalized," *Chicago Tribune*, February 25, 1985, 3:5.

18. "Knight Banned One Game," *Chicago Tribune*, March 3, 1985, 4:3.

19. Cooper Rollow, "Indiana Stays Alive in 2 Overtimes," *Chicago Tribune*, March 25, 1985, 4:10.

20. Bill Jauss, "Indiana Finally Wins at Home," *Chicago Tribune*, January 16, 1986, 4:3.

21. Bob Logan, "Iowa Fails to Net Iowa in Trap," *Chicago Tribune*, March 3, 1986, 2:3.

22. Bob Logan, "6 Officials in Big 10 Face the Ax," *Chicago Tribune*, April 12, 1986, 4:3.

23 Logan, "6 Officials in Big 10 Face the Ax," 4:3.

24. "T Time in Indiana: Bobby Calls Quick Foul on Officials," *Chicago Tribune*, November 13, 1986, 4:2.

25. Fred Mitchell, "Ailing Indiana Chills Purdue," *Chicago Tribune*, February 1, 1987, 3:1.

26. Robert Markus, "Big 10 Officials React to Calls against Them," *Chicago Tribune*, February 27, 1989, 3:4.

27. "Ohio State Escapes Scare at Home," *Chicago Tribune*, February 24, 1991, 3:3; Skip Mylenski, "Indiana Tops MSU in the 4th Dimension," *Chicago Tribune*, March 1, 1991, 4:3.

28. Knight with Hammel, *Knight*, 179.

29. Ed Sherman, "Stiffer Penalties Sought for Abusing Big 10 Refs," *Chicago Tribune*, March 3, 1991, 3:6.

30. "NCAA Adopts no Jump Ball Rule," *Chicago Tribune*, April 3, 1981, 4:4.

31. Skip Mylenski, "We've Only Seen the Tip of the Jump-Ball Controversy," *Chicago Tribune*, February 7, 1982, 4:1.

9. The Big Ten in the Mid-1980s

1. Peter Kendall, "Penn State Has Plenty to Offer the Big 10," *Chicago Tribune*, December 15, 1989, 4:1.

2. "Big Ten Didn't Exactly Warmly Welcome MSU," *Chicago Tribune*, December 15, 1989, 4:7.

3. Ed Sherman, "Penn State Will Ease into the Big 10," *Chicago Tribune*, December 16, 1989, 2:1; Ed Sherman, "Pitt, Rutgers Next in Line for Big 10?," *Chicago Tribune*, December 19, 1989; Ed Sherman, "Looks Like Penn State Won't Count in Big 10," *Chicago Tribune*, December 20, 1989, 4:1.

4. "Atlantic 10 May Boot Penn State," *Chicago Tribune*, December 22, 1989, 4:2.

5. John Coyle, personal interview with author, June 21, 1989, State College, PA. Coyle was Penn State's faculty athletic representative from 1970 to 2000.

6. Ron Smith, *Wounded Lions; Joe Paterno, Jerry Sandusky and the Crises in Penn State Athletics* (Urbana: University of Illinois Press, 2016), 92.

7. Skip Mylenski, "On College Basketball," *Chicago Tribune*, Janaury 12, 1990, 4:3.

8. Coyle interview.

9. Smith, *Wounded Lions*, 94.

10. Coyle interview.

11. Smith, *Wounded Lions*, 95.

12. Smith, *Wounded Lions*, 95.

13. Smith, *Wounded Lions*, 96.

14. Brad Faldute, "Shalala Expects Council of Ten Will OK Addition of Penn State," *Wisconsin Capital Times*, May 31, 1990 clipping, President Thomas Papers, Box 10435, Folder "Big Ten Con.," Penn State University Archives; quoted in Smith, *Wounded Lions*, 97.

15. Ed Sherman, "Opposition to Penn St. Still Strong in Big 10," *Chicago Tribune*, April 15, 1990, 3:9.

16. "Briefs," *Chicago Tribune*, April 19, 1990, 4:2.

17. Smith, *Wounded Lions*, 99.

18. Smith, *Wounded Lions*, 99.

19. "Big 10 BB Schedule," *Chicago Tribune*, November 2, 1983, 4:6.

20. *Sporting News* poll, *Chicago Tribune*, October, 4, 1983, 4:5.

21. "AP Top 20," *Chicago Tribune*, November 17, 1983, 4:6.

22. Robert Markus, "Coaches Like Iowa, Mich. St," *Chicago Tribune*, November 21, 1983, 4:12.

23. Robert Markus, "Miami Upsets Indiana's Schedule," *Chicago Tribune*, November 27, 1983, 3:4.

24. Mike Conklin, "Sharp Illinois Settles a Score with Utah," *Chicago Tribune*, November 26, 1983, 2:1.

25. Conklin, "Miami Upsets Indiana's Schedule"; Steve Alford with John Garrity, *Playing for Knight* (New York: Simon and Schuster,1989), 36.

26. Robert Markus, "MSU, Iowa Rate 1-2 in Big Ten Chase," *Chicago Tribune*, November 27, 1983, 3:4.

27. Mike Conklin, "The Illini Can't Wait for Winter," *Chicago Tribune*, November 27, 1983, 3:4.

28. Mike Conlkin, "Welch Out of Illini Plans," *Chicago Tribune*, November 28, 1983, 4.

29. Mike Conklin, "Purdie Guard Ricky Hall Leads Upset of Louisville," *Chicago Tribune*, December 4, 1983, 3:3.

30. "Kentucky Squeezes by Indiana," *Chicago Tribune*, December 4, 1983, 6:3.

31. "Unbeaten Michigan Stuns Georgia," *Chicago Tribune*, December 6, 1983, 4:3.

32. "Indiana Classic," *Chicago Tribune*, December 18, 1983, 3:2. "Hoosier Classic," *Chicago Tribune*, December 31, 1983, 4:3; "Texas-El Paso Dump Michigan," *Chicago Tribune*, December 28, 1983, 4:3; "Sun Bowl Tournament," *Chicago Tribune*, December 29, 1983, 4:3.

33 "Purdue 65 Youngstown St. 54," *Chicago Tribune*, December 18, 1983, 3:2; Mike Kiley, "Purdue Suffers 1st Loss," *Chicago Tribune*, December 20, 1983, 4:2.

34. Mike Conklin, "Kentucky Ices Illini," *Chicago Tribune*, December 25, 1983, 4:3.

35. "Texas-El Paso Dumps Michigan," *Chicago Tribune*, December 28, 1983, 4:3; Bill Jauss, "Kentucky Overwhelms Purdue," and "Sun Bowl Tournament," *Chicago Tribune*, December 29, 1983, 4:3.

36. Roy Damer, "Michigan St. Slips by Iowa," *Chicago Tribune*, January 5, 1984, 4:1.

37. Mike Conklin, "A Rosy Opener," *Chicago Tribune*, January 6, 1984, 4:1; "Rowinski, Purdue Rip Wisconsin," *Chicago Tribune*, January 6, 1984, 4:3; Roy Damer, "NU Gets Lost Again," *Chicago Tribune*, January 6, 1984, 4:3.

38. Mike Conklin, "Illini Escape Wisconsin in Overtime," *Chicago Tribune*, January 8, 1984, 3:1.

39. Roy Damer, "Berg, Northwestern shock Michigan St.," *Chicago Tribune*, January 8, 1984, 3:1.

40. Mike Conklin, "Absentees Costly to Big 10 Teams," *Chicago Tribune*, January 14, 1984, 2:3; Roy Damer, "Purdue Sneaks Past a Stunned Indiana," *Chicago Tribune*, January 15, 1984, 4:1; Steve Alford with John Garrity, *Playing for Knight* (New York: Simon & Schuster, 1989), 51.

41. Mike Kiley, "Overtime Work Pays Off for Indiana," *Chicago Tribune*, January 20, 1984, 4:3.

42. Mike Conklin, "Illini Shot Down, but Stay on Top," *Chicago Tribune*, February 17, 1984, 4:1; "Bobby, Nobody's Perfect," "MSU 63 Purdue 53," *Chicago Tribune*, February 17, 1984, 4:3.

43 Mike Conklin, "Heavy Traffic," *Chicago Tribune*, February 28, 1984, 4:7; Mike Conklin, "It's the Cut of the Stat," *Chicago Tribune*, February 29, 1984, 4:1.

44. Mike Conklin, "Purdue Elects to Tighten Race," *Chicago Tribune*, March 1, 1984, 4:1.

45. Mike Conklin, "Illini landslide," *Chicago Tribune*, March 5, 1984, 4:1.

46. Mike Conklin, "Illini Hope Refs Won't Take Over," *Chicago Tribune*, March 14, 1984, 4:2. "Alford Named Big 10 Freshman of Year," *Chicago Tribune*, March 15, 1984, 4:2.

47. "Michigan Rolls, Ohio State Falls," *Chicago Tribune*, March 16, 1984, 4:2.

48. Cooper Rollow, "Michigan Tops Irish in NIT," *Chicago Tribune*, March 29, 1984, 4:1.

49. "Time for a Clock," *Chicago Tribune*, March 30, 1984, 4:2; "NCAA Stalls on Shot Clock," *Chicago Tribune*, April 5, 1984, 4:2.

50. Bob Logan, "Memphis State Shackles Purdue," *Chicago Tribune*, March 18, 1984, 4:1; Don Pierson, "Alford Sets Indiana Free at Foul Line," *Chicago Tribune*, March 18, 1984, 4:3.

51. Mike Conklin, "Illini Beat Jitters, Drill Villanova," *Chicago Tribune*, March 19, 1984, 4:3.

52. Don Pierson, "This Morning, Indiana Is Finer," *Chicago Tribune*, March 23, 1984, 4:1.

53 Mike Conklin, "Illini Stay Alive, May Lose Winter," *Chicago Tribune*, March 23, 1984, 4:1. Mike Conklin, "All Illini Get Is Heartbreak," *Chicago Tribune*, March 25, 1984, 4:1; Don Pierson, "Against All Odds, Virginia in Final 4," *Chicago Tribune*, March 25, 1984, 4:1; Mike Kiley, "Knight: It's My Fault," *Chicago Tribune*, March 25, 1984, 4:2.

54. Bob Knight with Bob Hammel, *Knight: My Story* (New York: Thomas Dunne, 2002), 239.

55. "Big 10 Approves Shot Clock," *Chicago Tribune*, April 26, 1984, 4:9.

56. Mike Conklin, "Sterling Effort," *Chicago Tribune*, May 20, 1984, 4:5.

57. "Heathcote at Home," *Chicago Tribune*, October 12, 1984, 4:2.

58. Mike Conklin, "Some Added Ingredients," *Chicago Tribune*, November 18, 1984, 3:1; Mike Conklin, "Beefed-up Big 10 Set for a Gold Medal Year," *Chicago Tribune*, November 18, 1984, 3:8.

59. Rich Lorenz, "Knight Skips Big 10 Meeting," *Chicago Tribune*, November 19, 1984, 4:3.

60. "No. 400 Easy for Knight," *Chicago Tribune*, December 9, 1984, 3:3.

61. "Boston College Ends Mich. St. Winning Streak," *Chicago Tribune*, December 29, 1984, 2:3; "Tennessee 81 Michigan 77," and "Hoosier Classic," *Chicago Tribune*, December 30, 1984, 4:7; "Roundup," *Chicago Tribune*, December 31, 1984, 2:8.

62. "Indiana by a Landslide," *Chicago Tribune*, January 3, 1985, 4:3; "Illinois is Off and . . . Oops," *Chicago Tribune*, January 4, 1985, 4:1.

63 "Guards Spark Iowa," *Chicago Tribune*, January 4, 1985, 4:3; Mike Conklin, "Iowa Makes Illinois Look Sick," "Unforeseen Star Upends Indiana," *Chicago Tribune*, January 6, 1985, 6:4.

64. "Minnesota 81 Michigan State 75," and "Purdue 72 Wisconsin 68," *Chicago Tribune*, January 20, 1985, 4:8.

65. Mike Conklin, "Purdue Puts a Lid on Indiana," and "Michigan 86 Michigan State 75," *Chicago Tribune*, January 25, 1985, 4:1 and 4:3.

66. Knight with Hammel, *Knight*, 240.

67. "Hey, Bobby, Did You Know Alford's Gonna Start?," *Chicago Tribune*, January 31, 1985, 4:1. Giomi announced that he would transfer the next day and he did, subsequently, to North Carolina State; Alford with Garrity, *Playing for Knight*, 158.

68. Mike Conklin, "Iowa Dumps the A-Team," *Chicago Tribune*, February 1, 1985, 4:1.

69. Mike Conklin, "Illini Reach a New Low," *Chicago Tribune*, January 31, 1985, 4:1.

70. "Wisconsin Surprises Iowa," *Chicago Tribune*, February 21, 1985, 4:3; Bob Logan, "NU Leaves Iowa, Raveling in Shock," *Chicago Tribune*, February 24, 1985, 4:1; Mike Conklin, "Illinois Bombs Indiana's Best," *Chicago Tribune*, February 22, 1985, 4:1; "Knight Ejected during Indiana Loss," *Chicago Tribune*, February 24, 1985, 4:3.

71. Chad Carlson, *Making March Madness, the Early Years of the NCAA, NIT and College Basketball Championships, 1922–1951* (Fayetteville: University of Arkansas Press, 2017), 315.

72. "Indiana Rolls into Title Game," *Chicago Tribune*, March 28, 1985, 4:3; Mike Conklin, "UCLA Is a Champ Once More," *Chicago Tribune*, March 30, 1985, 2:1.

73 "Klein, Arkansas Defense Knock Out Iowa," *Chicago Tribune*, March 15, 1985, 4:2; Phil Hersh, "Auburn Alive and Well—Just Ask Purdue," *Chicago Tribune*, March 15, 1985, 4:3.

74. Reid Hanley, "Seniors Give Ohio State a Well-Guarded Triumph," *Chicago Tribune*, March 15, 1985, 4:3; Robert Markus, "Illinois Satisfies Its Tourney Hunger," *Chicago Tribune*, March 16, 1985, 2:1; Mike Conklin, "Michigan Survives, Somehow," *Chicago Tribune*, March 16, 1985, 2:2.

75. "Michigan State Tumbles to Alabama-Birmingham," *Chicago Tribune*, March 16, 1985, 2:2.

76. Mike Conklin, "Michigan Falls to Villanova," *Chicago Tribune*, March 18, 1985, 4:3.

77. Robert Markus, "Surging Illini in Final 16," *Chicago Tribune*, March 18, 1985, 4:1.

78. "One-Man Show for Illini Not Enough," *Chicago Tribune*, March 22, 1985, 4:1. Ultimately, the Big East had three of the four Final Four teams: Georgetown, Villanova, and St. John's.

79. Phil Hersh, "Falk Ponders His Future at Northwestern," *Chicago Tribune*, March 14, 1985, 4:3; "Knight's New Strategy," *Chicago Tribune*, April 2, 1985, 4:2; "NCAA Rules Committee Voted to Adopt 45-Second Clock," *Chicago Tribune*, April 3, 1985, 4:2.

80. Shon Morris email to the author, January 12, 2020. Tarpley was the #7 selection in the 1986 NBA draft and won the Sixth Man Award from the NBA in 1988, but he was banned from the league in December 1995 for violating his court-ordered after-care program and using alcohol. He died of liver failure in 2015 at the age of fifty.

81. "Street & Smith's All America," in *Street and Smith's Basketball Official Yearbook*, ed. Jim O'Brien (New York: Conde Nast 1985), 18.

82. Bob Logan, "Michigan, Illinois Lead the Conference's Better Half," *Chicago Tribune*, November 17, 1985, 4:6.

83 Jody Homer, "No Knight at Big 10 Media Show," *Chicago Tribune*, November 18, 1985, 3:6.

84. "College Roundup," *Chicago Tribune*, November 30, 1985, 2:3; "Oklahoma Jars Illini in Final Seconds," *Chicago Tribune*, December 1, 1985, 4:2.

85. "Michigan Bumps Past Ga.Tech," *Chicago Tribune*, December 1, 1985, 4:3; "Rice's Surge Saves Michigan Victory," *Chicago Tribune*, December 3, 1985, 4:3.

86. "Alford Suspended for a Game," *Chicago Tribune*, December 7, 1985, 2:2; "Kentucky Overcomes Indiana," *Chicago Tribune*, December 8, 1985, 4:3; "Knight Faults NCAA, Not Rule," *Chicago Tribune*, December 9, 1985, 3:2.

87. "Iowa State 74 Iowa 61," and "Tennessee Topples Illinois," *Chicago Tribune*, December 11, 1985, 4:3; "Wagner Leads Louisville Past Indiana," *Chicago Tribune*, December 19, 1985, 4:3.

88. "Indiana 87 Idaho 82," and "Michigan State 93 Massachusetts 45," *Chicago Tribune*, December 28, 1985, 2:3; "Indiana 74 Mississippi 43," and "Michigan State 76 New Mexico 61," *Chicago Tribune*, December 29, 1985, 4:3.

89. "Purdue 67 Lamar 56," and "Colleges," *Chicago Tribune*, December 28, 1985, 2:3; "Purdue 84 Santa Clara 56," and "Princeton 54 Wisconsin 49," *Chicago Tribune*, December 29, 1985, 4:3.

90. Bill Jauss, "Michigan Edges Indiana," *Chicago Tribune*, January 3, 1986, 4:1; Jody Homer, "Perfect Illinois Routs Minnesota," *Chicago Tribune*, January 3, 1986, 4:3.

91. "Minnesota Shocks Michigan," *Chicago Tribune*, January 17, 1986, 4:1.

92. "Indiana Feels Lost at Home," *Chicago Tribune*, January 6, 1986, 3:8; "Indiana Loses Guard Brooks," *Chicago Tribune*, January 9, 1986, 4:2; Knight with Hammel, *Knight*, 246.

93 Steve Perlstein, ed., *Gopher Glory* (Minneapolis: Layers, 1985), 117.

94. Lynn Henning, "Embarrassment Got to Dutcher," *Detroit News*, January 31, 1986, 7C.

95. "Minnesota Back on Practice Floor," *Chicago Tribune*, January 27, 1986, 4:3; "Minnesota Will Play Out Season," *Chicago Tribune*, January 28, 1986, 4:3; "2 Kick in at Minnesota," *Chicago Tribune*, January 29, 1986, 4:3; Mike Kiley, "Gophers Suspend 2 More," *Chicago Tribune*, January 30, 1986, 4:1; "It's a Sweet Victory for Minnesota," *Chicago Tribune*, January 31, 1986, 4:1.

96. Mike Kiley, "Minnesota Moves Away from Low-Grade Image," *Chicago Tribune*, February 2, 1986, 4:4.

97. "Miller, Ohio State Part Ways," *Chicago Tribune*, February 4, 1986, 4:2; "I Was Fired, Miller Says," *Chicago Tribune*, February 5, 1986, 4:3.

98. "Short-Term Deal at Ohio State," *Chicago Tribune*, February 8, 1986, 2:2.

99. "Knight Staying at Indiana," *Chicago Tribune*, February 13, 1986, 4:2.

100. "Skiles Scorches Illini," *Chicago Tribune*, February 7, 1986, 4:1.

101. "Michigan on Target for Consecutive Titles," *Chicago Tribune*, February 5, 1986, 4:3; Bob Logan, "Michigan Has a Tough Time," *Chicago Tribune*, February 7, 1986, 4:3.

102. "Michigan Guards Keep Iowa at Bay," *Chicago Tribune*, February 16, 1986, 4:4.

103 Bob Logan, "Michigan Rolls to Big 10 Title," *Chicago Tribune*, March 9, 1986, 4:1.

104. Jody Homer, "Hard Work Helps Skiles to Big 10 MVP," *Chicago Tribune*, April 28, 1986, 3:4.

105. Shon Morris email to the author, January 12, 2020.

106. "Illini's Douglas Honored," *Chicago Tribune*, April 24, 1986, 4:2.

107. "NIT Roundup," *Chicago Tribune*, March 18, 1986, 4:2. "Ohio State in Garden party," *Chicago Tribune*, March 22, 1986, 2:1. "Ohio St., Wyoming in Final," *Chicago Tribune*, March 25, 1986, 4:2; "Ohio State Sends Miller Out a Champ," *Chicago Tribune*, March 27, 1986, 4:2; "Ohio State Gets BC Coach," *Chicago Tribune*, March 16, 1986, 4:13.

108. Bob Logan, "Purdue Boils over Pairings," *Chicago Tribune*, March 10, 1986, 3:1; Gene Keady with Jeff Washburn, *The Truth and Nothing but the Truth* (Champaign: Sports Publishing LLC, 2005), 62–63.

109. "LSU Staggers Purdue in 2 OTs," *Chicago Tribune*, March 4, 1986, 4:3.

110. "Michigan State Wins on Skiles' Free Throws," *Chicago Tribune*, March 14, 1986, 4:3; Bill Jauss, "Indiana Bumped Off," *Chicago Tribune*, March 15, 1986, 2:3; Robert Markus, "Welch, Illini Fend off Fairfield," *Chicago Tribune*, March 15, 1986, 2:3; Bob Logan, "N.C. State Walks

by Faltering Iowa," *Chicago Tribune*, March 15, 1986, 2:3; Bob Logan, "Sluggish Michigan Zaps Stubborn Akron," *Chicago Tribune*, March 15, 1986, 2:3.

111. "MSU Shocks Georgetown," *Chicago Tribune*, March 16, 1986, 4:3.

112. Robert Markus, "Illini, Michigan Get the Boot," *Chicago Tribune*, March 17, 1986, 3:1.

113 "Michigan St. Fails in OT," *Chicago Tribune*, March 22, 1986, 2:1.

114. Bill Jauss, "NU Basketball Job Rejected: 'I Don't Do Miracles,'" *Chicago Tribune*, April 2, 1986, 4:2; Bill Jauss, "NU Picks a Coach," *Chicago Tribune*, April 5, 1986, 2:1.

115. "Iowa's Raveling among Coaches Traveling," *Chicago Tribune*, March 28, 1986, 4:3. "Minnesota Hires Clem Haskins," *Chicago Tribune*, April 2, 1986, 4:1; "Friday Briefs," *Chicago Tribune*, April 4, 1986, 4:1; "No Surprise: Iowa Hires Davis," *Chicago Tribune*, April 7, 1986, 3:8.

116. "Wisconsin Coach Dealt a Reprimand," *Chicago Tribune*, April 23, 1986, 4:2.

117. Sam Smith, "Strange Doings in the Collegiate Ranks," *Chicago Tribune*, March 30, 1986, 4:3.

10. Ending the 1980s: The Big Ten Renewal

1. "Big 10 Nets ESPN for Basketball: ABC May Be Next Catch," *Chicago Tribune*, May 6, 1986, 4:3.

2. "Friday Briefs," *Chicago Tribune*, May 9, 1986, 2:4.

3. Shon Morris email to the author, January 12, 2020.

4. Bob Logan, "It's Il to the Illini or Reno for NIU's Battle," *Chicago Tribune*, May 11, 1986, 4:9; "NIU's Battle Chooses Illinois," *Chicago Tribune*, May 15, 1986, 4:2.

5. Jerry Schnay, "Illinois Nets Kings' Liberty," *Chicago Tribune*, November 7, 1986, 4:1.

6. Bob Hammel, *Beyond the Brink with Indiana* (Bloomington: Bloomington Herald-Telephone and Indiana University Press, 1987), 14.

7. "Darryl Thomas Returns to Help Indiana Squeak Past Soviets," *Chicago Tribune*, November 16, 1986, 4:13; Jody Homer, "Thomas: Great to Be Back in Indiana Lineup," *Chicago Tribune*, November 17, 1986, 3:4.

8. "Soviets Hold Off Iowa in Exhibition," *Chicago Tribune*, November 17, 1986, 3:4. Marciulionis, a Lithuanian, starred on the 1988 Soviet Gold Medal team at the Olympics in Seoul, for the bronze-medal winning Lithuanian teams in 1992 in Barcelona, and in 1996 in Atlanta. He played in the NBA from 1989 to 1997 and was voted into the Naismith Basketball Hall of Fame in 2014.

9. Neil Milbert, "5-Year Rides Suggested in Big 10," *Chicago Tribune*, November 17, 1986, 3:3; "Odds and Ends," *Chicago Tribune*, November 20, 1986, 4:2.

10. "Albeck's Debut Mangled by Michigan," *Chicago Tribune*, November 22, 1986, 2:2; "Memphis State Ousts Michigan in NIT 2d Round," *Chicago Tribune*, November 25, 1986, 4:7.

11. "Blackwell Rallies Illinois Past Duke," *Chicago Tribune*, December 1, 1986, 3:3.

12. "3-Pointers Power Maine over Mich. St," *Chicago Tribune*, December 5, 1986, 4:3.

13. Hammel, *Beyond the Brink*, 8.

14. Jody Homer, "Indiana Tip Kentucky, Chapman," *Chicago Tribune*, December 7, 1986, 4:6.

15. "Illini Hold on to Beat Pitt," *Chicago Tribune*, December 7, 1986, 4:8.

16. "Vanderbilt Comeback Staggers Indiana," *Chicago Tribune*, December 10, 1986, 4:1; Robert Markus, "Moe's 28 Carry Iowa over BYU," *Chicago Tribune*, December 10, 1986, 4:3.

17. W. Michigan Topples Michigan," "Purdue 77 Wichita State 61," *Chicago Tribune*, December 9, 1986, 4:7.

18. Jody Homer, "Illini Run Down by N. Carolina," *Chicago Tribune*, December 21, 1986, 3:1; Jody Homer, "No. 9 Illini Humbled by Loyola," *Chicago Tribune*, December 28, 1986, 3:1.

19. "North Carolina Topples Purdue," *Chicago Tribune*, December 30, 1986, 4:1.

20. Jody Homer, "Blackwell's Magic Lifts Illini," *Chicago Tribune*, January 4, 1987, 4:1. "Minnesota Gives Haskins 1st Big 10 Win," *Chicago Tribune*, January 4, 1987, 4:3.

21. "Purdue 87 Michigan State 72," "Iowa 80 Northwestern 44," *Chicago Tribune*, January 4, 1987, 3:3.

22. "Indiana's Alford Blunts Ohio State Rally," *Chicago Tribune*, January 5, 1987, 4:4.

23. Steve Alford with John Garrity, *Playing for Knight* (New York: Simon & Schuster, 1989), 258.

24. "Alford Rescues Indiana," *Chicago Tribune*, January 13, 1987, 4:3; Jody Homer, "Iowa Rally Stuns Illinois," *Chicago Tribune*, January 15, 1987, 4:1.

25. Robert Markus, "Iowa Wears Its No.1 Well," *Chicago Tribune*, January 20, 1987, 4:1; Jody Homer, "Iowa's Road Power Impresses Coaches," *Chicago Tribune*, January 21, 1987, 4:3.

26. Robert Markus, "Iowa Battles to Big 10 Lead," *Chicago Tribune*, January 23, 1987, 4:1.

27. Hammel, *Beyond the Brink*, 49–50; John Laskowski with Stan Sutton, *Tales from the Indiana Locker Room* (New York: Sports Publishing), 123.

28. Jody Homer, "Tough Indiana Defense Blocks Illini," "*Chicago Tribune*, January 29, 1987, 4:1; Fred Mitchell, "Purdue Rips Ohio State," *Chicago Tribune*, January 30, 1987, 4:1; "Iowa Strikes Early to Top Michigan State," *Chicago Tribune*, January 30, 1987, 4:3.

29. Fred Mitchell, "Ailing Indiana Chills Purdue," *Chicago Tribune*, February 1, 1987, 3:1; Jody Homer, "Rice, Michigan Thunder Past Iowa," *Chicago Tribune*, February 1, 1987, 3:6.

30. Jody Homer, "Illinois Rushes Past Ohio St.," *Chicago Tribune*, February 3, 1987, 4:1.

31. Bill Jauss, "Big 10 Coaches Say 6 Belong in Tourney," *Chicago Tribune*, February 4, 1987, 4:3.

32. "Alford's 42 Lifts Indiana Past Mich. St.," "Iowa 78 Minnesota 47," *Chicago Tribune*, February 5, 1987, 4:8. "Mitchell Rallies Purdue Past Wisconsin," and "Ohio State 95 Michigan 87," *Chicago Tribune*, February 6, 1987, 4:3.

33. "Indiana's Alford Shoots Back on Michigan," *Chicago Tribune*, February 9, 1987, 3:3; "Hopson's 34 Paces Ohio St.," *Chicago Tribune*, February 10, 1987, 4:3.

34. Mike Kiley, "NU Frustrates, Falls to Indiana," *Chicago Tribune*, February 12, 1987, 4:1.

35. "Indiana Needs 3 OTs to Subdue Wisconsin," *Chicago Tribune*, February 17, 1987, 4:1; "Another Squeaker for Indiana," *Chicago Tribune*, February 20, 1987, 4:3.

36. Robert Markus, "Purdue Triumphs," *Chicago Tribune*, February 27, 1987, 4:1; "Iowa Sets School Mark with No. 24," *Chicago Tribune*, February 27, 1987, 4:3.

37. Bob Logan, "Purdue Free Throws Hold Off Ohio State," *Chicago Tribune*, March 1, 1987, 3:7. "Iowa Snaps Michigan's Mastery," and "Michigan State 77 Minnesota 67," *Chicago Tribune*, March 1, 1987, 3:8; Jody Homer, "Illini Bend, Don't Break This Time," *Chicago Tribune*, March 2, 1987, 3:1.

38. Robert Markus, "Purdue Clinches Big 10 Title Tie," *Chicago Tribune*, March 5, 1987, 4:1; Jody Homer, "Illini Play Full Time, Work over Michigan," *Chicago Tribune*, March 5, 1987, 4:7; Bill Jauss, "Iowa Strength Overpowers NU," *Chicago Tribune*, March 6, 1987, 4:1.

39. Robert Markus, "Purdue Routed by Michigan," *Chicago Tribune*, March 8, 1987, 3:1; Bill Jauss, "Calloway's Late Steal Helps Save Indiana," *Chicago Tribune*, March 8, 1987, 3:8.

40. Jody Homer, "It's Tough on Illini Who Could Only Sit, Wait," *Chicago Tribune*, March 10, 1987, 4:1.

41. Jody Homer, "Illinois Spoils Big 10 Party," "Indiana Waltzes Past Punchless Fairfield," and "Michigan Outguns the Navy," *Chicago Tribune*, March 13, 1987, 4:1.

42. "Kentucky Humbled by Hopson," and "For Iowa, an Opener to Savor," *Chicago Tribune*, March 14, 1987, 2:1; Bill Jauss, "Purdue Beats Northeastern to the Punch," *Chicago Tribune*, March 14, 1987, 2:3.

43. Mike Kiley, "Indiana Surge Chills Auburn," *Chicago Tribune*, March 15, 1987, 3:1; "North Carolina Comes Out Smoking, Then Holds Off Michigan," *Chicago Tribune*, March 15, 1987, 3:5.

44. Bill Jauss, "Florida Surge Ousts Purdue," *Chicago Tribune*, March 16, 1987, 3:1; Michael Perry, "Gators Chew Boilers Defense," *Lafayette Journal and Courier Presents Most Memorable Moments in Purdue Basketball History* (Champaign, IL: Sports Publishing, 1998), 150. Robert Markus, "Georgetown Survival Course," *Chicago Tribune*, March 16, 1987, 3:6.

45. Sam Smith, "Iowa Uses Bomb Squad to Overcome Texas-El Paso," *Chicago Tribune*, March 16, 1987, 3:6; "Briefs: Davis Named Big 10 Coach of the Year," *Chicago Tribune*, March 18, 1987, 4:2.

46. Hammel, *Beyond the Brink*, 92.

47. Phil Hersh, "Indiana's Offense Jolts Duke," *Chicago Tribune*, March 21, 1987, 2:1; Mike Kiley, "Gamble Guns Iowa Past Oklahoma in OT." *Chicago Tribune*, March 21, 1987, 2:1.

48. Phil Hersh, "Indiana teaches LSU a lesson." *Chicago Tribune*, March 23, 1987, 3:1.

49. Mike Kiley, "UNLV Junks Strategy, Runs Down Iowa," *Chicago Tribune*, March 23, 1987, 3:1.

50. Hammel, *Beyond the Brink*, 102.

51. Bob Logan, "Indiana Slips by UNLV," *Chicago Tribune*, March 29, 1987, 3:1. The Indiana victory was Knight's 365th at Indiana, the most ever by a coach at a Big Ten school, breaking his tie with "Piggy" Lambert at Purdue (1917–1945) and Branch McCracken at IU (1938–1965).

52. Alford with Garrity, *Playing for Knight*, 281.

53. Robert Markus, "Winner is . . . Indiana," *Chicago Tribune*, March 31, 1987, 4:1.

54. Bob Hammel, *Beyond the Brink*, 117.

55. Hammel, *Beyond the Brink*, 119.

56. "This Wasn't a Dominant Team," *Chicago Tribune*, April 1, 1987, 4:1; Bob Logan, "With Big 3, Syracuse Could Return to Final 4," *Chicago Tribune*, April 1, 1987, 4:4.

57. Jody Homer, "Alford Named Big 10's Best," *Chicago Tribune*, April 28, 1987, 4:1.

58. Jody Homer, "The I's Have It Again," *Chicago Tribune*, November 16, 1987, 3:14.

59. "Mitchell Leads Purdue over Arkansas-Little Rock in Big Apple-NIT," *Chicago Tribune*, November 21, 1987, 2:3.

60. "Indiana Forfeits to Soviets," *Chicago Tribune*, November 22, 1987, 3:3.

61. "Iowa St. Upsets Purdue to Reach NIT Semifinals," *Chicago Tribune*, November 25, 1987, 4:3; Gene Keady with Jeff Washburn, *The Truth and Nothing but the Truth* (Champaign, IL: Sports Publishing, 2005), 67.

62. Robert Markus, "'Oh No' Shot Features Kentucky's OT Victory," *Chicago Tribune*, December 6, 1987, 3:6; "George Washington 65 Michigan State 64," *Chicago Tribune*, December 6, 1987, 3:8.

63. "Grant Helps Michigan Romp; Purdue Knocks Off Colorado," *Chicago Tribune*, December 8, 1987, 4:7.

64. Linda Kay and Mike Conklin, "Odds and Ends," *Chicago Tribune*, December 15, 1987, 4:2.

65. "Eastern Michigan 84 Michigan State 80," *Chicago Tribune*, December 18, 1987, 4:3; Linda Young, "N. Carolina Melts Illinois," *Chicago Tribune*, December 20, 1987, 3:1; "Iowa St. Downs Iowa in OT as Rhodes Scores Record 54," and "Louisville 81 Indiana 69," *Chicago Tribune*, December 20, 1987, 3:11.

66. "Big 10 Tightens Academic Rules," *Chicago Tribune*, December 26, 1987, 2:6.

67. Linda Young, "Purdue Cruises Past Illini," *Chicago Tribune*, January 5, 1988, 4:1; Robert Markus, "Iowa's Point Well Taken," *Chicago Tribune*, January 7, 1988, 4:1; Bob Logan, "Grant, Michigan Teach NU a Lesson," *Chicago Tribune*, January 7, 1988, 4:3.

68. Robert Markus, "Purdue Escapes Pesky Ohio State," *Chicago Tribune*, January 8, 1988, 4:3. Linda Young, "Illinois Staggers but Nips Minnesota," *Chicago Tribune*, January 8, 1988, 4:1.

69. Robert Markus, "Purdue Survives Scare by Iowa," *Chicago Tribune*, January 10, 1988, 3:6; Linda Young, "Illinois Relies on Charity," *Chicago Tribune*, January 10, 1988, 3:6.

70. Bill Jauss, "NU Leaves 'em Cheering," *Chicago Tribune*, January 12, 1988, 4:1. In what we might call an "Indiana aside," the NCAA passed Proposition 66 at the annual convention the next day, which allowed players to pose for calendars if they were for charity: this was what had caused Steve Alford to be suspended for a game in the 1985–86 season.

71. Shon Morris email to author, January 12, 2020.

72. Neil Milbert, "Northwestern Can't Escape from Iowa's Stranglehold," *Chicago Tribune*, January 17, 1988, 3:6; Linda Young, "Illinois Breezes Past Wisconsin," *Chicago Tribune*, January 17, 1988, 3:6; "Purdue 82 Minnesota 74," and "Michigan St. Finds New Life by Beating Indiana in Overtime," *Chicago Tribune*, January 17, 1988, 3:7.

73. Robert Markus, "Michigan's Defense Leaves Indiana in the Twilight Zone," *Chicago Tribune*, January 25, 1988, 3:1.

74. Ohio State Dunks Michigan," *Chicago Tribune*, January 19, 1988, 4:3; "Purdue Pushes Streak to 15 Wins in a Row," *Chicago Tribune*, January 21, 1988, 4:3.

75. Neil Milbert, "Iowa by a Landslide over Illini," *Chicago Tribune*, January 22, 1988, 4:1; Linda Young, "Replaying a Sad Story at Illinois," *Chicago Tribune*, January 24, 1988, 3:1.

76. "Knight Benches 2; Indiana Responds," *Chicago Tribune*, January 28, 1988, 4:3; Robert Markus, "Indiana Holds Off Purdue," *Chicago Tribune*, January 31, 1988, 4:1.

77. "Michigan Outmanned Seikaly, Syracuse," *Chicago Tribune*, February 1, 1988, 3:3; Linda Young, "Big 10 Coaches Find National TV Exposure Isn't 'Indecent,'" *Chicago Tribune*, February 3, 1988, 4:3.

78. Robert Markus, "Michigan Snowballs Past Iowa," *Chicago Tribune*, February 4, 1988, 4:1; "Purdue's Big First Half Is too Much for Wisconsin," *Chicago Tribune*, February 4, 1988, 4:4.

79. Ed Sherman, "OSU Trips Misfiring Illinois," and "Hillman's Shooting Puts Indiana on the Offensive," *Chicago Tribune*, February 5, 1988, 4:3.

80. Neil Milbert, "Indiana Rallies to Tip Illinois," and "Iowa Balance too Much for Michigan St.," *Chicago Tribune*, February 7, 1988, 4:3.

81. Robert Markus, "Revenge Sweet in Purdue Win," *Chicago Tribune*, February 8, 1988, 3:1. Michael Perry, "Purdue Earns Big Road Victory," *Lafayette Journal and Courier Presents Most Memorable Moments in Purdue Basketball History* (Champaign, IL: Sports Publishing, 1998), 153.

82. Linda Young, "Illini Erase Bad Memory with Romp over Ohio State," and "Mills, Michigan Turn Back Comeback Bid by Minnesota," *Chicago Tribune*, February 18, 1988, 4:6; "Hot-Shooting Indiana Blasts Michigan State," *Chicago Tribune*, February 19, 1988, 4:3.

83. "Purdue Drives Home the Points," *Chicago Tribune*, February 22, 1988, 3:1.

84. "Indiana Turns Back Wisconsin," *Chicago Tribune*, February 25, 1988, 4:9.

85. Linda Young, "Illini Take Lumps from Purdue," *Chicago Tribune*, February 26, 1988, 4:1; "Marble, Iowa Get Revenge," *Chicago Tribune*, February 28, 1988, 3:9.

86. Linda Young, "Illinois Gives Henson 500th," *Chicago Tribune*, March 1, 1988, 4:1.

87. "Ohio State Stuns Purdue, Keeps NCAA Hopes Alive," *Chicago Tribune*, March 10, 1988, 4:1; Robert Markus, "Surging Illini Batter Michigan," *Chicago Tribune*, March 10, 1988, 4:8.

88. "NU Loses 12th in a Row," "Iowa 103 Wisconsin 70," "Indiana 91 Minnesota 85," and "UPI All Big 10 Team Selected by Coaches," *Chicago Tribune*, March 11, 1988, 4:3; John Laskowski with Stan Sutton, *Tales from the Indiana Locker Room* (New York: Sports Publishing), 123.

89. "Keady COY in District IV of USBA," *Chicago Tribune*, March 1, 1988, 4:2; Robert Markus, "Purdue Cautious Big 10 King," *Chicago Tribune*, March 6, 1988, 3:1; "Indiana's

Free-Throw Shooting Gives Knight Milestone Victory," *Chicago Tribune*, March 6, 1988, 3:11. Lambert was head coach at Purdue from 1916–17 and 1918–46.

90. "Minnesota is Put on Probation," *Chicago Tribune*, March 8, 1988, 4:3.

91. "Carter Leads Ohio St. over Old Dominion," *Chicago Tribune*, March 17, 1988, 4:11; "Mateen, Ohio State Advance," *Chicago Tribune*, March 23, 1988, 4:4; "NIT: OSU 68 UNM 65," *Chicago Tribune*, March 26, 1988, 2:3; "Ohio State, Connecticut in NIT Final," *Chicago Tribune*, March 30, 1988; "Connecticut Tops OSU for Crown," *Chicago Tribune*, March 31, 1988, 4:7.

92. Mike Conklin, "Purdue Off to Fast Start," *Chicago Tribune*, March 18, 1988, 4:4; Skip Mylenski, "Michigan Tops Boise St.," *Chicago Tribune*, March 18, 1988, 4:5; Robert Markus, "Indiana Only a Pretender," *Chicago Tribune*, March 19, 1988, 2:1.

93. Linda Young, "Illinois Sheds Ugly Memory," and "Armstrong, Iowa Thwart Florida State Rally," *Chicago Tribune*, March 19, 1988, 3:1; Skip Mylenski, "Rice's Magic Means Victory for Michigan," Michael Conklin, "Purdue Buries a Jinx—and Memphis St," *Chicago Tribune*, March 20, 1988, 3:1.

94. Linda Young, "Free Throws Cost Illinois," *Chicago Tribune*, March 21, 1988, 3:1; Fred Mitchell, "Iowa Makes It Look Easy against UNLV," *Chicago Tribune*, March 21, 1988, 3:7.

95. "Disgruntled Calloway Reportedly to Leave Indiana," *Chicago Tribune*, March 22, 1988, 4:4. "Purdue's Keady Chosen Coach of Year in the Big 10 by Big Margin," *Chicago Tribune*, March 24, 1988, 4:8; "Keady to Texas? Wants the Job?" *Chicago Tribune*, April 2, 1988, 4:2. Mark Montieth, *Passion Play* (Chicago: Bonus, 1988), 323.

96. Skip Mylenski, "Arizona Proves Its Point in Rout of Iowa," and "North Carolina's Strength is Too Much for Michigan," *Chicago Tribune*, March 26, 1988, 2:1; Bob Logan, "Kansas St. Roars Back to End Purdue Dreams," *Chicago Tribune*, March 26, 1988, 2:1; John Millman, "Kansas State Shocks Purdue," *Lafayette Journal and Courier Presents Most Memorable Moments in Purdue Basketball History* (Champaign, IL: Sports Publishing, 1998), 157.

11. The End of the 1980s and into the 1990s

1. Skip Mylenski, "NCAA Calls 3-Year Foul on Kansas," *Chicago Tribune*, November 2, 1988, 4:2; "Cincinnati Programs Placed on Probation," *Chicago Tribune*, November 4, 1988, 4:6.

2. Barry Temkin, "Big 10 Rule Dries Up Junior College Pool," *Chicago Tribune*, November 7, 1988.

3. Bill Jauss, "Notebook," *Chicago Tribune*, November 8, 1988, 4:3. And later this group would be given the nickname of "Flyin' Illini" for this ability to run and dunk with aplomb.

4. Linda Young, "Illini Defense Shreds Florida," *Chicago Tribune*, December 6, 1988, 4:3; Linda Young, "Down by 18, Illinois Rallies to Top Missouri," *Chicago Tribune*, December 20, 1988, 4:1.

5. "Syracuse Stomps Indiana," *Chicago Tribune*, November 24, 1988, 4:3; "Syracuse Tops Mizzou in OT for Big Apple," *Chicago Tribune*, November 26, 1988, 2:2.

6. Robert Markus, "Rest of League Wise to Purdue, Mature McCants," *Chicago Tribune*, November 30, 1988, 4:4; "Ball State Downs Purdue," *Chicago Tribune*, December 11, 1988, 3:11.

7. Andrew Bagnato, "Louisville Press Unravels Indiana," *Chicago Tribune*, December 4, 1988, 3:5; "Hillman, Anderson Spark Indiana," *Chicago Tribune*, December 21, 1988, 4:3.

8. "Iowa Beaten by 3-Pointers," *Chicago Tribune*, December 26, 1988, 3:3; "Conference Boasts 3 Unbeatens," *Chicago Tribune*, December 26, 1988, 3:3.

9. "Burson Scores 37 Points, Ohio State Routs Florida," *Chicago Tribune*, December 28, 1988, 4:3; "Ohio State Slips by St. John's to Win Title," *Chicago Tribune*, December 30, 1988, 4:3.

10. "Far West Classic," *Chicago Tribune*, December 30, 1988, 4:3; "Michigan State 76 Oregon 61," *Chicago Tribune*, December 31, 1988, 2:2; "Battle Leads Illini to Pot of Gold at End of Rainbow," *Chicago Tribune*, January 1, 1989, 3:8.

11. Robert Markus, "Indiana Stops Ohio State Cold," *Chicago Tribune*, January 5, 1989, 4:1.

12. "Indiana Tips Purdue for Knight Record," *Chicago Tribune*, January 10, 1989, 4:3.

13. "NCAA Convention Reverses Itself, Strengthens Eligibility Rule," *Chicago Tribune*, January 12, 1989, 4:5; Barry Temkin, "Partial Qualifier Rule Sets Up New Reasons to Cheat," *Chicago Tribune*, January 13, 1989, 4:3.

14. Skip Mylenski, "Illini KO Michigan for 15th Win," "Minnesota Tips Iowa on a Tap-In," *Chicago Tribune*, January 15, 1989, 3:1; Robert Markus, "Indiana Gives Knight No. 500, but He's Unimpressed," "Burson's Last-Second Shot Lifts Ohio St.," and "Purdue 68 Wisconsin 62," *Chicago Tribune*, January 15, 1989, 3:3.

15. Robert Markus, "Illini Stay Jump Ahead of Wildcats," *Chicago Tribune*, January 20, 1989, 4:1; "Wisconsin Surprises Michigan," *Chicago Tribune*, January 22, 1989, 3:1; "Edwards Carries Indiana in Overtime," and "Iowa 67 Purdue 66," *Chicago Tribune*, January 22, 1989, 3:12; "Indiana Edges Michigan for 13th in a Row," *Chicago Tribune*, January 24, 1989, 4:1.

16. "Illinois Soars to No. 1, but Gill Injury Mars Joy," *Chicago Tribune*, January 23, 1989, 3:1; Linda Young, "Illinois Will Have to Adjust," *Chicago Tribune*, January 23, 1989, 3:20; "Illinois Enjoys the View from the Top," *Chicago Tribune*, January 24, 1989, 4:1.

17. Linda Young, "Illini Roar Back to Trip Indiana," *Chicago Tribune*, January 29, 1989, 3:1.

18. "Michigan's Rice too Hot to Handle," "Louisville Misses Shot at No. 1," *Chicago Tribune*, January 30, 1989, 3:3.

19. Ed Sherman, "Indiana, Jadlow, Rip Iowa," *Chicago Tribune*, January 31, 1989, 4:1.

20. "Minnesota Pulls Off Still Another Upset," *Chicago Tribune*, February 1, 1989, 4:1; Linda Young, "Purdue Too Hot for Illini," *Chicago Tribune*, February 3, 1989, 4:1; "Hillman Helps to Rally Indiana over Minnesota," *Chicago Tribune*, February 5, 1989, 3:4.

21. Linda Young, "Bardo's Defense Rescues Illinois," and "Michigan Turns Back Iowa in a 2-OT War," *Chicago Tribune*, February 10, 1989, 4:1; "Minnesota, Wisconsin Stun Michigan, Iowa," *Chicago Tribune*, February 12, 1989, 3:6.

22. "Ohio State's Burson Hospitalized with Neck Injury," *Chicago Tribune*, February 16, 1989, 4:3; "Burson's Neck Injury Ends Ohio St. Career," *Chicago Tribune*, February 17, 1989, 4:3.

23. "Edwards' 3-Pointer Lets Indiana Escape," *Chicago Tribune*, February 20, 1989, 3:1; Bill Jauss, "Wisconsin Could Find Way Back to NCAA Tourney," *Chicago Tribune*, February 20, 1989, 3:3.

24. "Final 4 Ticket Brokers Put on Happy Face," *Chicago Tribune*, February 22, 1989, 4:2; Skip Mylenski, "Big East or Big 10," *Chicago Tribune*, February 22, 1989, 4:10.

25. "Indiana Wins 6th Straight," and "Michigan 89 Ohio State 72," *Chicago Tribune*, February 24, 1989, 4:1; Robert Markus, "Indiana Unleashes Jadlow, Rolls On," and "Michigan Rolls Behind Rice's 38 Points," *Chicago Tribune*, February 26, 1989, 3:3; Linda Young, "Illini Get a Big Lift from Smith," *Chicago Tribune*, February 27, 1989, 3:1; "Michigan Doubles Up MSU," *Chicago Tribune*, February 28, 1989, 4:3; "Edwards Burns Ohio St.; Indiana Clinches Title," *Chicago Tribune*, March 2, 1989, 4:3.

26. Skip Mylenski, "Michigan Buries Iowa Early," *Chicago Tribune*, March 5, 1989, 3:3; Linda Young, "Illini Upend Michigan Again," *Chicago Tribune*, March 12, 1989, 3:1.

27. "Indiana Wraps Up Big 10," *Chicago Tribune*, March 10, 1989, 4:1; "Indiana Takes a Rest in Loss to Iowa," *Chicago Tribune*, March 12, 1989, 3:5.

28. "Indiana Wraps Up Big 10," *Chicago Tribune*, March 10, 1989, 4:1.

29. Robert Markus, "Frieder Regrets the Timing," *Chicago Tribune*, March 16, 1989, 4:1.

30. "Frieder Set to Leave Michigan for Arizona State," *Chicago Tribune*, March 15, 1989, 4:2; Robert Markus, "Frieder 'Regrets the Timing,'" *Chicago Tribune*, March 16, 1989, 4:1.

31. Linda Kay and Mike Conklin, "Odds and Ins," *Chicago Tribune*, March 16, 1989, 4:2.

32. "Wisconsin, Ohio State Advance," *Chicago Tribune*, March 16, 1989, 4:1; "Hawkeye Fever," *Chicago Tribune*, March 16, 1989, 4:2.

33. "Freshman Helps in Michigan St. Win," *Chicago Tribune*, March 17, 1989, 4:4.

34. Linda Young, "Illinois' Victory Isn't Pretty," *Chicago Tribune*, March 17, 1989, 4:1; "Masked Man Helps Minnesota Advance," *Chicago Tribune*, March 17, 1989, 4:3; Robert Markus, "Hoyas Squeak, Hoosiers Roar," *Chicago Tribune*, March 18, 1989, 2:1; Skip Mylenski, "Armstrong Grows Up in Iowa Win," *Chicago Tribune*, March 18, 1989, 2:3.

35. Linda Young, "Illini Soar, but DePaul Falls," *Chicago Tribune*, March 19, 1989, 3:1; "Minnesota Doesn't Waste Its Last Lead," *Chicago Tribune*, March 19, 1989, 3:5; "Indiana Climbs to Peak Form," and "Michigan Survives to End a Fairy Tale," *Chicago Tribune*, March 20, 1989, 3:1; Skip Mylenski, "Monroe's 40 Heroics Carry N.C. State Past Iowa," *Chicago Tribune*, March 20, 1989, 3:3.

36. "St. Louis Erases Big Deficit to Beat Wisconsin in NIT," *Chicago Tribune*, March 21, 1989, 4:1; "Ohio State Tops Nebraska; Michigan State Advances," *Chicago Tribune*, March 21, 4:3; "Michigan State Earns NIT Semi-Final Berth," *Chicago Tribune*, March 23, 1989, 4:3; "St. John's Wins in OT at Ohio St," *Chicago Tribune*, March 24, 1989, 4:4.

37. "Knight Named Big 10 COY," *Chicago Tribune*, March 22, 1989, 4:3.

38. Robert Markus, "Michigan, UNLV Pull Surprises," *Chicago Tribune*, March 24, 1989, 4:1; "Michigan Rolls Past Virginia," *Chicago Tribune*, March 26, 1989, 3:1.

39. Skip Mylenski, "Illini Battered, but Not Beaten," *Chicago Tribune*, March 25, 1989, 2:1; Skip Mylenski, "Illinois Battles to Final Four," *Chicago Tribune*, March 27, 1989, 3:1.

40. 'Hoosiers Find Out That the Hall Can Be a Tough Place, Indeed," *Chicago Tribune*, March 24, 1989, 4:1; "Duke Teaches Minnesota a Tough Lesson," *Chicago Tribune*, March 25, 1989, 2:3.

41. Skip Mylenski, "Terrific 2 Will Emerge from Kingdome Showdowns," *Chicago Tribune*, April 1, 1989, 2:1.

42. "Knight, Elliott Win Top Honors," *Chicago Tribune*, April 1, 1989, 2:3.

43. Skip Mylenski, "It's Michigan, Seton Hall," *Chicago Tribune*, April 2, 1989, 3:1.

44. Mylenski, "It's Michigan, Seton Hall," 3:1.

45. Skip Mylenski, "Michigan Tops Seton Hall," *Chicago Tribune*, April 4, 1989, 4:1.

46. "Fisher to Be Named Coach at Michigan," *Chicago Tribune*, April 10, 1989, 3:3.

47. Ed Sherman, "Big 10's New Chief Wants Scholars Put First," *Chicago Tribune*, April 6, 1989, 4:1.

48. Mike Conklin, "Odds and Ins," *Chicago Tribune*, January 1, 1990, 3:9.

49. Gene Keady with Jeff Washburn, *The Truth and Nothing but the Truth* (Champaign, IL: Sports Publishing, 2005), 78.

50. Skip Mylenski, "Arizona Gets Physical in Win over Michigan," *Chicago Tribune*, November 26, 1989, 3:6; "Wolverines Rebound with Nervous Victory," *Chicago Tribune*, November 28, 1989, 4:3.

51. Skip Mylenski, "Indiana Barely Tops Kentucky," *Chicago Tribune*, December 3, 1989, 3:1. Joseph Tybor, "Indiana Freshmen Take Irish to School," *Chicago Tribune*, December 6, 1989, 4:3. "Funderbunke Quits IU after Being Kicked Out of Practice," *Chicago Tribune*, December 16, 1989, 2:2.

52. "Michigan Topples Duke in Overtime," *Chicago Tribune*, December 10, 1989, 3:1.

53. "Unbeaten Iowa Drops N. Carolina to 4–4," and "Michigan State 88 Austin Peay 76," *Chicago Tribune*, December 10, 1989, 3:4; Gary Reinmuth, "Patient UIC Surprises Michigan St." *Chicago Tribune*, December 13, 1989, 4:1.

54. Robert Markus, "Illini Defense Get the Job Done," *Chicago Tribune*, December 17, 1989, 3:1; "Indiana 69 UTEP 66," *Chicago Tribune*, December 17, 1989, 3:3; "Mills Powers Michigan to Win," *Chicago Tribune*, December 17, 1989, 3:4; Robert Markus, "Illini Remove All Doubts," *Chicago Tribune*, December 21, 1989, 4:1; Bill Jauss, "Knight's Hoosiers Beginning to Look a Lot Like Champions," *Chicago Tribune*, December 26, 1989, 4:4.

55. "N. Iowa Stuns Iowa Before State-Record Crowd," *Chicago Tribune*, January 4, 1990, 4:2.

56. Robert Markus, "Gill Leads Illini Past Wisconsin," *Chicago Tribune*, January 5, 1990, 4:1; "NCAA Clears Gill, Bardo Hours Before Game," *Chicago Tribune*, January 5, 1990, 4:3.

57. Robert Markus, "Gill Leads Illini Past Wisconsin," and "Ohio State Upsets Knight's Best Plan," *Chicago Tribune*, January 5, 1990, 4:1.

58. Neil Milbert, "Indiana-Michigan, Clash of 2 Tough, Title Teams," *Chicago Tribune*, January 8, 1990, 3:11; Neil Milbert, "Indiana Shocker," *Chicago Tribune*, January 9, 1990, 4:1.

59. Ed Sherman, "NCAA Softens Stance on Proposition 42," *Chicago Tribune*, January 9, 1990. 4:1; "NCAA Notebook," *Chicago Tribune*, January 9, 1990, 4:3; Ed Sherman, "Presidents Muscle NCAA into Reforms," *Chicago Tribune*, January 10, 1990, 4:1.

60. "Purdue Ends Minnesota Streak," and "Wisconsin Edges Iowa in Overtime," *Chicago Tribune*, January 12, 1990, 4:3.

61. "Purdue Tops Indiana in Overtime," *Chicago Tribune*, January 14, 1990, 3:1; "Michigan 87 Minnesota 83," *Chicago Tribune*, January 4, 1990, 3:3.

62. Robert Markus, "Michigan Holds off Illinois," *Chicago Tribune*, January 16, 1990, 4:1. "Purdue Makes It a Big 10 Fivesome," *Chicago Tribune*, January 16, 1990, 4:3.

63. Robert Markus, "Liberty Ignites Illinois," *Chicago Tribune*, January 19, 1990, 4:1; "Calip's Guiding Hand Helps Michigan Win," *Chicago Tribune*, January 19, 1990, 4:3.

64. Robert Markus, "Illinois No Match for Purdue Muscle," and "Iowa Stuns Michigan," *Chicago Tribune*, January 21, 1990, 3:1; Neil Milbert, "Michigan State 91 Northwestern 80," *Chicago Tribune*, January 21, 1990, 3:3.

65. Neil Milbert, "Big 10 Notebook," *Chicago Tribune*, January 24, 1990, 4:7.

66. Jack Saylor, "Michigan State Buries Indiana," *Chicago Tribune*, January 25, 1990, 4:3.

67. Robert Markus, "Illini Edge Wisconsin," *Chicago Tribune*, January 26, 1990, 4:2; Ed Sherman, "Illinois May Avoid NCAA's Noose," *Chicago Tribune*, January 26, 1990, 4:2; "Purdue Registers Key Road Victory," *Chicago Tribune*, January 26, 1990, 4:3.

68. "Purdue 80 Iowa 59," "Robinson's Clutch Shot Lifts Michigan," *Chicago Tribune*, January 28, 1990, 3:2; "Minnesota's Manpower Mangles Indiana," *Chicago Tribune*, January 29, 1990, 3:3.

69. Neil Milbert, "Purdue Unstoppable? Don't Tell That to Keady," *Chicago Tribune*, January 29, 1990, 4:2; Neil Milbert, "Purdue Knocks Michigan Flat," *Chicago Tribune*, February 1, 1990, 4:1.

70. Andrew Bagnato, "Mich. St. Bursts Purdue's Bubble," *Chicago Tribune*, February 4, 1990, 3:1.

71. Robert Markus, "Illinois Unable to Handle Michigan's Heavyweights," and "Minnesota Closes in on Purdue," *Chicago Tribune*, February 12, 1990, 3:1.

72. "Michigan St. Has Iowa Outmanned," *Chicago Tribune*, February 13, 1990, 4:3.

73. Neil Milbert, "Purdue 'D' Dominates Indiana," *Chicago Tribune*, February 20, 1990, 4:1; Skip Mylenski, "Big 10 Nation's Big Shots," *Chicago Tribune*, February 21, 1990, 4:3; Robert Markus, "Illini Show They're Far from Dead," *Chicago Tribune*, February 22, 1990, 4:1.

74. "Michigan St. Beats Indiana; Loses Manns," *Chicago Tribune*, February 26, 1990, 3:3; Robert Markus, "Ohio State Freshman Floors Illini," *Chicago Tribune*, February 27, 1990, 4:1.

75. Neil Milbert, "Purdue Jolted by Iowa," *Chicago Tribune*, March 1, 1990, 4:1; Skip Mylenski, "Say Yes to Michigan. .. State," *Chicago Tribune*, March 2, 1990, 4:1; Neil Milbert, "Smith Lifts Mich. State," *Chicago Tribune*, March 4, 1990, 3:1.

76. Keady with Washburn, *The Truth and Nothing but the Truth*, 81.

77. Robert Markus, "Illinois Checks Out Painfully," and "Cal Shoots Down Indiana," *Chicago Tribune*, March 16, 1990, 4:1.

78. "Mich. St. Averts U-P-S-E-T; LSU Advances," and "Buckeyes Get Past Providence in OT," *Chicago Tribune*, March 16, 1990, 4:3; Andrew Bagnato, "Michigan Survives Illinois State Scare," "Purdue Wakes Up in Time to Overcome Northeast Louisiana," and "Minnesota 64 Texas El-Paso 61," *Chicago Tribune*, March 17, 1990, 3:3.

79. Keady with Washburn, *The Truth and Nothing but the Truth*, 81.

80. "Michigan State 62 UC Santa Barbara," and "Johnson Sparks the Rebels over Ohio State," *Chicago Tribune*, March 18, 1990, 4:3; "NCAA's Upsetting 'Upstarts,'" and "Texas Roadblock Stops Purdue," *Chicago Tribune*, March 19, 1990, 3:1; "Marymount Star Gathers Dies," *Chicago Tribune*, March 5, 1990, 3:1; Joseph Tybor, "Minnesota, Syracuse Stay Alive—Barely." *Chicago Tribune*, March 19, 1990, 3:3.

81. Robert Markus, "MSU Falls in OT; Minnesota Wins," *Chicago Tribune*, March 24, 1990, 3:1.

82. Robert Markus, "The Final (Fab) Four," *Chicago Tribune*, March 26, 1990, 3:1.

83. Neil Milbert, "Big 10 a Little Red-Faced over NCAA Misfortune," *Chicago Tribune*, March 28, 1990, 3:3.

84. Barry Temkin, "Illini Lose All-Stater Martin to Purdue," *Chicago Tribune*, April 12, 1990, 4:7; "Ray Thompson Drops Out of Iowa," *Chicago Tribune*, April 18, 1990, 4:2; "Michigan's Higgins to Turn Pro," *Chicago Tribune*, April 12, 1990, 4:6; Bill Jauss, "NU's Walters to Kansas," *Chicago Tribune*, April 20, 1990, 4:3.

85. "NCAA Rule Changes Retain 3-Point Range," *Chicago Tribune*, April 4, 1990, 4:2; "NCAA Changes 1-and-1 Free Throw Rule," *Chicago Tribune*, April 5, 1990, 4:3.

12. The Last Years of Just Ten: 1990–92

1. "How the Tribune Sees the Big 10," *Chicago Tribune*, November 14, 1990, 4:6; "Overall Tribune Top 20," *Chicago Tribune*, November 14, 1990, 4:8.

2. Melissa Isaacson, "Youth Served (Up) at Illinois," *Chicago Tribune*, November 6, 1990, 4:8.

3. Ed Sherman, "NCAA Dunks Illini Program," *Chicago Tribune*, November 7, 1990, 4:1.

4. Bob Knight with Bob Hammel, *Knight: My Story* (New York, St. Martin's Press, 2002), 266.

5. "Briefs," *Chicago Tribune*, November 12, 1990, 3:3; "Briefs," *Chicago Tribune*, November 13, 1990, 4:3; Skip Mylenski, "Mr. Smith Goes to the Top," *Chicago Tribune*, November 14, 1990, 4:5.

6. "MSU 78 Furman 73," *Chicago Tribune*, November 24, 1990, 3:3; "Nebraska Shocks Michigan State," *Chicago Tribune*, November 29, 1990, 4:12; "Bowling Green Surprises No. 5 Michigan State," *Chicago Tribune*, December 2, 1990, 3:5.

7. Robert Markus, "UIC Shakes Its Way Past Stunned Illini," *Chicago Tribune*, November 30, 1990, 4:3; Robert Markus, "40 Points 'Cure' Kaufmann, Illini," *Chicago Tribune*, December 2, 1990, 3:3; "It's Wild! Irish Fall to Butler; Illini Barely Survive," *Chicago Tribune*, December 4, 1990, 4:1. "Penn State Rips Sloppy Illinois," *Chicago Tribune*, December 6, 1990, 4:1.

8. Skip Mylenski, "NCAA Sets the Formula for Getting TV Money," *Chicago Tribune*, December 7, 1990, 4:4; Chad Carlson, *Making March Madness, the Early Years of the NCAA, NIT, and College Basketball Championships* (Fayetteville: University of Arkansas Press, 2017), 316.

9. Melissa Isaacson, "Illinois Finally Displays Defense," *Chicago Tribune*, December 8, 1990, 3:1; Melissa Isaacson, "Illini Classic Kings-Naturally," *Chicago Tribune*, December 9, 1990, 3:3.

10. "Indiana Classic," *Chicago Tribune*, December 8, 1990, 3:3; "Indiana 91 San Diego 64," and "Indiana Holds Off Kentucky," *Chicago Tribune*, December 19, 1990, 4:3; "Indiana Pounds Iowa St.," *Chicago Tribune*, December 22, 1990, 3:3.

11. "Michigan St. 83 Detroit 61," *Chicago Tribune*, December 9, 1990, 3:5; "Michigan State Survives at Buzzer," *Chicago Tribune*, December 14, 1990, 4:3; "UNLV's Johnson Takes Over, Leads Rout of MSU," *Chicago Tribune*, December 16, 1990, 3:3.

12. "Purdue Shocks No.17 Georgia," *Chicago Tribune*, December 30, 1990, 3:5; Skip Mylenski, "Wonder What Keady's Up To?" *Chicago Tribune*, January 2, 1991, 4:1.

13. Dennis Bracken, "Minnesota, Holtz Facing Major NCAA Violations," *Chicago Tribune*, December 15, 1990, 3:1.

14. Melissa Isaacson, "Indiana Shows Illini a Lesson," *Chicago Tribune*, January 3, 1991, 4:1. "Buckeyes Stay Unbeaten After Getting Past Iowa," *Chicago Tribune*, January 4, 1991, 4:6; "Michigan State 85 Michigan 70," *Chicago Tribune*, January 4, 1991, 4:6.

15. "Ohio State Still Standing at Bell," *Chicago Tribune*, January 22, 1991, 4:1.

16. "Ohio State Remains Unbeaten," *Chicago Tribune*, January 25, 1991, 4:8.

17. Skip Mylenski, "Indiana Blitz Leaves MSU Stunned," *Chicago Tribune*, January 27, 1991, 3:3.

18. "Jackson, Ohio State Trip Purdue," and "Indiana Bumps Off Minnesota," *Chicago Tribune*, February 4, 1991, 3:3.

19. "Hall of Fame Elects Knight," *Chicago Tribune*, February 8, 1991, 4:1; Neil Milbert, "Surging Indiana Finishes Off NU," *Chicago Tribune*, February 8, 1991, 4:3.

20. Neil Milbert, "2d Chance Rescues Wisconsin," *Chicago Tribune*, February 10, 1991, 4:2.

21. "NU's Skid Hits 12 as OSU Rolls," and "Iowa Fails Again at Michigan," *Chicago Tribune*, February 10, 1991, 4:3.

22. "Indiana Moves in Front in Big 10," *Chicago Tribune*, February 11, 1991, 3:3; "Bank's Open as Ohio St. Edges Wisconsin," *Chicago Tribune*, February 15, 1991, 4:3; "Ohio State Wins One for the Ages," *Chicago Tribune*, February 18, 1991, 3:1.

23. Melissa Isaacson, "Ohio St. Survives a Scare," *Chicago Tribune*, February 21, 1991, 4:3; "Iowa Rally, Missed Fts Stop Indiana," *Chicago Tribune*, February 22, 1991, 4:3.

24. "Ohio State Escapes Scare at Home," *Chicago Tribune*, February 24, 1991, 3:3; "Arizona Squeaks By; Indiana Rolls," *Chicago Tribune*, February 25, 1991, 3:3.

25. Skip Mylenski, "Indiana Tops MSU in the 4th Dimension," *Chicago Tribune*, March 1, 1991, 4:3.

26. "Free Throw Gives Ohio St. a Share of Big 10 Title," *Chicago Tribune*, March 4, 1991, 3:3.

27. Neil Milbert, "Big 10 Also-Rans Join Rush for NCAA Bids," *Chicago Tribune*, March 8, 1991, 4:7.

28. "Michigan St. 66 Michigan 59," *Chicago Tribune*, March 10, 1991, 3:4; "Michigan St. Set for Tournament; Wisconsin Falls," *Chicago Tribune*, March 10, 1991, 3:6; Skip Mylenski, "Buckeyes Have It—a Top Seed," *Chicago Tribune*, March 11, 1991, 3:1; Linda Young, "Iowa Dumps Struggling Ohio State," *Chicago Tribune*, March 11, 1991, 3:6.

29. Melissa Isaacson, "Knight, Henson Square Off," *Chicago Tribune*, March 11, 1991, 3:6.

30. Neil Milbert, "Badgers, Michigan Earn Trips to NIT," *Chicago Tribune*, March 11, 1991, 3:8; "Big 10 Censures Knight, Henson," *Chicago Tribune*, March 14, 1991, 4:3.

31. "Simms, Tompkins Power Wisconsin Past Bowling Green in OT," and "Colorado 71 Michigan 64," *Chicago Tribune*, March 14, 1991, 4:8; Joseph Tybor, "Stanford Handles Wisconsin with Ease," *Chicago Tribune*, March 18, 1991, 4:4.

32. "Indiana Beats 1st Round Jinx," *Chicago Tribune*, March 15, 1991, 4:1; Melissa Isaacson, "Iowa Finds Itself in Nick of Time," *Chicago Tribune*, March 15, 1991, 4:3; Richard Finn, "Kilgore Key as Temple Shreds Purdue Defense," *Chicago Tribune*, March 15, 1991, 4:4.

33. "Michigan St. Ousts Green Bay at Buzzer," *Chicago Tribune*, March 16, 1991, 3:2.

34. Rich Strom, "Jent Gives Ohio St. Much-Needed Spark," *Chicago Tribune*, March 16, 1991, 3:3; Skip Mylenski, "Ohio State Wins Ugly," *Chicago Tribune*, March 18, 1991, 3:1.

35. Bill Jauss, "Knight Hits Right Switch for Indiana," *Chicago Tribune*, March 17, 1991, 3:1; Melissa Isaacson, "Duke Makes Routing Iowa Look Easy," *Chicago Tribune*, March 17, 1991, 3:3.

36. Andrew Bagnato, "Utah KOs Spartans in 2-Overtime Slugfest," *Chicago Tribune*, March 18, 1991, 3:5.

37. Knight with Hammel, *Knight*, 269.

38. Bill Jauss, "Kansas' Punch Floors Indiana," *Chicago Tribune*, March 22, 1991, 4:1; Melissa Isaacson, "Ohio State Rudely Dismissed," *Chicago Tribune*, March 23, 1991, 3:1.

39. "Big Ten Notes," *Chicago Tribune*, November 4, 1991, 3:15.

40. Knight with Hammel, *Knight*, 268.

41. Skip Mylenski, "New-Look UCLA Destroys Indiana," *Chicago Tribune*, November 16, 1991, 3:1.

42. "Henson Upgrades Illinois," *Chicago Tribune*, November 20, 1991, 4:8; Paul Sullivan, "Illini Collapse Irks Henson," *Chicago Tribune*, November 26, 1991, 4:1.

43. "Something Old, New Lead MSU Upset," *Chicago Tribune*, November 29, 1991, 4:6; "Arkansas Rescued by Miller," *Chicago Tribune*, November 26, 1991, 4:2; "Maui Classic," *Chicago Tribune*, November 28, 1991, 4:6.

44. "Mich. St. Improves to 9-0," *Chicago Tribune*, December 28, 1991, 3:3; Skip Mylenski, "Michigan St. Runs Silent, Runs Deep," *Chicago Tribune*, December 29, 1991, 3:1; Skip Mylenski, "Star Lost, Team Is Found," *Chicago Tribune*, January 3, 1992, 4:1.

45. Neil Milbert, "NU Hits Boards, Topples Columbia," and "Ohio State Hammers Chicago State," *Chicago Tribune*, December 1, 1991, 3:3 and 3:5; Neil Milbert, "NU Era: 3-0 After Comeback," *Chicago Tribune*, December 3, 1991, 4:1.

46. "Indiana 97 Butler 73," *Chicago Tribune*, December 1, 1991, 3:4; Joseph Tybor, "Irish No Match for Indiana," *Chicago Tribune*, December 4, 1991, 4:1; Skip Mylenski, "Kentucky Puts Indiana Down—to the Last Shot," *Chicago Tribune*, December 8, 1991, 3:1; Skip Mylenski, "Knight Still Doing It His Way," *Chicago Tribune*, December 6, 1991, 4:1.

47. Paul Sullivan, "Illinois Gets a Move On, Streaks Past NE Louisiana," *Chicago Tribune*, December 2, 1991, 3:5; Paul Sullivan, "Tennessee St. No Sweat for Illini, Thomas," *Chicago Tribune*, December 4, 1991, 4:4; Paul Sullivan, "Illinois Wins, but It's No Classic," *Chicago Tribune*, December 7, 1991, 3:3; Paul Sullivan, "Thomas Held in Check, but Illini Cruise," *Chicago Tribune*, December 8, 1991, 3:5; Paul Sullivan, "Temple Feasts on Cold Illini," *Chicago Tribune*, December 11, 1991, 4:3.

48. Jim Spadafore, "U-M Puts Up Dukes, Falls in OT," *Detroit News*, December 15, 1991, E1.

49. Skip Mylenski, "Michigan Recruits a Winning Combo," *Chicago Tribune*, December 18, 1991, 4:1; "Webber, Michigan Edge BYU," *Chicago Tribune*, December 29, 1991, 3:3; "Citrus Bowl Tournament," *Chicago Tribune*, December 31, 1991, 4:2.

50. Skip Mylenski, "Ohio St. Takes the Bows," *Chicago Tribune*, January 8, 1992, 4:1; "Illini Barely Get By in Opener," *Chicago Tribune*, January 9, 1992, 4:1.

51. Skip Mylenski, "Michigan Frosh Pass 1st Exam," *Chicago Tribune*, January 10, 1992, 4:1.

52. "Hoosiers Whip Gophers," *Chicago Tribune*, January 10, 1992, 4:4; "Minnesota Upstages Michigan," *Chicago Tribune*, January 12, 1992, 3:3.

53. Skip Mylenski, "Indiana Counter-Punch Floors Ohio St.," *Chicago Tribune*, January 15, 1992, 4:1; "Funderbunke Wants to Shed Past," *Chicago Tribune*, January 11, 1992, 3:1.

54. "Purdue Wins Again at Michigan," *Chicago Tribune*, January 16, 1992, 4:3; Paul Sullivan, "Michigan Holds Off Illinois," *Chicago Tribune*, January 19, 1992, 3:3.

55. "Michigan Finally Finds Mark at Home," *Chicago Tribune*, January 26, 1992, 3:3; "Indiana Quiets Purdue," *Chicago Tribune*, January 29, 1992, 4:7; "Michigan's Talent Tops MSU in Overtime," *Chicago Tribune*, January 30, 1992, 4:3; Terry Cabell, "Youth Wins Out over Experience," *Detroit News*, January 30, 1992, 1D.

56. Paul Sullivan, "MSU Demolishes Indiana's Streak," *Chicago Tribune*, February 2, 1992, 3:5; Paul Sullivan, "Indiana Wins, Peace Reigns," *Chicago Tribune*, February 5, 1992, 4:1.

57. "Jackson, OSU, Tip Michigan," *Chicago Tribune*, February 3, 1992, 3:5.

58. Jim Spadafore, "MSU Repays U-M," *Detroit News*, February 16, 1992, 1C.

59. "Indiana, Oklahoma Fall on Road," *Chicago Tribune*, February 13, 1992, 4:3; "NU Starts Fast, but Indiana Romps Away," *Chicago Tribune*, February 16, 1992, 3:2; "Mich. St. Punishes Michigan," *Chicago Tribune*, February 16, 1992, 3:5; "Indiana Rolls," *Chicago Tribune*, February 20, 1992, 4:2.

60. Neil Milbert, "Indiana Seizes Control of Big 10," *Chicago Tribune*, February 24, 1992, 3:1.

61. "Solidarity," *Chicago Tribune*, February 26, 1992, 4:7; "Wisconsin Buries No. 17 Michigan," *Chicago Tribune*, February 27, 1992, 4:1; Jim Spadafore, "Badgers Flatten U-M," *Detroit News*, February 27, 1992, 1C.

62. Neil Milbert, "Ohio St. Stays in Hunt, Jolts MSU," *Chicago Tribune*, March 1, 1992, 3:1.

63. "Ohio State Slips Past Michigan," *Chicago Tribune*, March 4, 1992, 4:3; Phil Hersh, "1-2 Punch Carries Indiana," *Chicago Tribune*, March 5, 1992, 4:1; Jim Spadafore, "Buckeyes Win in Walk After 31-Second Run at Wolverines," *Detroit News*, March 4, 1992, 1C.

64. Neil Milbert, "MSU Bulk Subdues Wildcats," *Chicago Tribune*, March 6, 1992, 4:3; Paul Sullivan, "Illini Carve Another Notch on Payback Belt," *Chicago Tribune*, March 8, 1992; "Mich. St. Runs Past Minnesota," *Chicago Tribune*, March 12, 1992, 4:2; Skip Mylenski, "Michigan Passes Indiana's Test," *Chicago Tribune*, March 9, 1992, 3:1.

65. "Media All Big 10 Team," *Chicago Tribune*, March 17, 1992, 4:3.

66. Neil Milbert, "Purdue Proves There's No Place Like Home, Overpowers Butler," *Chicago Tribune*, March 20, 1992, 4:7; "NIT, Pitt 67 Penn State 65," *Chicago Tribune*, March 19, 1992, 4:6.

67. Neil Milbert, "Purdue Refuses to Go by the Boards," *Chicago Tribune*, March 24, 1992, 4:3; Fred Mitchell, "Florida Knocks Purdue Out of NIT," *Chicago Tribune*, March 26, 1992, 4:3.

68. Paul Sullivan, "Jackson Will 'Run' Wisconsin," *Chicago Tribune*, March 26, 1992, 4:3.

69. Skip Mylenski, "Big 6 in NCAA Power Play," *Chicago Tribune*, March 16, 1992, 3:1.

70. Skip Mylenski, "Rejuvenated Ohio State in Command," and "Indiana's Banquet Circuit Starts with EIU," *Chicago Tribune*, March 20, 1992, 4:1; "Iowa Earns Shot at Duke," *Chicago Tribune*, March 20, 1992, 4:4.

71. Jack Saylor, "Comeback for Seconds," *Detroit News*, March 21, 1992, B1.

72. Fred Mitchell, "Indiana Survives Shaq Attack," *Chicago Tribune*, March 22, 1992, 3:1; Skip Mylenski, "Ohio St. Heats Up at Last, Burns UConn," *Chicago Tribune*, March 22, 1992, 3:1; "Davis Surprise Leader of Duke Win over Iowa," *Chicago Tribune*, March 22, 1992, 3:1.

73. "Michigan Polishes Off E. Tennessee St.," *Chicago Tribune*, March 23, 1992, 3:1; Skip Mylenski, "Cincinnati Wins Duel of Bumblers," *Chicago Tribune*, March 23, 1992, 3:4.

74. Neil Milbert, "Anderson, Indiana Rebound," *Chicago Tribune*, March 27, 1992, 4:1.

75. "Rose in Bloom for Michigan," *Chicago Tribune*, March 28, 1992, 3:1; Robert Markus, "Ohio State KO's Carolina," *Chicago Tribune*, March 28, 1992, 3:1.

76. Neil Milbert, "Hoosiers Make Short Work of UCLA," *Chicago Tribune*, March 29, 1992, 3:1; Robert Markus, "Michigan's Kids Come of Age," *Chicago Tribune*, March 30, 1992, 3:1.

77. Neil Milbert and Skip Mylenski, "In the End: Michigan and Duke," *Chicago Tribune*, April 5, 1992, 3:1.

78. Skip Mylenski, "Duke Reigns Once More," *Chicago Tribune*, April 7, 1992, 4:1.

79. "Michigan Kids Crushed but Howard Sees Title in '93," *Chicago Tribune*, April 7, 1992, 4:7.

INDEX

Page locators in italics indicate photographs

237

MURRY R. NELSON is an author and has written several books about the history of American sports, basketball, and America's school curricula. He is Emeritus Professor of Education and American Studies at Penn State University. Nelson graduated from Grinnell College with a BA, Northwestern University with a master's in teaching, and Stanford University with a master's in anthropology and a PhD. He lives in State College, Pennsylvania.

FOR INDIANA UNIVERSITY PRESS

Lesley Bolton *Project Manager/Editor*

Tony Brewer *Artist and Book Designer*

Brian Carroll *Rights Manager*

Dan Crissman *Trade and Regional Acquisitions Editor*

Samantha Heffner *Trade Acquisitions Assistant*

Brenna Hosman *Production Coordinator*

Katie Huggins *Production Manager*

Dan Pyle *Online Publishing Manager*

Leyla Salamova *Book Designer*

Stephen Williams *Marketing and Publicity Manager*